# The history of Royal Holloway College
## 1886–1986

By the same author

*The Making of a King: the early years of James VI and I* (1968)
*James V, King of Scots* (1970)
*Life and Times of Edward II* (1972)
*The Stewart Kingdom of Scotland 1371–1603* (1974)
*The Crowned Lions: The Early Plantagenet Kings* (1978)
*James VI of Scotland* (1979)
*James I of England* (1981)
(two volume biography)
*Land of the Scots* (1983)

# The
# history of
# ROYAL
# HOLLOWAY
# COLLEGE
# 1886–1986

—— :>:> <:<: ——

Caroline Bingham

Constable · London

First published in Great Britain 1987
by Constable and Company Limited
10 Orange Street, London WC2H 7EG
Copyright © 1987 by Caroline Bingham
Set in Linotron Ehrhardt 11pt by
Rowland Phototypesetting Limited
Bury St Edmunds, Suffolk
Printed in Great Britain by
St Edmundsbury Press Limited
Bury St Edmunds, Suffolk

British Library CIP data
Bingham, Caroline
The history of Royal Holloway College
1886–1986
1. Royal Holloway College – History
I. Title
378.422′11   LF449.R6

ISBN 0 09 468200 3

To my parents,
with love and gratitude

# CONTENTS

# CONTENTS

# ILLUSTRATIONS

Royal Holloway College cricket team, 1890's (*RHC Archives*)

An early game of hockey (*RHC Archives*)

Band, conductor Miss Emily Daymond (*RHC Archives*)

The Classics Department production of Antigone, 1905 (*RHC Archives*)

Royal Holloway College, the library, 1937 (*RHC Archives*)

Miss E. C. Higgins, Principal of Royal Holloway College, 1907-1935 (*RHC Archives*)

The interior of Royal Holloway College Chapel (*RHC Archives*)


*between pages 256 and 257*

The Picture Gallery (*RHC Archives*)

Professor Hilda Johnstone, with a group of research students, 1937 (*RHC Archives*)

Royal Holloway College Jubilee, 1937 (*RHC Archives*)

Princess Alice, Countess of Athlone, at the presentation of the Powell Gates, 1958 (*RHC Archives*)

Miss Fanny Street, Acting Principal, 1944-45 (*RHC Archives*)

Dinner in honour of Miss Dorothy Hustler (*RHC Archives*)

Professor Tolansky shows 'Moondust' to Queen Elizabeth the Queen Mother, November 1970 (*Photo: Richard Burton, RHC Archives*)

Students taking their finals in the Picture Gallery (*RHC Archives*)

The Department of Zoology at Alderhurst, with Professor Jewell's Soay sheep in the foreground (*RHC Archives*)

Dr Lionel Butler, Principal of Royal Holloway College, 1973-1981 (*RHC Archives*)

The Partnership agreement between Royal Holloway College and Bedford College, 26 July 1982 (*Photo: Michael Harris, RHC Archives*)

# ACKNOWLEDGEMENTS

Writing the *History of Royal Holloway College* was a very pleasurable task, greatly facilitated by the friendly spirit with which the College welcomed me. Many members of the staff, academic and adminstrative, helped me in many ways, and I am particularly grateful to my colleagues in the Department of History.

The chronological structure of this book is based on the principalships. Dr Roy Miller, Principal 1982-1985, was kind enough to give me a great deal of valuable information on recent years. Dr Lionel Butler, Principal 1973-1981, had most regrettably died before my connection with the College began; therefore I owe very appreciative thanks for information on him to his widow, Mrs Gwendoline Butler, to Dr Roy Miller, Professor Katharine Worth, Dr Geoffrey Alderman, Miss Janet Christie, Mr Richard Hardy, Miss J. L. Hurn and numerous others. Dame Marjorie Williamson, Principal 1962-1973, was kind enough to give me a valuable and entertaining account of her years at RHC, both as a student and as a Principal. I was fortunate to meet Dr Edith Batho, Principal 1945-1962, during the last months of her life, and I am very grateful to Mrs Pat Fowles for the introduction, and for her own information on Dr Batho's years as Principal. For information on Miss J. R. Bacon, Principal 1935-1944, I am particularly indebted to Miss A. A. Divine and the late Dr J. M. S. Tompkins, and to Dr Mary Bradburn for her valuable comments on life at RHC during the Second World War. Many people, including past students, provided reminiscences of Miss E. C. Higgins, Principal 1907-1935. Miss Janet Adam Smith gave me a delightful account of Miss Higgins in retirement. Mrs Amy Mummery, once Miss Higgins' personal maid, provided unique reminiscences. No RHC alumnae remembered the principalship of Miss Emily Penrose, 1897-1907, but I contacted informants who remembered her as Principal of Somerville. For these personal recollections I am indebted to Miss Janet Adam Smith, Lady Dalrymple-Champneys, Professor Dominica Legge, Miss Hester Thomas and Dame Janet Vaughan. Miss M. E. Bishop,

[ 9 ]

Principal 1887-1897, has passed beyond the reach of memory, and my sources of information on her will be found in the Notes and References.

In researching the life and business interests of Thomas Holloway I am particularly indebted to Miss Jeannie Chapel, author of *Victorian Taste: The Complete Catalogue of Paintings at the Royal Holloway College*, who generously lent me her own research material, including much information on the Holloway, Martin-Holloway and Driver-Holloway families. Descendants of those families, from whom I received the utmost help and kindness, were Mr and Mrs Gerald Oliver, Dr A. W. Harrison-Barbet, himself the author of a short biography of Thomas Holloway, Mrs Pamela Mumford, Miss Betty Driver-Holloway and Mrs C. Held (who generously donated £100 to assist in preparing the College History). Mr R. G. Davis generously shared with me his research on the Holloway family, and Mrs Elizabeth Staziker of Surrey Record Office was helpful in providing access to the Holloway papers. Professor Elizabeth A. Daniels, Vassar Historian, was immensely helpful in assisting me to research the influence of the example of Vassar College on the foundation of Royal Holloway.

Many members of Royal Holloway College staff, both past and present, have helped me with information: I particularly wish to thank the following: Dr Geoffrey Alderman, Mr Douglas Barge, Dr Caroline Barron, Dr N. L. Biggs, Mr A. J. Boog, Professor R. C. Bowen, Dr Mary Bradburn, Miss Mary Burton, Miss Ursula Burton, Professor P. M. Butler, Miss Janet Christie, Professor J. Mordaunt Crook, Miss Julian Chryostomides, Professor Rodney Dales, Miss A. A. Divine, Professor John Dodge, Mrs Pat Fowles, Dr Vera Fretter, the late Miss Josephine Fuller, Mr Richard Hardy, Professor Alan G. Hill, Miss J. L. Hurn, Mr Robert Latham, Miss B. P. Legge, Professor Dominica Legge, Professor C. T. Lewis, Mr K. F. Livesey, Mr Roger Lockyer, Mrs Margaret Majumdar, Miss Norma Miller, Dr A. Moreton Moore, Sister M. G. Moss, Mrs Pat New, Dr Lionel Pike, Dr Elizabeth Prichard, Mr Peter Rado, Dr Francis Robinson, Dr Joan Thomas, the late Dr J. M. S. Tompkins, Dr Helmut Weigel, Professor Katharine Worth.

Many past students of the College answered my advertisements for reminiscences of their student days, and my debt to them will be obvious in the ensuing pages. The letters and memoirs of the following alumnae/alumni will be collected in the College Archives: Miss Eleanor Barnes (1928-1931), Mr Mike Bayliss (1965-1969), Mrs Lucy Ben-Levi, née Fowles (1942-1945), Mrs Catherine Bowden, née Watson (1923-1926), Dr Mary Bradburn (1935-1940), Mrs K. M. Broomhall, née Balding (1928-1932), Mrs Betty M. Brown, née Chittleburgh (1935-1938), Dr Ida Busbridge (1926-1932), Miss Alison Chard (1978-1981), Mrs Doris Chennells, née Feather (1931-1934), Mrs Doreen

Coker, née Stableton (1944-1947), Mrs Elsie Cook, née Moudy (1919-1921), Miss Irene Coombs (1926-1929), Miss Margaret M. H. Cross (1930-1933), Miss Marian Crout (1912-1915), Miss Elizabeth Edwards (1931-1933), Miss Janet Fookes MP (1954-1957), Mrs Patricia Garner, née Cooke (1931-1935), Dr Mary Gedye, née Scott (1918-1921), Miss Muriel Glyn-Jones (1919-1922), Miss Gillian E. Harris (1940-1943), Mrs K. Hawkes, née Griffits (1930-1933), Miss Helen Heather (1927-1931), Mrs Eileen Horsfall-Turner, née Jenkins (1929-1932), Mrs Charmian Humphreys, née Hollyoak (1943-1946), Mrs Margaret Hutchings, née Pike (1920-1923), Mrs Isabelle Kenny, née Frost (1970-1973), Mrs Mary Kennedy, née Charlesworth (1950-1953), Mrs Kathleen Lathbury, née Culhane (1918-1922), Miss I. B. Leggett (1929-1932), Lady Linstead, née Marjorie Walters (1933-1936), Miss Felicity Lott (1965-1968), Miss Marjorie Lunt (1930-1933), Professor Doireann MacDermott (1947-1950), Mrs E. M. Nash, née Valentine (1945-1948), Mrs Molly Neal, née Lilley (1918-1922), Mrs Helen Parry, née Russell (1944-1948), Miss Joyce Pentelow (1938-1942), Miss Mildred Perfect (1929-1933), Mrs Jeanne Pingree, née Bennett (1946-1949), Miss Margaret A. Selby (1952-1955), Mrs Patricia Spurrin, née Lisk (1951-1954), Mrs Veronica Sydenham, née Denny (1923-1926), Mrs Annice Szrajbman, née Taylor (1941-1943), Mrs Rachel Teschemaker, née Davison (1918-1921), Miss A. D. Thompson (1937-1940), Mrs Yvonne Tomes, née Mayhew (1946-1949), Miss Doreen Urwick (1923-1926), Miss Kathleen Vinall (1923-1926), Mrs M. C. Vincent, née Pitman (1927-1933), Mrs Gladys Wade, née Barber (1907-1910), Mrs Elizabeth Warner, née Strahan (day student 1930s), Dr Grace Waterhouse (1924-1928), Mr P. Vianney Waters (1965-1968), Mrs Honor Westmacott, née De Salis (1944-1947), Mrs Jill Williams (1962-1965), Miss Frieda Winter (1920-1923).

I am indebted for information on past students to Mr Philip Tregarthen Asdell for memoirs of his mother, née Miss Muriel Mannack (1914-1917); to Mr William Barnes for memoirs of his mother, née Miss Adelaide Ward (1898-1902); to Mr Reginald T. Coe, for memoirs of his late wife, née Miss Mary Bickley (1922-1925). Mrs Christine Hague, Secretary of RHCA/ RHESUS provided me with correspondence from members of these associations.

Some former members of the ATS who attended No. 2 OCTU and the Junior Officers Training School at RHC during the Second World War were kind enough to send me memoirs. I am very grateful to Miss Kathleen N. Edwards, MBE, TD, JP, Mrs D. M. Ellery, Mrs Audrey Everett, Miss Joyce Lunniss, Miss Rosemary Shaw, Miss Elisabeth Wheat and also to Major (Retired) D. R. M. Parker, Curator of the WRAC Museum, Guildford.

Many individuals beyond the circle of the College and the former students have given me information and assistance of various kinds. I should like to express my gratitude to Sir Thomas Armstrong, Mr Ian Bradley, Mrs Margaret Brereton, Mr T. A. B. Corley, Mr Greg Ernest, Dr Babette Evans, Professor Douglas Johnson, Mr David Kennard, Sir Philip Powell, Miss Eve Saville, MBE, Dr Janet Sondheimer, Mrs Hilary Spurling and Dr Gillian Sutherland.

Recent history, the period leading to the merger of Royal Holloway College and Bedford College, presented its own problems. For assistance in achieving a balanced view of this period I am particularly indebted to Dr Roy Miller for information on the Royal Holloway viewpoint, and for additional information to Dr Geoffrey Alderman and Miss J. L. Hurn. Professor R. E. D. Bishop and Mr David Neave gave me very full information on the negotiations for a merger between Royal Holloway College and Brunel University. Sir Randolph Quirk gave me a lucid explanation of recent events in London University which led to the merger of RHC and Bedford. Miss Marigold Packenham-Walsh wrote *A Bedford View of the Merger*, and Professor Dorothy Wedderburn added her personal comments to it.

In conclusion, there are some particular debts of gratitude which I should like to acknowledge: to Dr and Mrs Roy Miller, Mr and Mrs Gerald Oliver and Mr and Mrs A. J. Boog for their generous entertainment; to Mr Roger Lockyer for my introduction to the history of RHC, and to Dr Francis Robinson for his constant support while I have been writing it; to Mr Negley Harte for generously lending me the manuscript of *The University of London 1836-1986*, to which my debt will be obvious; to Chrys Salt, author of the RHC Centenary play *College Voices*, for her stimulating encouragement and for sharing her research; to Mrs Elizabeth Bennett, Archivist of Royal Holloway and Bedford New College, for her friendship and untiring help on which I could always rely, and to the continuing assistance of her successor, Mrs Clare Daunton. I owe a very great debt to Frances Bingham and Liz Mathews for their care and support of me during recent months. I am grateful, as always, to Mrs Sheila Collins for her expertise in typing the manuscript.

My hope is that from the mass of information at my disposal I have achieved a fair and accurate *History of Royal Holloway College*: while I acknowledge my indebtedness to many informants I accept that any errors are my own.

CAROLINE BINGHAM
30 July 1987

PART ONE


# THOMAS HOLLOWAY
# AND THE FOUNDATION OF
# ROYAL HOLLOWAY COLLEGE
# 1800–86

# 1

## DESERVED CELEBRITY

What manner of man was Thomas Holloway? The
answer is written plainly in his long career, which is
marked by two main features. He was one of those
who with dauntless courage plunge boldly into life's
conflict . . . and who, attaining to success, achieve and
deserve celebrity. On the labours of such men the
original impress always remains.[1]

'WHO can deny that he is one of the wonders of the nineteenth
century?' an admiring journalist wrote of Thomas Holloway
in 1877, when his plans to found a sanatorium and a women's
college had captured the public imagination.[2] He was hailed as a wonder
before either of his foundations had been opened, presumably because
he had spent a long life amassing wealth and had turned in his old age
to expending it with astonishing liberality for the public good. By 1877
he was famous as the manufacturer of two patent medicines, Holloway's
Ointment and Holloway's Pills, which had made his name in the exact
sense of the term a household word. Advertisements for his products
appeared in newspapers throughout the world, and on hoardings beside
the Niagara Falls and at the foot of the Great Pyramid. When Mr
Gladstone received Thomas Holloway, to discuss his philanthropic
projects, he referred to him in his diary as 'Mr Holloway (of the
pills)'. [3]

Thomas Holloway's origins were contrastingly obscure; he was the
son and namesake of a sailor from Devon. The elder Thomas Holloway
was born in 1764, and served in the Navy on board HMS *Defence*, a ship
of the line of seventy-four guns, on which he claimed to have fought at
the Battle of Ushant on 'The Glorious 1st of June' 1794, though the
ship's muster makes no mention of him. Three years later he married
Mary Chellew, the daughter of a Cornish farmer, whose family had lived
in the parish of Lelant since 1520. This must have been an advantageous
marriage, for he left the Navy and became the landlord of an inn, the

[ 15 ]

Robin Hood and Little John in Devonport, where he also opened a bakery business. At the inn, on 22 September 1800, his eldest son Thomas was born, to be followed by a second son Henry, and three daughters, Caroline, Mary Jane and Matilda. Some years later the family moved to Penzance, first to the Turk's Head inn, Chapel Street, and afterwards to a grocery shop in the Market Place.

This modest prosperity enabled the young Thomas Holloway to be sent to school, first in Camborne and then in Penzance, until he was sixteen, when he was apprenticed to a chemist.[4] The acquaintance with *materia medica* which Thomas acquired during his apprenticeship seems to have been the sole basis of what he later advertised as 'Holloway's Healing Genius'. Thomas Holloway left no reminiscences of his childhood or youth, but he was obviously dissatisfied with the limitations of Penzance and the dull prospect of a career as a provincial chemist for in his late twenties he turned his back upon both, and left England in search of fortune and adventure.

In 1828 he went first to Dunkirk, where he and a group of light-hearted young friends formed a group which they called the Société de l'Étoile; in old age he recalled this period as 'some of the happiest days of my life'.[5] Later he moved to Roubaix, a growing textile town near Lille, where he lived 'with only just money enough to support an extremely frugal existence', and formed at least one lifelong friendship;[6] but he became bilingual, so that when he returned to England, after some three years abroad, he was able to find employment in London as an interpreter and 'secretary to a gentleman'. From this employer Holloway may have acquired his social polish, for in later years it was said that 'there was nothing in his manner to denote a humble origin'.[7] On the evidence of a portrait painted in early middle age his appearance was both dignified and dandified. He was a strikingly handsome man with dark curly hair, hazel eyes, and an expressive face on which the artist captured an attractive suggestion of a smile.

By 1835 Thomas Holloway had prospered sufficiently to start his own business as a foreign commercial agent with offices at 8 Wood Street, Cheapside, from which he moved two or three years later to 13 Broad Street Buildings, also in the City. It was probably at the first address that he was approached by an Italian, Felix Albinolo, who sold leeches and wanted to market an ointment alternatively called Albinolo's Ointment or

[ 16 ]

The St Cosmas and Damian Ointment after the saintly brother physicians. For this purpose Holloway had apparently acquired potentially useful contacts. He introduced Albinolo to a Mr Travers, a surgeon at St Thomas's Hospital. The ointment was tried in the hospital, but as it was similar to the 'cerate of wax and olive oil' already in use, Travers refused to write a testimonial for it. However, another surgeon, Mr Joseph Henry Green, whose dressers tried the ointment, wrote a letter concerning it, from which a passage was taken out of context and quoted as a testimonial in a newspaper advertisement. Mr Green responded by threatening to apply to the Court of Chancery to forbid further use of his name.[8]

The experiment had scarcely been successful, but it inspired Holloway to attempt the same method of advertisement for his own benefit. On 15 October 1837 the first advertisement for Holloway's Ointment appeared, and on 16 June 1838 the advertisement, in a paper named *Town*, was accompanied by a testimonial from Mr Herbert Mayo, senior surgeon at the Middlesex Hospital. Albinolo responded by inserting a notice in *Town*, on 4 August 1838, which stated that Mayo's testimonial had been given to Albinolo's Ointment, of which the formula had been kept secret.

'After this,' according to one of Mr Travers' dressers, who many years later remembered the dispute, 'the ointment was advertised as Albinolo's ointment for some time, and then the name of Holloway was substituted.'[9]

To Holloway's lasting advantage, Albinolo was imprisoned for debt in 1839, and thenceforward Holloway was free to market the ointment under his own name.[10] For many years he guarded the secret of its formula, but when at last it was analysed it proved to be a very simple ointment which Holloway's early pharmaceutical experience would have enabled him to concoct if Albinolo had kept his secret to the last. It was made of yellow and white beeswax, resin, lanolin and olive oil, a soothing but certainly not a miraculous recipe.[11] Holloway's genius lay not in healing but in advertising.

At first Holloway's advertising costs outstripped his profits. He was unable to pay for his advertising, and was forced to declare himself bankrupt. *The Times* was the newspaper which foreclosed on him, and it has been frequently stated that he refused to read *The Times* for the rest of his life. In fact his *Letter Book* of 1867-72 and his diary of 1877 both provide evidence that he did not persist in boycotting *The Times*, for both contain references to articles and advertisements in it.[12] However, he may have harboured a temporary resentment against it, because as a result of the action of *The Times* he spent a short period in Whitecross Street debtors' prison, which probably is now chiefly remembered because it is mentioned in *Pickwick Papers*. When Mr Pickwick is faced with imprisonment, it may be recalled, he is told by his lawyer, Mr Perker, 'You can't go to Whitecross Street, my dear sir. Impossible! There are sixty beds in a ward; and the bolt's on, sixteen hours out of the four-and-twenty.' Horrified by this description, Mr Pickwick elects to go to the Fleet instead. Thomas Holloway endured the discomfort and humiliation of Whitecross Street, from which he was liberated on the payment of £600 by his mother, who by this time was a widow, living with him in London.[13]

Once at liberty, Holloway arranged with his creditors the payment of a composition, and some years later he gave a dinner at which he paid them all in full, and added a bonus of ten per cent. He determined that he would never again incur debts, and in later years when he had many employees he insisted on paying them daily instead of weekly. On resuming his business Holloway began to manufacture his pills, which had a more complex formula than the ointment. They contained aloes, rhubarb root, cinnamon, cardamoms, ginger, saffron, Glauber's salt and potassium sulphate, 'plus confection of roses in sufficient quantity'. This formula, which was presumably Holloway's own invention, would have produced a mildly laxative effect.[14]

Thomas Holloway dated his business from his first efforts in 1837 and, ignoring his bankruptcy and imprisonment, referred to the date of his first advertisement as 'The Glorious 15th October' (no doubt an echo of paternal references to 'The Glorious 1st of June'). On the eve of the fortieth anniversary of his business, in 1877, he wrote to his brother-in-law Henry Driver (who at this date was in charge of the day-to-day running of the business) and instructed him to read the letter aloud to Holloway's assembled employees. It is worth quoting at length.

Tomorrow forty years ago my advertisement appeared for the first time, in three Sunday papers, the *Weekly Dispatch, The Sunday Times,* and another paper, the name of which I have forgotten. I have, I believe, told you, that the first Ointment that I made was in my mother's saucepan, which held perhaps six quarts, an extra jump was in a long fish kettle, and after that her little copper, which would hold about 40 lbs.

The Pills were not started until two years after the Ointment had come into existence. Hibberd, an old clerk, and myself used to take turn and turn about and go into the cellar at 13 Broad Street Buildings, and make a few Pills with a small machine we had, and we used to put them into one of the little drawers of the desk which was about six inches long, indeed, we used to count them. This was my first beginning, and for many years, as you know, we used to have a little supper and singing, to commemorate the event. But when I left for America in 1853 this was discontinued.

Now tomorrow I wish you to call together in my back office, all the Clerks and the Porters, and read them the beginning of this paragraph, and then present to each Clerk a sovereign in gold, to the porters five shillings each in silver, and when you have done this send for the Forewoman and all the Girls, and read to them the same extract, and then give to each of the Girls two shillings, and sixpence, and to the Forewoman five shillings ...

You will tell them that my object in communicating to them my early beginning is merely for their edification, as showing what small beginnings may lead to, by ability, perseverance, and industry.[15]

The conclusion of the letter illustrates two of Thomas Holloway's most strongly marked characteristics, both of which were typical of the Victorian self-made man: his readiness to acknowledge his humble origins, and his immense pride in his achievements.

Some years earlier, in 1863, Holloway had published an account of his beginnings in business, in which greater stress was laid upon his difficulties. ' ... my task was very difficult and disheartening,' he wrote. ' ... I expended in one week the sum of £100 in advertising ... and all I sold in that time was two small pots of Ointment. In fact no person would then have accepted the Medicine as a gift. I had to practise the most rigid economy and to work most assiduously. By four o'clock in the morning I had generally commenced my day, not to cease until ten at night ...'[16]

It is rather amusingly told that Thomas Holloway employed his brother Henry to go from shop to shop asking for Holloway's Pills and Ointment, and then evincing great surprise and contempt when these medicines had not been heard of. Thomas himself would visit the shops later as 'Holloway's representative' and, Henry having created demand, the shopkeepers would then order a good stock![17] The story may be apocryphal, but Thomas Holloway certainly would not have despised such methods. He is said to have paid £1,000 in 1838 for having his remedies illustrated by scenes and tricks, and mentioned by name in London pantomimes.[18]

Continuing his account of his early struggles he wrote:

So strong are the fetters of prejudice, that my Pills and Ointment for a considerable time obtained little or no favours. But I did not suffer my energy to be readily daunted; I went on advertising, not only with determination, but judiciously and carefully, and in the end succeeded in creating for my preparations a limited reputation throughout the British Isles. This might have satisfied me at one time, but, as our desires increase with our success, I made up my mind to be content with nothing less than girdling the Globe with depots of my remedies. For this purpose I used to go down to the docks to see captains of ships and passengers sailing to all parts of the world, collecting from them such information as was necessary.[19]

Growing prosperity enabled Holloway to move from Broad Street Buildings (where someone contemptuously described his office as 'a little cupboard') to more spacious premises. He appears in the London Directory of 1841 as 'Thomas Holloway, Patent Medicine Warehouse, 244 Strand'. His new offices are said to have had a very ornate interior, but they have long since disappeared, for the building was requisitioned in 1867 and demolished to provide part of the site of the new Law Courts. To 244 Strand Thomas Holloway brought his mother, who lived there until her death in 1843, having survived long enough to see him become a wealthy and happily married man.

It was probably in the course of his visits to the London docks that Thomas Holloway met Miss Jane Driver, the eldest daughter of a shipwright, of 22 King Street, Rotherhithe. She had been born in 1814, and was therefore in her middle twenties when Thomas, who was approaching forty, began to pay court to her. According to her portrait Jane was a rather plain young woman with a round face and an incipient double chin; but she had a gentle expression and appealing dark brown eyes. Thomas fell deeply in love with her, and remained devoted to her for the rest of her life. A charmingly absurd little note from him survives as a souvenir of their courtship:

> If Grace Darling can have the permission of her Parents to go to Drury Lane Theatre this evening she must be here by half past five o'clock.
>
> Grace will find that plenty of tea and toast stored away in her lighthouse before she leaves King Street will enable her lamp to be in good trim all the evening.
>
> Holloway's umbrella will be as useful to him this evening as a Pot of Ointment to a Bad Leg.[20]

They were married at the Church of St Mary Magdalen, Bermondsey, on 12 January 1840. Thenceforward there was little time for visits to the theatre or dalliance under an umbrella. Jane Holloway joined her husband at the tedious tasks of making pills and ointment, and worked the same long hours as he did. Their only recreations were a late evening walk along the Strand, or a weekend expedition to Hampstead Heath. Occasionally there would be a drive out into the country in a pony-trap, when Thomas would make a round of villages, selling his medicines from door to door. A householder who remembered his visits recalled that 'the impression he made was not in the least that of the pushing canvasser, but of a quiet, kindly man convinced of the merits of the goods he recommended.'[21] This, of course, was precisely the impression he would have wished to make. Jane was fully convinced of their merits, for she used to give pots of Ointment to the poor of their neighbourhood, 'together with more substantial gifts'.[22]

In the years which followed his marriage Thomas Holloway adopted his wife's family as his own. Jane was the eldest of several children. Her younger sister Mary Ann Driver remained unmarried, and eventually became Thomas's sole heiress; her brother Henry Driver was a Master Mariner before he joined Holloway's business; her youngest sister Sarah

Ann Driver married George Martin, who was closely associated with Holloway in the building of the Sanatorium and the College. George Martin, who was several years younger than his wife, was of German extraction. At the time of his marriage, in 1857, he called himself Viscount d'Altenburg, a name borrowed from his grandfather's place of origin, Saxe-Altenburg.[23] It is easy to imagine the embarrassment which must have resulted when his false claim to nobility was revealed; but it was conveniently forgotten, and the desire for title which had given rise to it was in the end partly fulfilled by a knighthood. Holloway's affection for his brothers-in-law is witnessed, and his disappointment that he was childless suggested, by the fact that Henry Driver and George Martin at his request adopted the surnames Driver-Holloway and Martin-Holloway after his death.

Holloway's adoption of his wife's family did not imply alienation from his own. He provided a home for his unmarried sister Matilda until her death in 1867, and he did his best to establish his nephew William Young (the son of his other sister, Caroline) in a satisfactory career. Since William showed a strong disinclination to apply himself to anything, and was in turn a law student, a bank clerk, an actor and a butcher, it is scarcely surprising that he was not taken into Holloway's business. Caroline's daughter and namesake married a Dr Lee, who attended Holloway during a serious illness in 1877.[24] The only internecine quarrel among the Holloways took place in 1850, when Henry Holloway set up in competition with his brother, selling medicines also called Holloway's and also in the Strand, and litigation was required to put a stop to his enterprise. On 9 November the Master of the Rolls granted an injunction against Henry Holloway, with the words, 'I think this as clear and plainly avowed a fraud as I ever knew, defendant will not be allowed to practise a fraud like that here complained of.'[25] Fortunately this unpleasant episode did not lead to a permanent breach between the brothers, as Henry later joined Thomas's business and remained on good terms with him until his death in 1875.

Thomas Holloway was no stranger to litigation. Frequent attempts to infringe his rights in his trade marks and his name made him 'a very good friend to the legal profession'.[26] Nonetheless, he is said to have harboured a strong prejudice against lawyers, together with doctors and clergymen. Prejudice against lawyers is not uncommon among those who make frequent use of their services, high fees and the suspicion that law and justice do not always go together being the usual causes. With the medical profession Holloway's relations were inevitably ambiguous. His remedies were claimed to be panaceas, far surpassing conventional medicines in efficacy; yet he retained a doctor to care for the health of his employees, and reluctantly consulted him during an illness of his own. The origin of his prejudice against clergymen is obscure, and the evidence of it is merely negative. In 1877, the only year for which a complete diary of his survives, he did not once attend church; and in an age when many men held strong and partisan religious views, he decreed that the College he founded should be non-denominational.

From 1840 onwards Holloway's prosperity increased with astonishing rapidity, accompanied by growing expenditure on advertising. In his own words:

> It was a rule with me from the commencement to expend judiciously all the money I could spare in publicity, which went on increasing, when in the year 1842, I expended about £5,000 in advertising. Time rolled on, and from the hitherto unthought-of yearly outlay of £5,000, I increased it to £10,000 in the year 1845.[27]

By 1848 he could well afford to spend some months abroad, and he travelled extensively in Belgium, the Netherlands, Germany and France. Jane was left behind, probably to manage the business, but she joined her husband for three short periods during his travels.

On 28 May he sailed from London to Antwerp and toured the Netherlands arranging agencies for the sale of his medicines and placing advertisements for them in local newspapers. On 30 May he noted in his diary, 'Made an arrangement with the *Nouvelle Gazette* in Rotterdam for two insertions weekly or 26 times at 65 florins', and at Leeuwarden which he reached on 6 June 'made an arrangement with the *Provincial Courant* for 80 florins *per ann* twice a week.'[28] However, Holloway had not come abroad only to do business. He was an indefatigable sightseer and a traveller of enviable stamina. He usually paused only a day or two in each town, before moving on by train, diligence or steamer. He never mentioned delays, and seldom discomfort, but he always noted the cost of his journeys. As one might expect of him, he spent his money carefully, but ungrudgingly so long as he was satisfied that he was receiving good value. At Deventer, on 9 June, he wrote, 'Went to the theatre, a Dutch troop from Amsterdam. Their travelling theatre cost about £1,000, and they have two.' He had obviously got into conversation with the actors after the performance and questioned them about their costs, which seem to have interested him more than the play itself.

On 24 June he was joined by Jane at Rotterdam. They went on to stay at The Hague, Amsterdam, Antwerp and Brussels, whence they made an excursion to the field of Waterloo. Holloway made no comment on the battle or the battlefield, but praised the good local guide and added some criticism of an English guide, Serjeant Major Cotton: 'I should recommend persons who want to see the field not to employ him, as he cuts you off very short so as to get back and take others.'

'Poor Jane', as Thomas always sentimentally called her, left for England on 9 July. He escorted her to Antwerp, and when the steamer had sailed he returned to Brussels in a despondent mood. 'When I arrived in my room at the hotel without her,' he wrote, 'where we had both been together only a few hours before, I could hardly believe that she was no longer with me. God bless her, she is one of the best of wives any man ever had.' This expression of his attachment to Jane is the only revelation of Thomas Holloway's feelings which his diary contains. Jane paid him a second visit from 24 July to 1 August, a period which was spent entirely in Brussels. After her second departure Holloway travelled in Germany, partly for pleasure and partly for the good of his health, concerning himself no further with agencies or advertisements.

In Germany he visited the Spa of Boppard, where he met his old acquaintance Herbert Mayo of the Middlesex Hospital, and paid him £1 for a consultation. He also experimented with taking a cure: 'On Sunday morning I was swaddled in blankets for an hour and a quarter and then sprinkled all over with cold water which caused me to spring out of the tub. I was served this way for three mornings . . . but feeling it did not suit my case I gave it up.'

There cannot have been much wrong with him as he resumed his travels with his accustomed energy, and visited Hamburg, Frankfurt, Heidelberg and Baden-Baden, where he sampled the spa water with some scepticism. 'There is a house called the "Drink-Hall" where you go to drink the water which is brought there in a pipe . . . in my opinion it has an artificial look. I had a glass of it, like unto a glass of warm whey. It is good for the nerves, they say . . .'

By 30 September he had made his way to Ostend, to meet Jane. They spent a fortnight sightseeing in Paris, before sailing from Boulogne to Folkestone. Holloway concluded his diary by noting that his absence had been 'five months all but six days'.[29] Holloway's diary is full of references to his visits to palaces, public buildings and picture galleries, churches and synagogues, theatres, circuses and casinos (as an onlooker and not a gambler). But his diary is more tantalising for its omissions than rewarding for its contents. No doubt an Englishman in 1848 who remained abroad for five months and avoided all political turmoil would have regarded himself as a fortunate traveller, but posterity must regret that he was not a witness of any of the great events of the Year of Revolutions.

A few years later Holloway renewed his efforts at 'girdling the globe with depots of his remedies'. An early entry in his travel diary for 1853 reads: 'May 12. *This day twelve months I left England* and have not been home since.'[30] As the rest of 1853 was occupied by travels in Europe this absence must have been the visit to America to which he referred in his letter to Henry Driver, so that in fact he had left England in 1852, not 1853 as he stated in the letter. He was initially successful in establishing markets in North America, where his medicines sold particularly well during the Civil War; but in the years that followed it he suffered from pirating of his name on such a large scale that his American profits were severely diminished.

Holloway's 1853 diary, which was bought in France and begun in Milan, contains little except notes of his arrivals and departures, comparisons between the currencies of different countries, and brief memoranda of his business transactions, which are of interest for the light which they shed upon his methods. A typical entry, made on 13 May at Bologna reads: 'Occupied all the day in making arrangements to obtain permission of the Commission de Santé to sell our remedies. Made the acquaintance of a Doctor Ottavio Pancerasi . . . I saw Professor Alessandrini and Professor Sgorzi, Professor of Chemistry, who promise me their protection in getting permission to sell my remedies.' The following day he wrote: 'Avvocardo Carlo Monte Editore della *Gazetta di Bologna*. Agreed to give him 140 fr. for two insertions weekly – he not to send the paper.' The explanation of the concluding words is that Holloway was accustomed to insist that he was sent a copy of every newspaper in which his advertisement appeared, with the result that he collected in the course of years one of the most extensive libraries of English, colonial and foreign newspapers in existence.[31]

From Bologna he travelled by way of Leghorn to Rome, where he visited the Vatican; thence to Naples, from which he made an excursion to Pompeii, and from there to Messina, whence he sailed to Trieste. He travelled on to Vienna, Dresden and Stettin. On 23 August he noted: 'St Petersburg. Arrived this day by steamer at Cronstat at 9.30 and left at 11.30 by a small steamer for St Petersburg. Got there in one hour and a half.' Two days later he noted the name 'Joseph Peters, druggist. St Petersburg', who presumably was the agent commissioned to sell his remedies. He visited Moscow, and then returned to Stettin. By 29 September he was in Hamburg, where he was joined by Jane. They remained in Hamburg until 14 October, when 'Poor Jane' sailed again for England. Holloway remained abroad until early December, but the remainder of the diary is composed entirely of the names of the cities he visited, continuing to place advertisements and arrange agencies.[32]

So successful was Holloway in establishing the sales of his medicines abroad that by 1863 he was able to record that his yearly expenditure had reached £40,000 in advertising his remedies 'in every available manner throughout the Globe'.

'For the proper application of their use,' he continued, 'I have had the most ample directions translated into almost every known tongue; such as Chinese, Turkish, Armenian, Arabic, Sanskrit, and most of the vernaculars of India, and all the languages spoken on the European Continent.'[33]

The advertisements which proclaimed 'Holloway's Healing Genius' or promised 'Health for All' continued to be supported by medical testimonials, and were also accompanied by letters from sufferers who had been restored to health. A particularly striking example was a letter from an Irish farmer, printed on a broadsheet beneath an engraving of a crowd of suffering humanity suppliant at the feet of Aesculapius, god of healing. The letter, dated 20 May 1866 and addressed to 'Professor

Holloway', declared that the sufferer had lost the use of his limbs, his sight and hearing were failing, and pains which had plagued him for twenty years were growing worse. He had taken Holloway's remedies for a month: 'I am now, thanks to God and your invaluable Pills and Ointment, quite recovered, and able to follow my usual avocations with comfort.'[34] The lucid and literate style of this letter, and others selected for quotation, is somewhat similar to Holloway's own, which suggests that Holloway improved the letters he chose to use, if indeed he did not compose some of them.

Besides his advertisements, broadsheets and leaflets accompanying his medicines, Holloway also published *Holloway's Almanac and Family Friend, Holloway's Abridged Medical Guide for the use of Missionaries and others, Holloway's Atlas* and a series of *Holloway's National Drawing Books*. In 1857 he issued currency tokens, which were the size of the old penny and halfpenny pieces; they bore Holloway's profile and the legend 'Professor Holloway, London' on the obverse, and on the reverse a seated figure of Hygeia, goddess of health, with the legend 'Holloway's Pills and Ointment'. These tokens were used as currency in London, but for some unexplained reason most of them were sent to Australia, where they are thought to have formed part of the early currency of the colony.[35]

The adoption of the style 'Professor Holloway' was intended to impress the more ignorant purchasers of the medicines, but it brought Holloway some public ridicule and he was wise enough to abandon it, though not everyone else did so. The hint of charlatanism created by the bogus title, and by the well publicised but closely guarded secrecy of the remedies, led to the invention of all kinds of legends concerning his origin and theirs. In general he ignored these stories, but one of them annoyed him sufficiently to elicit a dignified rebuke. On 9 October 1871 he wrote to the editor of the *Kentish Observer*:

> I read in your *London Corresp*[ondent's] *Letter* in your paper of 5th inst, that I was once Butler to a Gentleman's family, and that I obtained from my master the formula for my Pills and Ointment. I beg you will be good enough in your next issue to contradict this statement, as I never was Butler or servant in any capacity, but have always independently carried on business for myself.[36]

[ 27 ]

Whatever may have been said about him, Holloway was generally admired by those who met him. Though in later life he became white-haired and rather stout, he retained a handsome and dignified appearance. An anonymous friend wrote of him:

> Mr Thomas Holloway could not have been said to be the imitation of any man. In character he stood alone. Apart from his commanding stature (he stood well over six feet), in conversation he invariably impressed his hearers with the accuracy of his judgment, to the extent that people were not only ready to follow his lead but were anxious to acquire information from him.[37]

The whole course of his life illustrated how ready others were to follow his lead, and in financial matters alone his information would have been worth having. As the 1860s progressed his fortune was rapidly augmented by skilful investment in stocks and shares: 'he dared to deal in the most risky stocks, yet his speculations were uniformly successful, so that he made large sums to be added to the profits of his business.'[38] He had an astute adviser in his stockbroker, Walpole Lloyd Greenwell, who later became one of the Governors of the College. He also founded Holloway's Bank, which is said to have made a loan to the French Government during the Franco-Prussian War.

In 1867, when his premises in the Strand were requisitioned, he moved to 533 Oxford Street (later renumbered as 78 New Oxford Street), a corner building which he called Holloway House. Here he and Jane had rooms above the business in which to stay when they were in London, but by this time Holloway had bought a house in the country, Tittenhurst Park at Sunninghill, near Ascot, which became his main residence. It was a Georgian house which had been refaced in the 1830s, a modest choice for a man of immense wealth, whose taste inspired such ostentatious buildings as the Sanatorium and the College. The household at Tittenhurst comprised Thomas and Jane Holloway, Jane's sister Sarah Ann and her husband George Martin, together with her unmarried sister Mary Ann Driver and Thomas's unmarried sister Matilda Holloway, who had long been an invalid and died soon after the move had taken place. They had few visitors apart from other members of the family, and made no attempt to be accepted in local society. Their amusements were to drive out in one of their four carriages when the weather was fine or to play billiards when it was not. In the evenings the ladies would play the piano and sing, or George Martin would read aloud. Their life was the respectable and unassuming existence of any prosperous middle-class family.[39]

After his move to the country Thomas Holloway became an early commuter, travelling to London almost every day by train to attend to his business. On one of these journeys, in 1869, he fell into conversation with a Captain Joseph Dingwall, who told him that the breakdown of his marriage had decided him to sell his property in England and go to Turkey. Dingwall's house, Broomfield Hall, was not far from Tittenhurst, and must have been known to Holloway, at least by sight, for he immediately made an officer of £25,000 for the house and its contents, which Dingwall thankfully accepted.[40] It was an excellent bargain, for the contents were valued at £10,000 and included a fine collection of pictures, which steadily appreciated in value. Holloway removed the collection to Tittenhurst, pulled down Broomfield, and built a new house in its place, which he sold in 1872. With characteristic thoroughness, when Holloway put the rebuilt Broomfield on the market, he wrote a description of it which he sent to ninety-six agents. The new house sold for £20,000 which may have been a modest profit, but Holloway probably regarded the main profit as being represented by the pictures, which were Dutch, Flemish, French and Italian Old Masters. Among them were Giovanni Bellini's *St Francis in Ecstasy* and Gerard David's *Deposition from the Cross*, both of which are now in the Frick Collection, New York.[41]

To most men who had passed the normal age of retirement, the purchase, demolition, rebuilding and sale of Broomfield would have been a major preoccupation; to Thomas Holloway Broomfield was only one of many new interests, which included the purchase of forty acres of farmland adjacent to Tittenhurst, and a profitable sideline in breeding and selling cattle. As he entered the last decade of his life, while he continued to control his vast business, Holloway brought unimpaired energy and new vision to the planning of his greatest enterprises, the Sanatorium and the College.

Towards the end of his life Holloway told the architect of both these buildings that he had 'worked harder to spend his money than he ever did to make it'.[42] His decision to devote the greater part of his fortune to philanthropy arose from the fact that he was childless and had no relative to whom he was willing to bequeath so much.

The turning point of his life seems to have been 19 April 1861, when he attended a public meeting in the Freemasons' Hall and heard Lord Shaftesbury make a speech on the care of the insane. The background of this event was that a few years previously there had been a widespread scare that insanity was increasing, and that existing lunatic asylums were inadequate. In 1859 Parliament appointed a Select Committee to examine the question, and Shaftesbury, who had constantly laboured to improve the unhappy condition of the insane, was summoned as its principal witness. According to his first biographer, Edwin Hodder, Shaftesbury's evidence before this Committee gave 'a succinct history of the whole *régime* of lunatic asylums since 1828'.[43] This evidence revealed that while pauper asylums provided, however imperfectly, for the insane of the poorer classes, and private establishments, at a price, for the rich, the middle-class insane fell into what is now termed a 'poverty trap'. Shaftesbury crusaded enthusiastically for the foundation of an asylum to provide for them; fund-raising for this enterprise was the purpose of his speech in the Freemasons' Hall. Shaftesbury was a magnificent orator, and he developed his theme by sketching some imaginary case histories.

> Take first the case of the small tradesman . . . He begins by some strangeness of conduct; he is queer, he is moody, he neglects his business. He enters perhaps into profligate, dissipated and extravagant habits. At first his relatives do not see whence this arises; and when they do discover the malady, they try to keep him at home as long as possible, to avoid the expense of an asylum . . . And see how it affects the business. It soon transpires that the man is . . . supposed to be mad; and people begin to shrink from his house, the customers fall off, the decrease in the receipts tends to the augmentation of the disorder, and the whole family is plunged in distress.

This imaginary but all too realistic disaster was well calculated to move the mind of a businessman such as Thomas Holloway, who had once been a small tradesman himself. Shaftesbury went on to imagine the effects of insanity upon the families of poor clergymen, half-pay officers, doctors, law students and bank clerks, and of people dependent on small salaries, such as governesses and tutors. 'What', he demanded, 'can be worse or more miserable, than the condition of those persons under the affliction of insanity?'[44]

Lord Shaftesbury was appealing for £5,000 to finance the first experiment, and his audience immediately contributed £760. Holloway was probably not among those who made a contribution, for he was not a man who handed out money without preliminary calculation, but he went home and gave long thought to Shaftesbury's proposals. Shaftesbury may have been disappointed by the initial response to his appeal, but he must have been astonished when, three years later, he received the following letter:

My Lord,
A gentleman who is possessed of nearly a quarter of a million, is about to make a settlement of it (after providing for his relatives) for charitable uses.

Knowing your great philanthropy and your experience in such matters, I advised him to be guided by your Lordship as to the disposal of his property, if you would condescend to take an interest in the subject. If your Lordship assents, might I ask for him the favour of an audience?

I have the honour to be Yr Lordship's very obedient servant,
J. Bowen May.[45]

The writer was Thomas Holloway's solicitor. His letter was favourably received, and the result was a meeting between Shaftesbury and Holloway on 25 May 1864.

No greater contrast could be imagined than between these two men. Shaftesbury was an austere aristocrat and a devout Evangelical; Holloway was a confident and outgoing self-made man, and a nominal though scarcely a practising Anglican. Shaftesbury was a Tory; Holloway was non-political, though most of his political contacts were Liberals. Shaftesbury had dedicated his entire adult life to philanthropy (a word which he thoroughly disliked); Holloway had dedicated his to making money, though he always maintained that he had done well by doing good. Despite their differing characters and backgrounds, their meeting led to a fruitful collaboration of ideas. Both of them believed that charity demeaned its recipients, and that so far as possible people should be assisted to help themselves. Neither would have been an unconditional supporter of the Welfare State. The Holloway Sanatorium reflected their views, in that it was not intended to be an asylum for the permanently insane, but a refuge in which the temporarily deranged should be assisted to resume their working lives. When the Sanatorium was opened in 1885 by the Prince of Wales, George Martin Holloway handed him a statement which asserted that 'the design and completion of this noble work belongs to two men, Lord Shaftesbury and Mr Thomas Holloway.'[46] At their first meeting Holloway told Shaftesbury that he intended to spend his fortune on a single building and a single benefaction; but from this plan Shaftesbury, fortunately for the future of the College, dissuaded him.

Plans for the Sanatorium went forward very slowly, and in the meantime Thomas Holloway made a Will, on 1 September 1864, in which he made provision for what was presumably to be a second benefaction. By the terms of this Will £150,000 was to be given to the Lord Mayor and Common Councilmen of the City of London 'for the erection of a hospital for reception of convalescent patients from the London Hospitals upon such terms as my widow shall direct'. (The plans were to be submitted to Jane Holloway). The Will also provided for her to receive an income of £2,000 a year, to be reduced to £300 should she remarry, and there were some small bequests to members of his own family. This Will was eventually superseded by another, and the hospital was never built.[47]

It was not until 1872 that plans for the Sanatorium were advanced by the launching of a limited competition to find an architect. In judging the ten entries invited Thomas Holloway consulted three experts: Thomas Leverton Donaldson, emeritus Professor of Architecture at University College, London, and founder of the Royal Institute of British Architects, who was regarded as 'the father of the architectural profession'; George Godwin, editor of the *Builder*, who had himself designed a lunatic asylum in 1847; and Thomas Henry Wyatt, Consulting Architect to the Lunacy Commissioners. Donaldson was 'a Classicist, Greek, Roman and Renais-

Thomas Holloway, *c.* 1875.

Jane Holloway, *c.* 1875.

Statue of the Thomas and Jane Holloway by Count Gleichen in the Founder's Quad.

The official opening of Royal Holloway College by Queen Victoria, 30th June 1886.

Royal Holloway College photographed from the North Tower.

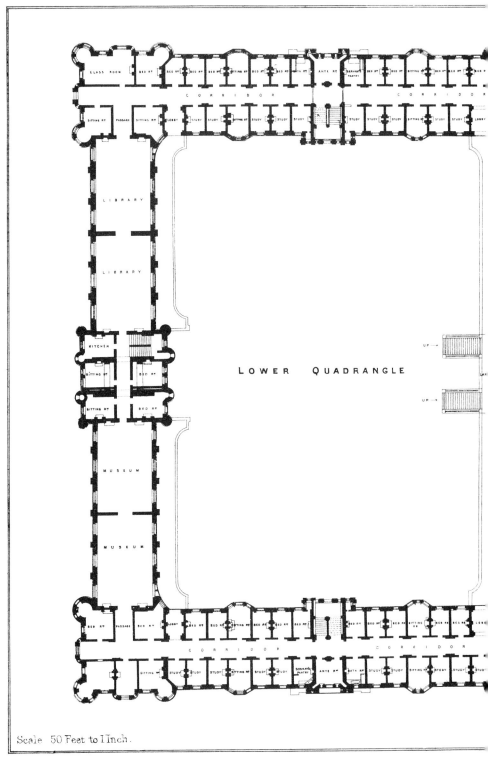

Scale  50 Feet to 1 Inch.

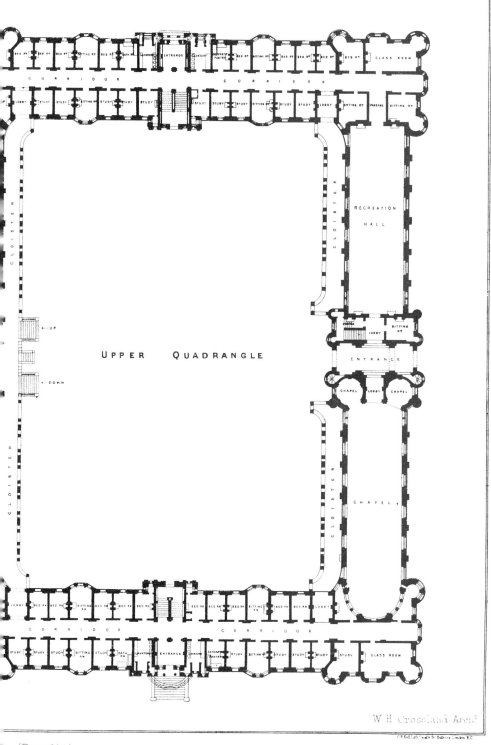

W H Crossland Arch?

The College in summer: the
South Tower reflected in the
lake.

The College in winter: the
building from the south east.

Miss M.E. Bishop, Principal
of Royal Holloway College,
1887–1897.

Miss Emily Penrose, Principal
of Royal Holloway College,
1897–1907.

Miss Bishop with staff of Royal Holloway College (back row, standing: Professor
W.R. Cassie, Professor S.L. Loney, Professor E.H. Donkin, Miss M.E. Bishop,
Miss C. Frost, Dr M.J. Benson; second row, seated: first two unidentified; third
from left Miss T. Dabis; fourth Miss N. Pechinet, fifth unidentified; sixth Miss
E.M. Guiness; third row, seated on ground: first, Miss E.E. Field; second, Miss
E. Daymond, third unidentified.

sance. He despised the Middle Ages, and only tolerated Gothic and Tudor forms *faute de mieux*.' The other two were less prejudiced: Godwin favoured 'rational' architecture, regardless of style, and Wyatt 'could turn his hand to most styles'.[48] After consultation with them Holloway chose the plans submitted by William Henry Crossland, together with a collaborator who died before the building was begun.

W. H. Crossland was a pupil of Sir George Gilbert Scott. He practised in Yorkshire, first at Huddersfield and later at Halifax, where he designed the industrial estate of Ackroyden, one of the earliest examples of its kind, begun in 1861. He also built and restored a number of churches in Yorkshire and Lanchasire, and won the competition for Rochdale Town Hall (1866-71). In 1867 he was elected FRIBA, and he had recently moved to London when he submitted the plans for Holloway Sanatorium.

Crossland was on holiday when he received a telegram from his collaborator, John Philpot Jones, to announce that they had won the competition. 'When the adjudication was given in our favour,' he wrote. 'I was up in the north of Nova Scotia, thinking a great deal more of salmon and moose than of Sanatoria . . . On my return matters had progressed rapidly and I found Mr Jones in almost daily communication with Mr Holloway, submitting to him plans and views of designs in great variety . . . The elevations followed, and showed a building, the characteristics of which were façades of plain and ornamental brick throughout.'[49]

Holloway had expressed a preference for 'the grand old Flemish style', and Crossland complied with a design which was inspired by the Cloth Hall at Ypres, a building which Holloway must have seen and admired when he lived not many miles distant, at Roubaix. His choice of style was also influenced by the availability of appropriate material. 'I know that your taste is classical,' Holloway had written to Professor Donaldson, ' . . . but perhaps all things considered, the Gothic would be the most appropriate, as we can get red bricks in the neighbourhood.'[50] Holloway was determined that the Sanatorium should be visible from a railway, presumably because it would thereby advertise itself to the travelling public. Part of his own land, the Trotsworth Estate and Trumps Green Farm, fulfilled this condition; indeed, the site he chose was visible from two railways. The first brick was laid in June 1873 by Jane Holloway, and the second by Holloway himself. Thenceforward, despite the sudden death of John Philpot Jones, the work progressed rapidly, overseen by Holloway with a remorseless attention to detail.

In the late summer, when work on the Sanatorium was progressing well, Holloway 'mentioned casually that he had some idea of starting another great work' and asked Crossland if he thought that a style of architecture similar to the Sanatorium would be suitable for the purpose. Crossland wrote that the purpose was a college for the higher education of women, but in fact his account of events telescoped the stages by which Holloway reached this decision, for in September 1873 he was still thinking of a hospital, not for convalescents as he had stated in his Will of 1864, but for incurables. Crossland expressed the view that a return to Classical or Renaissance architecture was coming into favour, and suggested a building inspired by the châteaux of the Loire. He selected some views for Holloway to consider, giving preference to the Château of Chambord.

'The effect on Mr Holloway was somewhat startling,' Crossland continued. ' . . . he told me that he was advised to put the design to competition, but would like to hear from me the course I should take in the event of my becoming a competitor. I replied that I should visit the Touraine, and, with an assistant, sketch and measure Chambord in the completest way . . . He then said, "Will you do this Mr Crossland?" To which I answered most assuredly I would. He then patted me on the shoulder and said "My boy, you shall have the work; but mind, on the condition that you sketch and measure Chambord from bottom to top. No more competitions for me. I had too much trouble about the last"; and, he added, "When will you start?" My reply was that as soon as I could set matters quite straight at the Sanatorium I would start. In this way came to me the most important work of my life . . .'[51]

The immediate result of this conversation was that early in September 1873 Crossland and his assistant Mr Taylor set off to draw and measure Chambord with the exactitude that Holloway required. In the middle of the month Holloway joined them at the Hôtel St Michel, close to the Château, and later wrote an account of his visit.[52] In studying Chambord Holloway did not spare himself any more than he spared Crossland and

Taylor. They left the hotel at 9 a.m. each morning and remained at the Château until 12.30, when they took a lunch break: 'as it was very hard work going up and down so many flights of stairs we did not go to the Château again until 2, remaining there till about 6.30. It was tiring work, and we were always on the leg up and down.' Crossland and Taylor had been working for ten days before Holloway's arrival, so that his work, as he described it, consisted in referring to what they had done 'to determine how much of the Château I wanted for my purpose, as I intended at that time to take it as a model for building an Institution for incurables – but which idea I afterwards abandoned.

'I was engaged the whole of the 18, 19, 20 and 21 of Sept,' he continued, 'and up to one o'clock on my birthday the 22 of Sep [*sic*], and that afternoon Mr Crossland set about revising his plans upon a large scale and in accordance with my suggestion. The 23, 24 and up to 2 o'clock on the 25 the time was principally spent on these plans and running occasionally over the Château to compare our work with what we saw there – and on this afternoon we visited the Château for the last time, bidding it adieu, and we all left it with much regret.'

This was a demanding daily routine for a man of seventy-three, but Holloway's health was still robust, and his capacity for hard work and attention to detail astonished Crossland, who described him as 'a client who sent me to school'. They travelled home by way of Paris, where Crossland spent a day buying books on architecture, and Lille, where Holloway bought 'a small luncheon basket for Jane'. He also made a sentimental journey to Roubaix, before returning to England on 4 October.

Between the autumn of 1873 and the spring of 1874 Thomas Holloway abandoned his plan to found a hospital for incurables and decided to found a college for women. When the Foundation Deed of the College was executed on 11 October 1883, a few weeks before his death, he gave the credit to Jane with the words 'The College is founded by the advice and counsel of the Founder's dear Wife, now deceased . . .' There is no reason to doubt this statement, though there is no other evidence of Jane's interest in women's education.

Jane died on 26 September 1875, and in the two years between Holloway's return from Chambord and her death his correspondence on the subject of the College contains no mention of her. The only clue to the nature of her influence is to be found in the unpublished memoirs of Miss Marion Pick, who became a student of the College in 1903, and later returned to become Lecturer in Mathematics. She was told that Jane Holloway had entreated her husband to spend some of his fortune on a benefaction for women, 'because they are the greatest sufferers'.[53] Jane had been fortunate in the protection of a wealthy and devoted husband, but she had worked hard to assist him in the early years of their marriage, and she would have recognised how different her life might have been if his business had failed. Few women of Jane's generation had the opportunity to better their condition by their own efforts, and she may have seen that education would provide them with the best means to do so. If Holloway's inspiration is to be found in Jane's simple pity for women as 'the greatest sufferers', rather than in any active participation in his plans, the College has no less reason to be grateful to its Founder's wife.

On 12 May 1874 Holloway purchased the land on which the College was to be built, acquiring for £25,374 the 94-acre Mount Lee Estate, one mile from Egham and eighteen miles from London. The fact that the College was built relatively close to London was entirely fortuitous, as the Founder did not foresee or desire any future connection with London University. According to an early prospectus:

> The relative advantages of various sites for the College were maturely considered by him, and he decided in favour of Mount Lee, Egham, chiefly on account of the great healthfulness and beauty of the situation and the large extent of the grounds, which would enable the students to lead a thoroughly open-air country life.[54]

The hilltop site also ensured that the magnificent building which Holloway planned would dominate the surrounding countryside and be, like the Sanatorium, its own advertisement. At the time his choice was no doubt influenced by the fact that Mount Lee was only a few miles from Tittenhurst, which would enable him simultaneously to oversee the building of the College and watch the Sanatorium approaching completion. Regrettably, he died before either building was complete.

During the last decade of his life Holloway's celebrity ensured that all his activities would be news; accordingly, his philanthropic schemes aroused enormous interest throughout society. In 1873 Mrs Gladstone, who was full of enthusiasm for the Sanatorium, sought his acquaintance, and requested Mr Roger Eykyn, the Liberal MP for Old Windsor, to introduce Thomas Holloway to herself and the Prime Minister. Holloway called on them, but with irritating reticence merely noted in his diary that he found them 'extremely pleasant'.[55] Mr Gladstone, in a striking if indirect manner, was more forthcoming when, according to a contemptuous Irish journalist, he made a speech in which 'he compared the efficacy of his own political prescriptions to the purifying effect of the famous pills.' The Irishman also castigated Holloway for promptly sending Mrs Gladstone £500 for a charity, and added that had Mr Gladstone also mentioned the Ointment, doubtless Holloway would have sent £1,000![56]

With his unerring sense of publicity Holloway advertised the Sanatorium and the College in the same way as he had advertised the Ointment and the Pills. He sent notices concerning them to newspapers throughout the world, explaining that his two foundations were intended 'to make some acknowledgement to the public for the means which, through them, I possess'. Many papers printed his notice verbatim, and some also printed his letter à propos the College, which concluded: 'If I could think that the Ladies' College, when finished, should be the means of educating any of the daughters of your neighbourhood, I should deem myself extremely happy.'[57]

Though foreign girls were not among the first students of the College, news of its foundation was received with enthusiasm in the remotest parts of the world. The Lucknow newspaper *Oudh Akhbar* commented: 'Professor Holloway . . . has brought benefit to people all over the world. His "Holloway Pills and Balm" are well known . . . He is renowned for his spirit and dynamism . . . The building which Mr Holloway is constructing for female education (and we wish one such was here in Hindustan for the same purpose) is going to be a grand one. Indeed, it will be a rival to Oxford and Cambridge and the standard of education will be the same.'[58] The editorial in the St Helena *Guardian* expressed the same wish, in a laudatory and exclamatory style: 'Generous, noble-hearted Philanthropist! Would that we could find such a benefactor in St Helena as Happy England has found in Professor HOLLOWAY.'[59] The

Buenos Aires *Standard* mentioned the suggestion that the great exponent of advertising had turned to philanthropy for the sake of advertisement and dismissed it as a calumny, concluding simply: 'Holloway is a great and good man.'[60]

———————— :>·> 2 <·:<: ————————

# UNIQUE IN ENGLAND

> An extraordinary thing is happening in this district.
> Mr Holloway . . . is erecting in the fields of Egham a
> building which both in scale and style will be unique
> in England. It is intended for the higher education of
> women; but the question I am asking myself is whether
> any women with facilities open to them at both Oxford
> and Cambridge are ever likely to go to Egham to be
> educated.[1]

THOMAS HOLLOWAY'S decision to found a women's college was pioneering. Though newspapers throughout the world applauded his intention, higher education for women was a controversial issue in England, and the institutions which aspired to provide it were in their infancy.

The controversy centred on the propriety, or even the necessity, of upper- and middle-class women receiving more education than would endow them with attractive accomplishments and social graces, and of working-class women acquiring more than elementary literacy and domestic skills. Some opponents of women's education protested that the cultivation of intellect would make girls less feminine and mothers less maternal, while others cast doubt upon women's possession of intellect to be cultivated at all. Some members of the medical profession opined that mental work would adversely affect women's reproductive organs, render them unfit for motherhood, and so lead inexorably to the decline of the species. The pioneers of girls' schools and women's colleges required indomitable resolution in the face of prejudice and opposition, not all of which came from men.

Alfred, Lord Tennyson, focused on male prejudice when he wrote *The Princess* (1847), a narrative poem which tells of the foundation of a women's university by the Princess of an imaginary country. In the prologue to the poem a young English girl, Lilia, inspires her brother and his undergraduate friends to improvise the story by expressing a

[ 39 ]

passionate desire to have a university education like theirs, and telling them that modern women would easily equal the heroines of the past, if they were not kept in subjection.

> It is but bringing up, no more than that.
> You men have done it: how I hate you all!
> Ah, were I something great. I wish I were
> Some mighty poetess, I would shame you then
> That love to keep us children. O I wish
> That I were some great Princess I would build
> Far off from men a College like a man's
> And I would teach them all that men are taught.
> We are twice as quick.[2]

Tennyson recognised that many men wanted to do exactly what Lilia complained of, in the belief that uneducated women would make childlike and docile wives (overlooking the fact that throughout history women without formal education have made thralls of men by the power of sex or by innate force of character). However, according to the law, the Churches and tradition, women were subject to their husbands, and probably most of them did not question their condition, or thought it not so much subjection as protection. Such women were shocked and alarmed at the idea of abandoning the cocoon of gentility prescribed by convention, and of accepting new challenges. They were as prejudiced as any man against education for women. For example, Louisa, Duchess of Northumberland, refused to support the proposal to found a 'National Union for the Education of Girls of all Classes above the Elementary', in 1871, with the words, 'The object of all female education *ought* to be to enable a woman to fill her position in after-life – wife, mother, mistress or servant . . .' She added, for good measure, that to encourage girls to aspire to university education 'would be an unmixed evil'.[3]

In the mid-nineteenth century such girls' schools as existed sought only to equip their pupils with conventional accomplishments. They did not even equip them to become wives and mothers; as the pioneer educationist Maria Grey complained, they taught them only to catch husbands.[4] These 'Seminaries for Young Ladies' usually provided lessons in modern languages, drawing and water-colour painting, music and deportment. At the better establishments these subjects might be well taught, but all too frequently the young ladies entered adulthood with a smattering of some of these subjects and a mastery of none – except, perhaps, deportment. Most upper- and middle-class girls, however, were taught at home, by governesses who were following the only profession open to impoverished gentlewomen, and who were seldom very well educated themselves, since their own opportunities had been no better.

A girl's best chance of acquiring some education was to possess a liberal father who would permit her to share her brothers' early lessons, and would not discourage her from self-education thereafter. Some of the cultivated women who interested themselves in girls' education in the later nineteenth century were the products of autodidacticism and their fathers' libraries. Among such women were the daughters of Admiral Shireff, Emily Shireff and Maria Grey, who on the basis of their own experience wrote *Thoughts on Self Culture addressed to Women* (1850), the first of their many works on the subject. Elizabeth Wordsworth, daughter of Christopher Wordsworth, Bishop of Lincoln, and first Principal of Lady Margaret Hall, discovered the joy of learning through her scholarly father's need for an amanuensis. The fortunate few naturally desired to share their advantages with others, and they sought to create the opportunities by founding schools and colleges.

When Tennyson wrote *The Princess* the higher education of women was already a topic of ardent interest, but as yet no women's college existed. The following year Queen's College, Harley Street, was founded by The Revd F. D. Maurice and the Governesses' Benevolent Institution, with the aim of educating girls to become well qualified governesses and of raising the status of the profession. Then in 1849 the Ladies' College, Bedford Square, was founded by Mrs Elisabeth Reid, a remarkable Unitarian feminist. However, as both these institutions took girls from the age of twelve, neither was a women's college in the modern sense of the term. As the century ended their courses diverged, with Queen's College becoming a girls' school and the Ladies' College shedding its younger pupils and becoming Bedford College, a constituent school of London University.

The pioneers of women's education recognised that schools were as important as colleges, for the pupils of governesses and Ladies' Seminaries were not equipped to begin university education at the same standard as their brothers, who had attended boys' public schools and grammar schools. Beginnings were made with the founding of the North London Collegiate for girls in 1850 and Cheltenham Ladies' College in 1853. The Schools Inquiry Commission of 1864-8 revealed the generally abysmal condition of girls' education and stimulated the foundation of the Girls' Public Day School Company (later Trust), which from 1873 onwards established thirty-eight efficient High Schools for girls, which prepared them to university standard at fees within the reach of less prosperous middle-class parents. These schools presented a majority of the candidates for the women's colleges, and received many of their graduates back again as teachers.

The first women's college which attempted to provide its students with the same education as male undergraduates at Cambridge was the Women's College, Hitchin, which was founded by Miss Emily Davies with six students in 1869 and moved to Girton in 1873. Newnham College, Cambridge, was founded in 1871 by Professor Henry Sidgwick, also a great reformer of the whole system of education within the University. It began with five students, under the principalship of Miss Anne Clough, sister of the poet Arthur Hugh Clough, whose tongue-twisting but inspiring line 'say not the struggle naught availeth' might have seemed apposite to her own efforts. Women's colleges at Oxford followed, with Somerville and Lady Margaret Hall both founded in 1879, each with nine students.

Thomas Holloway doubtless followed these developments in women's education as they were reported in the newspapers, and may have discussed with Jane the foundations which were made before her death in 1875. But once he had resolved to found a women's college himself, he recognised his need for expert advice. He had no contacts with the academic world, and knew none of the pioneers of women's education. Wisely, he turned to a friend of his, James Beal, a successful auctioneer and estate agent, who had been active in local politics in Westminster for many years, and whose acquaintance included politicians and educationists. On Holloway's behalf, Beal invited a number of them to a meeting at Holloway's Oxford Street offices on 10 February 1875.

Among those who came were Millicent Fawcett, more famous for her work for women's suffrage, but also an enthusiast for women's education and at this time actively involved with the development of Newnham, and Maria Grey, of whose work Holloway was obviously ignorant, as he had asked James Beal, 'Will you have the goodness to let me know who and what she is?' Millicent Fawcett's sister, Dr Elizabeth Garrett Anderson, was also invited, and so was Emily Davies, who was their close friend. Thomas Holloway subsequently corresponded with Emily Davies, and even tried to tempt her away from Girton with an invitation to become the first Principal of his College. James Beal also invited some male supporters of women's education: Sir James Kay-Shuttleworth, whose chief interest was in the vocational training of teachers, and Joshua Fitch, who had assisted in the foundation of Girton and of the GPDST, and two MPs, Samuel Morley and David Chadwick, both of whom became Governors of the College. Chadwick brought The Revd William Hague, one of the Trustees of Vassar College which had opened ten years previously in North America, at Poughkeepsie in New York State.

Thomas Holloway, who was so confident in matters pertaining to his own business, addressed this distinguished gathering with some humility, freely admitting his ignorance of the work he had undertaken. 'I know nothing, or next to nothing,' he said, 'as to the requirements or the working of a College for ladies, and . . . it is for this reason that I invite your kind co-operation in furnishing suggestions, which, if I am wise enough to follow, I trust I shall leave behind me a monument not only of my work alone, but of your work also . . . I would wish that academic honours should be open to ladies in this College, and that they should have within their reach . . . either an MA, a DA, or earn a "Double First" . . .'[5]

He then spoke of the grand building which he planned, presented W. H. Crossland to his audience, and requested him to lay out his plan for their comments and suggestions. This plan must have undergone considerable changes after Thomas Holloway had abandoned his intention to found a hospital for incurables and decided to found a college. It was not the close copy of Chambord which Crossland and Holloway's accounts of their visit to the Château would suggest. In this prototype of the plan for the College Crossland had incorporated details from Blois, Fountainebleau, Azay-le-Rideau and the New Louvre, besides Chambord.[6]

If Crossland had misgivings at submitting his plans for general suggestions, he was fully justified. He later complained that 'certain highly educated ladies advised Holloway to do exactly what they would have done had they possessed the financial resources: to visit the men's colleges at Cambridge, and incorporate the lessons of their design into his plans. This advice Holloway initially accepted. In April he and Crossland spent a fortnight in Cambridge, when an entirely new plan was drawn, modelled according to Holloway on Trinity College, 'a pretty little gate with a belfrey on top which stands on the right side of St John's College', and 'some other interesting bits suitable to the period . . . taken from other colleges'.[7] But all this work was abortive because Holloway soon went down with a 'low fever', and while he was ill, Crossland recorded, 'the influence of the learned ladies lost its effect. At my earnest solicitation Mr Holloway returned to the Renaissance.'[8] Crossland had obeyed Holloway's temporary wishes with misgivings, and was obviously delighted to revert to his own ideas. In his final plans Crossland reinstated the ascendancy of Chambord and the other French châteaux, though one contribution made by a 'learned lady' was incorporated: this was Millicent Fawcett's suggestion that each student should have two rooms of her own, a generous provision for which students up to the Second World War owed her a debt of gratitude.

Of all those who attended the meeting on 10 February 1875, the one who impressed Holloway most profoundly was Dr Hague of Vassar. Holloway sought a second meeting with him on 13 February, before he returned to America. From him Holloway must have heard with astonishment some account of Matthew Vassar, the Founder of the American College, whose career bore an extraordinary similarity to his own. Vassar, Holloway's senior by a few years, had been born in England in 1794, the son of a Norfolk tenant farmer who emigrated with his family to America, where he encountered many tribulations and never attained more than a modest prosperity. Matthew Vassar aspired to real wealth, and after early vicissitudes he amassed an immense fortune as a brewer. Like Holloway he married and remained childless, and probably for this reason turned in later life to philanthropy. In his instance the inspiration came on a tour of England in 1845, when he visited Guy's Hospital, from whose Founder, Sir Thomas Guy, he claimed descent. His first intention was to emulate his ancestor and found a hospital, in his adoptive country; but later he decided to found a women's college, influenced in the first place by his niece, Lydia Booth, who kept a seminary for young ladies, and said to him, with a simplicity reminiscent of Jane Holloway's reported plea to her husband, 'Uncle Matthew, do something for women.'[9]

The deciding influence, however, was probably that of Professor Milo P. Jewett, who became the first President of Vassar College, a passionate advocate of the higher education of women, and a difficult and demanding colleague, who fell out with Vassar and was obliged to resign before the College opened. (Hague would no doubt have glossed over this distressing episode in his conversations with Holloway). Vassar, like Holloway, thought and planned slowly, appeared indecisive, but once he had reached a decision, acted with vigour. His College was founded in 1861, and the aspirations he expressed on that occasion will be discussed later in this chapter, in conjunction with the Foundation Deed of Thomas Holloway's College. Vassar donated an estate of 200 acres for the site of his foundation, and provided magnificent buildings designed by a distinguished architect, James Renwick Jnr, who derived his inspiration from French models, in this instance the Tuileries and the New Louvre. Vassar College opened in 1865 with some 300 students; by 1875 their numbers had risen to 420. The Founder secured from the New York State Legislature the right for his College to confer 'such honors, degrees and diplomas as are granted by any university, college or seminary of learning in the United States'.[10] It must have been a cause of great regret to Thomas Holloway that Matthew Vassar had died in 1868; to have exchanged ideas with him would have been of unrivalled value, but the College which embodied his ideas was an inspiration in itself.

In 1875 Vassar College was far in advance of existing English institutions, especially in the matter of degrees. The students of the embryonic women's colleges at Cambridge were grudgingly and unofficially permitted to take the degree examinations, but Cambridge did not officially confer degrees on women until 1948. The same situation applied when the Oxford women's colleges were founded, but Oxford adapted itself a little sooner, conferring degrees on women in 1920. London University, as a younger and more liberal foundation, opened its degrees to women in 1878. But when Thomas Holloway expressed the desire that 'academic honours should be open to ladies in this college', Vassar offered the precedent which inspired him, just as Vassar provided the working model of the large and opulent style of institution which he intended to create.

[ 45 ]

He was, naturally enough, rather envious of Vassar's success. 'I hope we shall be able to beat Vassar into fits,' he wrote to David Chadwick. 'It shall not be my fault if we don't.'[11]

At the very time when Holloway received his information from Dr Hague, George Martin was travelling in America on behalf of Holloway's business, and Holloway asked him to visit Vassar College and report on it. Since George Martin lived at Tittenhurst he must have reported verbally on his return. However, he may have been the author of *A Visit to Vassar College* by 'A Business Man out of Harness', which appeared in *The Queen, The Lady's Magazine*, in July 1875. This Business Man was very impressed at being taken to dine in Hall by one of Matthew Vassar's nephews, meeting the 'lady professors' and seeing 'long rows of snowy lawn, and brilliant crystal and fine flowers . . . bordered with young girls fifteen to twenty one years, and a flood of talk fills the great hall'. He admired the Museum, Library and Picture Gallery (all features which were reproduced in Thomas Holloway's foundation) and had an interview with the President of Vassar College, Dr John H. Raymond. The following year Dr Raymond sent Thomas Holloway a newly published *Historical Sketch of Vassar College*, with a personal inscription. George Martin, whether he wrote the piece in *The Queen* or not, was received by Dr Raymond, and returned full of enthusiasm. He suggested that Holloway should purchase a picture collection for his College, as Vassar had done for his; this suggestion Holloway ultimately accepted, but the smooth progress of his plans was disrupted by the death of his wife in September 1875.

Jane Holloway had suffered from a weak heart for some time, but the immediate cause of her death was bronchitis. Holloway was so deeply affected by it that for a time he seemed to lose interest in all his plans. He ceased to correspond with the educationists he had met in February, though hitherto he had maintained contact with several of them. Even his business correspondence was neglected, and Henry Driver wrote a number of letters on his behalf, apologising for Holloway's inability to answer them himself. Work on the Sanatorium was overseen by George Martin, but progress on the College came to a temporary halt. Crossland, however, may have been glad to work under less pressure than before. He took the opportunity of revisiting the French châteaux before completing his plans. In 1876 Holloway handed over the responsibility for completing the College to three trustees: George Martin, Henry Driver and David Chadwick.

At the beginning of 1877 he was still desolated by Jane's death, and on 12 January he wrote in his diary: 'This is the thirty-seventh anniversary of my marriage with poor, dear Jane . . . I kissed her marble bust today in memory of her.'[12]

During the ensuing weeks he was chiefly preoccupied with ordering Jane's tomb and arranging her final interment in the extension of Sunninghill churchyard. The tomb was a simple chest of red granite with side panels of white Portland stone on which the inscriptions were to be carved. It was intended for Jane, Thomas's sister Matilda Holloway, who had died in 1867, and ultimately for Thomas himself. After Jane's coffin had been disinterred and placed in it, Holloway and George Martin went to visit the tomb. 'We were both much affected,' wrote Holloway, 'in contemplating that the dear One's body was only a few yards from us.' Though the College was intended to be her memorial, it was some time before his interest in it revived.

Early in March he caught a bad cold which soon turned to bronchitis, and in his depressed condition he probably expected that it would kill him as it had killed 'poor, dear Jane'. He was cared for with remarkable devotion by George Martin who, he said, 'watched me night and day, feeling my pulse and giving me what is necessary'. In his diary he noted that he had swallowed beef tea, a preparation of horseradish, and a tonic prescribed by Dr Lee, the husband of his niece, Caroline. The fact that the doctor was a member of his extended family may have helped to overcome his suspicion of the medical profession, but the tonic did him no good. George Martin prescribed tumblersful of champagne, which were pleasanter if not more efficacious. Thomas dosed himself with morphia pills and Seidlitz powders. His own Pills he did not take, which may be his silent judgement of their efficacy.

Gradually he improved, and on his birthday, 22 September, he pro-claimed himself '77 years of age – in excellent health and spirits'. But this was a brave old man's optimism; he had not recovered his former vigour and did not regain it. Henry Driver took increasing responsibility for his business, and George Martin spent almost every day at the Sanatorium. The rich interior decoration of the Sanatorium's great hall was now being painted, and Holloway noted some details concerning it in his diary. His interest in his projects was reviving. During the autumn he spent several days going over the plans of the College with Crossland. The site on Mount Lee was not level, and a good deal of preparation was required before the building could begin. The first brick of the College was laid on 12 September 1879, but it was George Martin not Thomas Holloway who laid it. According to Crossland, during the building of the College Holloway only visited the site four times, though almost daily 'he was accustomed to drive past and view the progress from a distance'.[13] From that distance, however, he displayed his characteristically exacting attention to detail, and any outside interference with his plans irritated him intensely. For instance, Holloway decided that the College estate should be surrounded by a wall, and in order to help him decide on the design, he caused the contractor to build short samples of different styles of wall, one with railings, and the other a solid brick wall with a stone coping. Some residents of the neighbouring village of Englefield Green wrote to Holloway expressing the hope that he would not choose the ugly brick wall, but the more elegant one with railings. Holloway's response was to say to the contractor: 'Put the brick wall.'[14]

This illuminating little anecdote was remembered by Charles W. Carey, who met Thomas Holloway and George Martin in 1881 and also recorded his impression of the building as it appeared at that date:

> ... the walls were high enough to show its great size. With the surrounding forest of scaffolding it appeared larger than it really was. Only a partial view of the building could be obtained from the high road. The whole length of the front boundary ... was taken up with stonemasons' sheds, with machinery for cutting and carving the stone, operated by some of the nine hundred stonemasons employed there ...[15]

Carey was a young artist who had just finished his training at the Royal Academy Schools, and the meeting took place when he came to see Thomas Holloway's pictures at Tittenhurst. Young Mr Carey arrived at a fortunate moment for his future career: Thomas Holloway was about to begin buying the picture collection specifically intended for his College, and of this collection Carey was appointed curator in 1887, a post which he held until his death in 1943.

As previously mentioned, the suggestion that Holloway should purchase a picture collection for his College was made by George Martin
after his visit to Vassar, and he was probably inspired by the fact that
this was what Matthew Vassar had done. When Vassar first decided to
provide a picture collection for his College, he began by commissioning
copies of Italian Old Masters, but it was soon explained to him that a
collection of original paintings would have far greater aesthetic value
than one of copies, however well executed they might be. Accepting that
he had no knowledge of art, Matthew Vassar bought intact the collection
of The Revd Elias L. Magoon, the nucleus of which was a collection of
modern American landscape paintings, highly appropriate to ornament
his College and develop the artistic sensibilities of young American
women. This may have given Thomas Holloway the idea that his
collection, made for similar purposes, should be composed chiefly of
modern British paintings. Vassar's collection was listed in full in the
*Historical Sketch of Vassar College* sent to Holloway in 1876. There were
133 oil paintings, of which the American artists would doubtless have
been unfamiliar to Holloway. These were followed by a list of 254
water-colours and drawings, amongst which were works by a number of
British artists also included in Holloway's collections. These were Sidney
Cooper, Copley Fielding, Clarkson Stanfield and Turner. The favoured
subjects in Vassar's collection were landscapes and historical scenes, for
which Holloway also showed preference; but the Vassar collection also
contained some religious subjects, and these Holloway avoided in buying
for the College, though his personal collection included some religious
pictures.

Holloway, like Matthew Vassar, made no claim to be a connoisseur,
but he had always enjoyed looking at pictures, as his visits to galleries
on his foreign travels, and his purchase of Captain Dingwall's collection,
testified. He found a new interest in learning more about pictures as he
built up the collection for his College, a representative collection of
somewhat conservative Victorian taste. As his health was no longer robust
he chose the easiest method of collecting, which was to buy at auctions.
He would study Christie's catalogues and then send George Martin to
view the pictures for which he intended to bid.

'In May 1881 he made his first purchases at Christie's salerooms,'
wrote Mr Carey, in a short memoir. 'From that time he continued to

buy at every sale of note until the end of Christie's season 1883. Having first viewed the pictures and made his selection he sent Mr Martin to bid, giving him freedom to use his judgment in regard to price.'[16] Mr Carey often accompanied George Martin to Christie's, and no doubt his trained eye was helpful in assisting Holloway and Martin to choose good pictures, though he was too modest to claim that he had influenced them.

At the first sale in May 1881 Holloway paid £18,847 for five pictures. These were Millais' *The Princess in the Tower*, Creswick's *Trentside*, two pictures by Clarkson Stanfield, *View of the Pic du Midi d'Ossau, with Brigands* and *The Battle of Roveredo*, and Landseer's *Man Proposes, God Disposes*. It is pure speculation that Holloway may have been attracted to Clarkson Stanfield because he is represented in Vassar's collection; both the pictures by him are impressive mountain landscapes in which the foreground figures are dwarfed by the splendour of the scenery. The Landseer is a desolate arctic scene in which polar bears savage the remains of a shipwreck, tearing a tattered ensign and gnawing human bones. This picture was inspired by the loss of Sir John Franklin's expedition in search of the North West Passage, in 1845-7. Later expeditions discovered evidence of Franklin's fate, and the whole tragedy and its aftermath attracted a great deal of attention in the Press. Thomas Holloway had been fascinated by the story and had collected newspaper cuttings about it, so it seems likely that interest in the subject rather than aesthetic considerations led him to buy this impressive but unpleasant picture. The price was £6,615, and at that time a record price for a Landseer.

The *Art Journal* reported this purchase with great interest, declaring that the high prices of all the pictures 'were the result of a *carte blanche* having been given to the auctioneers, to buy them for a well-known philanthropist at any price'. Holloway concealed his identity for some time, while George Martin bid under the name of 'Thomas', 'Martin' or 'Mason', and excitement continued to be aroused by the high prices paid. £6,615 was reached again when Holloway bought *The Babylonian Marriage Market* by Edwin Long in May 1882. This picture, inspired by current interest in Babylonian antiquities and illustrating a passage from Herodotus, shows an auction of women. The Babylonian maidens, according to Herodotus, were auctioned to their husbands, the pretty girls being sold for high prices, in order of beauty, the ugly girls provided with dowries from the money the pretty ones had raised, thus ensuring that everyone was paired off – ugly girls and poor men, as well as the beautiful and the rich. When Holloway's identity and the purpose of his collection were revealed, *The Babylonian Marriage Market* was thought an extremely odd choice for a women's college.

Holloway received some adverse criticism for inflating the art market and for buying pictures at auction instead of from the artists themselves; but the fact that he had plenty of money, and little time left to him, were reasons enough. Edwin Long, at least, bore him no resentment. He wrote to Holloway 'to say how gratified I feel at the handsome way in which you have purchased my two pictures, and that they are to be placed in your noble collection'.[18] (The other picture by Long is *The Suppliants: Expulsion of the Gypsies from Spain*, bought in 1882 for £4,305).

When *The Babylonian Marriage Market* was first shown at the Royal Academy in 1875 (with accompanying explanation) it was ecstatically admired. Ruskin declared that it was worthy to be purchased by the Anthropological Society. Apart from choosing pictures for their interest, Holloway liked to rely on their good reception at the Academy. Both these considerations may have led him to choose Luke Fildes' great 'social realism' painting, *Applicants for Admission to a Casual Ward*, which aroused such intense excitement when it was exhibited at the Academy in 1874 that a barrier had to be placed round it and a policeman stationed beside it to protect it from the pressure of the crowd. Part of its fascination was that it was a shocking picture, in its unsparing depiction of poverty, but it was also a compassionate portrayal of the London poor, like some great descriptive passage by Dickens translated into paint. Frith's crowded panorama of modern life, *The Railway Station*, was not an Academy picture, but it had been hung in three international exhibitions before Holloway bought it for a mere £2,000. The comparatively low price was probably explained by the fact that Holloway could not secure the copyright of the picture, and a great number of engravings of it had been sold before it came into his hands. There are also other versions of it, as Frith had a penchant for repainting his favourite works.[19]

Besides buying these large-scale highly dramatic pictures, Holloway consistently chose landscapes and seascapes by a variety of distinguished English and Scottish artists, including Sidney Cooper, Copley Fielding,

Naysmith and MacWhirter. *Carthillon Cliffs* by John Brett is the only Pre-Raphaelite painting in the collection, but it is uncertain whether the absence of others is deliberate or fortuitous. Availability obviously had its effect on Holloway's purchasing. (Millais had been one of the original members of the Pre-Raphaelite Brotherhood, but the two Millais paintings in the Holloway collection, *The Princes in the Tower* and *Princess Elizabeth in Prison*, belong to his later style). In the end Holloway did not abide by his first plan of purchasing only works by British artists. Various European painters are represented in the collection, including Ludwig Munthe, Achille Noel, Constant Troyon and Tito Conti. Of Holloway's collection Mr Carey observed that it was remarkable how in the space of two years 'observation and experience soon broadened his view . . . [and] . . . he developed a proficiency for selecting pictures not only good in themselves but which raised the character of the whole Collection.'[20] A Constable, two Morlands, a splendid Turner sea painting, *Van Tromp Going About to Please his Masters*, and a lyrical Gainsborough, *Peasants Going to Market – Early Morning*, were all among his later purchases. The Gainsborough, which shows a procession of girls and young men, mounted on rough ponies, silhouetted against a luminous morning sky, was the last picture that he bought.[21]

The collection totalled seventy-seven pictures and, when hung, filled the Recreation Hall of the College, which became the Picture Gallery, though it had not been designed for that purpose. It has been conjectured that Holloway may have intended to build a separate Picture Gallery, as was done at Dulwich College, but there is no evidence to support this surmise, though it is often repeated. The Recreation Hall was not perfectly suited to its new use, as its walls were ornamented with pilasters which made the hanging of the large pictures difficult. The problem was solved by the artist Briton Riviere, who simply recommended the removal of the pilasters. Riviere is represented in the collection by two pictures, one of which is the famous and ever-popular *Sympathy*, which shows a little girl in disgrace, sitting on the stairs, her sympathetic dog resting its head on her shoulder.

By the summer of 1883 Thomas Holloway was a very frail old man and, perhaps with the premonition that time was running out for him, he turned his attention to drawing up the Foundation Deed of his College, which was executed on 11 October. He had had the opportunity of reading in *The Historical Sketch of Vassar College*, sent him in 1876, the speech made by the Founder to the Trustees of the projected College in 1861; and the Foundation Deed of his own College reveals his indebtedness to the ideas which Matthew Vassar had expressed.

It occurred to me [Matthew Vassar had said] that woman, having received from her Creator the same intellectual constitution as man has the same right to intellectual culture and development.

I considered that the mothers of a country mould the character of its citizens, determine its institutions, and shape its destiny.

Next to the influence of the mother is that of the female teacher, who is employed to train young children at a period when impressions are most vivid and lasting.

It also seemed to me, that if women were properly educated, some new avenues of useful and honourable employment . . . might be opened to her . . .

To be somewhat more specific in my views as to the character and aims of the College: I wish that the course of study should embrace at least the following particulars. The English Language and its Literature; other modern languages; the Ancient Classics, so far as may be demanded by the spirit of the times; the Mathematics . . . all branches of Natural Science . . . Intellectual Philosophy; the elements of Political Economy . . . Moral Science . . . Aesthetics . . . to be illustrated by an extensive gallery of Art . . . last, and most important of all, the daily, systematic Reading and Study of the Holy Scriptures . . .

All sectarian influences should be carefully excluded; but the training of our students should never be intrusted to the skeptical, the irreligious, or the immoral . . .

I desire that the College may be provided with commodious buildings, containing ample apartments for public instruction, and at the same time affording to the inmates the safety, quiet, privacy and purity of the family.[22]

There was much in this which evidently appealed to Thomas Holloway, and reinforced his ideas where it did not actually form them. For example, his own anti-clerical but not irreligious outlook accorded with that of the Baptist Vassar on the importance of avoiding sectarianism yet ensuring a Christian ethos. He was less confident than Vassar in giving his views on curriculum, but equally certain that courses of study should reflect both traditional and modern influences. According to his Foundation Deed:

> The Founder believes that the education of women should not be exclusively regulated by the traditions and methods of former ages; but that it should be founded on those studies and sciences which the experience of modern times has shown to be the most valuable and best adapted to meet the intellectual and social requirements of the students . . .

His religious views, and provisions, were summed up as follows:

> The Founder, during the whole of his life, has witnessed the hand of God in all things, and it is his earnest desire that the religious teaching of the College, though free from any sectarian influence, shall be such as to inspire most forcibly in the minds of the students their individual responsibility, and their duty to God.
>
> It is the Founder's desire that the domestic life of the College should be that of an orderly Christian household, and with this view he directs that the lady principal shall, every morning during the College sessions, conduct in the presence of the students a simple religious service, consisting of a psalm or hymn, and reading a portion of Holy Scripture . . .

Like Vassar, Holloway stressed the value of collegiate life and expressed, somewhat vaguely, some hope for the professional lives of the students thereafter:

> The Founder attaches just importance to the companionship and discipline of a collegiate life, and he has therefore made simple provision for the residence of the students in the College . . .
>
> It is the express and earnest desire of the Founder that the College shall neither be considered nor conducted as a mere training College for teachers and governesses . . .

[ 54 ]

Thomas Holloway made no reference to the maternal role in his Foundation Deed, where it would have been out of place, but he had written in a letter to David Chadwick: 'Most of us who do well, are greatly indebted, in early youth, to the teaching and training of our mothers – and how much better it might be to the human family if mothers of the next generation should possess a high class education.'[23]

Holloway's highest aspiration, expressed in the Foundation Deed, was that 'powers by Act of Parliament, Royal Charter, or otherwise, should ultimately be sought, enabling the College to confer degrees on its students'. This power Vassar College had possessed from the outset, and no women's college in Britain ever has possessed; it would have conferred upon Holloway's foundation the status of a women's university, which was what he desired. His generous intention was to provide for women a type of institution which hitherto had existed only for men; but most of the supporters of higher education for women doubted the benefits of such a development. They believed that if a women's university were founded and empowered to grant its own degrees, the intellectual equality of women with men would remain unproved, and their attainments, when not in competition with men, would still be dismissed as inferior. The controversy regarding the desirability of founding a women's university, and as an aspect of that controversy, the smaller question of the desirability of implementing the wish of Thomas Holloway, was not resolved until some years after his death.

Thomas Holloway died on 26 December 1883, and it is to be hoped that he died content, in the knowledge that his work would be completed under the capable direction of George Martin. In his last Will, dated on the same day as the Foundation Deed of the College, 11 October 1883, he left everything, his business, his freehold properties, and £550,061.8s.2d. to his sister-in-law, Mary Ann Driver. He had previously vested in the Trustees of the College £300,000, one third for the completion of the College and two thirds for its endowment. Henry Driver, who now assumed by Deed Poll the surname Driver-Holloway, took over the business, which, without Thomas's overseeing eye, began a slow decline.[24] George Martin took the name of Martin-Holloway, and dedicated himself to the completion of the Sanatorium and the College with a zeal and an ability little short of Thomas Holloway's own. After Holloway's death it was revealed that the Sanatorium and the College

[ 55 ]

were not the limits of his philanthropy: his obituary in *The Times* reported that he had given large, anonymous donations to many charities.

Holloway had lived long enough to see the College building completed, and Crossland recorded his satisfaction with it: 'He never, or perhaps very seldom, praised anyone. There was, however, one exception. When on his third visit to the College after its completion, he once again, after six years, patted me on the back and said *"Well* done, Mr Crossland, I am more than pleased".'[25]

He had every reason to be pleased with Crossland's masterpiece when the surrounding scaffolding was stripped away and the huge building stood revealed in its pristine splendour. When it was new the contrasting materials of white Portland stone and 'still flaming red brick . . . fairly scorched the eye'.[26] Mellowed by a century of weather and atmosphere pollution it is still astonishing, and the bold effect of its colouring is enhanced by its sheer size. The building forms a rectangle, 376 feet from east to west, by 526 feet from north to south. The longitudinal blocks are six storeys high, including the attics, and are connected at either end and in the middle by three latitudinal blocks, thus dividing the building into two quadrangles, each measuring 250 feet by 182 feet. The latitudinal blocks each comprise a central tower and two long, rectangular rooms. In the centre of the north block is the Clock Tower (or North Tower), which rises above the main entrance with the Chapel on the east and the Picture Gallery on the west; in the centre of the middle block is the octagonal Water Tower, with the Dining Hall on the east and the kitchen on the west; in the centre of the south block is the South Tower, which rises above the southern entrance, with the Library on the west and the Museum (now a continuation of the Library) on the east. As the site slopes to the south, there is a lower ground floor below the Library and Museum which, when the College was opened, was divided into twelve music rooms, beneath the Museum, and a Gymnasium, beneath the Library. The longitudinal ranges of the build-ing (known as East and West respectively) are traversed from end to end by corridors ten feet wide and one tenth of a mile in length. Three hundred sets of rooms, arranged in pairs, one on each side of the corridors, were designed to provide lodging of two rooms each – a study and a bedroom – for students and staff, besides space for bathrooms, sitting rooms, maids' rooms and pantries. Each room destined to be a

[ 56 ]

study had an open fireplace, while the bedrooms were unheated. (The College is said to have been designed with approximately one thousand rooms, but of course the number is constantly fluctuating as partitions are put up and taken down).

At the four corners of the building are Pavilions 'marked by circular projections – bastions we may call them in the case of the French château, turrets in that of Mr Crossland's College'.[27] The rooms inside the Pavilions are characterised by the delightful rounded extensions within these turrets, which in College parlance have always been known as 'bulges'. Beneath the south-western Pavilion is the main Lecture Theatre of the College, above which are the Principal's rooms. Other suites of rooms, intended for professors and heads of departments, were originally situated in the North and South Towers. The layout of the College is very simple, but inconvenient in two ways: it is impossible to traverse the College from east to west without going outside and through the cloisters which line the latitudinal blocks of the building on both quadrangles, or along the balconies above the cloisters; and it is imposs-ible to go from one quadrangle to the other without re-entering the building. In the early years of the College it was indeed possible to walk from west to east by way of the Library and Museum, but the disturbance of constant traffic through the Library increased as the community grew in size. The route is now closed, and as a result a latent fault in the design has become a positive inconvenience. An alternative east to west route, by way of the balcony above the south cloister of the north quadrangle, has been glassed-in to give protection from the weather.

This lack of thought for convenience in the design of the College is all the more curious in contrast with the care which Crossland expended in designing its service arrangments for the maximum convenience of the residents. The service buildings of the College – an engine house, laundry, gas works, coal and wood stores – were built approximately 300 yards to the east of it, and connected to the College by a tunnel through which all fuel and other supplies were to be brought.[28] An early description of the College gave this explanation.

The staff of porters and other workmen employed upon this service, upon the management of the steam heating apparatus – for the whole building is to be warmed by pipes as well as fire – upon the conveyance of linen to and from the laundry, upon the removal of refuse, and upon the introduction of provisions, will of course be of considerable strength, and the subway is intended to do away with the necessity of their continual presence in the quadrangle.[29]

With the seclusion of the service buildings and the concealment of their work-force, nothing detracted from the dramatic impression of the College building, isolated on its hilltop, where its 'countless mansardes, conical roofs, dormers, many-pinnacled towers, and tall elaborate chimneys'[30] were silhouetted against the sky. In the century of its existence the surrounding trees have grown so tall that the building is far less dominant than it was at first, and its details are only visible at close quarters. The closer the approach, the more remarkable the details appear, for the building is rich in sculpture and ornament.

'The subject which I have most at heart,' wrote Crossland, 'is the unity which should, I think, exist between architect and sculptor in all works of importance.'[31] Crossland found his ideal collaborator in the Italian sculptor Ceccardo Fucigna, who had previously worked with Crossland's old master, Sir George Gilbert Scott. Fucigna was responsible for designing all the sculpture and ornamentation, which was executed by himself and his assistants, in Portland stone.

Dominating the whole building is the openwork crown on the summit of the central tower, 'a renaissance parallel to the crown of St Giles' Cathedral in Edinburgh'.[32] On each rib of the crown a white stone crocodile pauses forever in the act of descent, and at the foot of each is poised a stork. Below these crouch eight winged lions, one at each angle of the octagon. 'These animals may not, perhaps, have any special fitness for their places beyond one of shape, but they are happily allied to the architecture . . .'[33] and this same blend of the bizarre and the fitting characterises the sculpture throughout the College.

The chief sculptures are the reliefs in the four pediments above the entrances to the residential parts of the College from the quadrangles. These are allegorical figures of Commerce and Medicine on the east of the north quadrangle, and of Poetry and Science on the west. In the south quadrangle Charity and Education on the west face a portrait bust of the Founder, supported by Surrey and Agriculture on the east. A series of heads form the keystones of the Chapel and Picture Gallery windows, and of the arches above the main entrance, through the North Tower. The heads above the central arch are, appropriately, Minerva, Goddess of Wisdom on the outside, and Hope on the inside. The keystones of the Chapel windows are, on the outside, Christ, St John, St Peter and St Paul, and on the inside Pope Julius II, Muhammad, Confucius and Savonarola. Above the outside windows of the Picture Gallery are heads of Handel, Rossini, Schiller and Machiavelli, and on the inside Dante, Aeschylus, Molière and Shakespeare. The scriptural and allegorical personages are obvious choices, but the other worthies are an odd selection. Most curious of all is that in a women's college, heads of famous women were not represented: the Mother of Christ and some female saints and Old Testament heroines might have adorned the Chapel, and, for example, Sappho, Hypatia, Boadicea and Queen Elizabeth I would have been as appropriate as the chosen men!

Men also predominate in Fucigna's scheme of decoration in the interior of the Chapel. The figures which adorn the ceiling, 'modelled in very bold relief, after the manner of the work of Primaticcio at Fontainebleau', in the words of Crossland's description, are 'on the south side Samuel and the four major prophets, with attendant figures, and on the north side St John the Baptist and the four evangelists with their emblems . . . The waggon vault of the ceiling . . . is divided into panels by longitudinal and transverse belts . . . and in the panel spaces thus formed are circular medallions containing figures of the six Archangels – the Saints Chamael, Gabriel, Michael, Raphael, Uriel and Zadkiel, with their distinctive attributes.'[34] The reliefs were coloured with oil paint, the colour being worked into the hollows of draperies and then rubbed off the more salient surfaces, to avoid an effect of heaviness. Crossland thought that 'the general scale of colour obtained by these means is not unlike that of the Sixtine Chapel'.[35]

A further attempt to imitate the Sistine Chapel was the relief in the semi-dome of the apse, showing the creation of Eve, the only subject with a woman as its principal figure. God the Father extends an omnipotent forefinger to summon Eve into existence, in a gesture reminiscent of Michelangelo's *Creation of Adam*; but with this gesture the resemblance ends, for the relief is a lamentable failure. Fucigna died before the work was finished, and the *Creation of Eve* was completed by his assistant,

Boldini, a markedly inferior artist, and coloured more crudely than the other reliefs. A woman journalist who visited the College a few years later voiced the ridicule which was a common reaction to it:

> Adam – in a state of extreme and painful leanness – is extended in the left corner, evidently far more astonished than pleased at the sight of a pink and portly Eve ... Whether he objects to Eve's super-abundance of adipose tissue, or whether he demurs at taking for his mate a lady with a canary-coloured wig ... is not explained; but the father of the human race ... evidently looks upon the whole affair as a somewhat doubtful joke. In the centre ... is a colossal white rabbit, sitting up in an attitude of the most blankly comical surprise and disapproval I have ever seen depicted in art ... [36]

Fortunately, in the course of a century, the colours have faded and the rabbit has won affection through familiarity.

After the College was completed, three more sculptures were added to its already plentiful supply. A statue of Queen Victoria was commissioned for the north quadrangle (thereafter known as the Queen's Quad), and of Thomas and Jane Holloway for the south quadrangle (thereafter called the Founder's Quad). The sculptor of both was Count Gleichen, the son of Queen Victoria's half-sister, Princess Feodore of Hohenlohe-Langenburg. These sculptures fitted admirably into the general scheme of the College, but the third addition has never been comfortably assimilated. It was *Erinna*, a semi-recumbent and semi-nude woman in white marble, with a distaff drooping from her hand. Erinna was a young Greek poetess, forbidden by her mother to join Sappho and her circle, and kept at home employed to weave and spin. Erinna died of anguish and frustration and the sculptor of the statue, H. S. Leifchild, expressed a dying wish that it should find a home at Royal Holloway College – presumably because it was a place where young women's aspirations would be satisfied. *Erinna* was presented to the College by the sculptor's widow and pupils, but unfortunately there is no natural place for it, and after many years in the Picture Gallery, and a few beside the tennis courts, it now rests, with an appearance of being unwanted, in the cloisters of the Queen's Quad.

The completion of the sculpture and interior decoration, and the furnishing of the College, were overseen by George Martin-Holloway, with as much attention as the Founder himself would have given. At the same time he attended to the last details of the completion of the Sanatorium, which was opened by the Prince and Princess of Wales (the future King Edward VII and Queen Alexandra) on 15 June 1885. The following month George Martin-Holloway wrote to Queen Victoria's private secretary, Sir Henry Ponsonby: 'I take the liberty to inform you that the "Holloway College" for women . . . founded by my late brother-in-law, Thomas Holloway, is now nearly completed, and I have been advised to ask for the Queen's most gracious consent, to open the same . . .'[37]

The advice was probably given by the sculptor Count Gleichen, with whom George Martin-Holloway formed a warm friendship, and who acted as an informal intermediary between himself and royalty. Martin-Holloway's formal request that the Queen should open the College at first met with a curt refusal. Early the following year Count Gleichen exerted his influence to persuade either the Queen or the Princess of Wales to open the College; he cleverly mentioned both, but it was the Queen's agreement he was attempting to obtain:

> It is perfectly unique in its way, being the *first* ladies' college of the sort and one man's work . . . and now that education is all the cry, something ought to be done to bring this magnificent gift before the public . . . it is much too great a thing to be opened by anyone but the Sovereign, or the Princess of Wales.[38]

In March George Martin-Holloway was informed that the Queen had graciously consented to open the College at the end of June. He was, of course, delighted, and when preparations were further advanced he wrote again to Ponsonby:

> It has been suggested to me that in consideration of her Majesty's condescension in opening the College that I should ask permission of the Queen to call it the Royal Holloway College. I should of course be very happy if her Majesty would permit it. Will you kindly help me in this?[39]

[ 61 ]

Perhaps this suggestion was made by Count Gleichen, and he may have used his influence with the Queen; but Martin-Holloway seems to have supposed that he owed her favourable response to the influence of Ponsonby, to whom he wrote elatedly:

> I do not know how to express my great sense of appreciation of this gracious honour but if you will kindly convey the same to the proper quarter you will fulfil my earnest desire and greatly oblige me.[40]

At that moment he was obviously a very happy man, but during the spring of 1886 he ran into unexpected difficulties when he began to seek a group of appropriately distinguished men to become Governors of the College. He had formed more exalted acquaintances than Thomas Holloway had ever possessed, and here again the friendship of Count Gleichen may have been useful to him. He approached Queen Victoria's son-in-law, Prince Christian of Schleswig-Holstein, who lived at Cumberland Lodge in Windsor Great Park, Sir Henry Thring (later Lord Thring), a Parliamentary draftsman who was reputed to have drafted all Mr Gladstone's legislation and who also lived in the locality, the Archbishop of Canterbury, Edward White Benson, and the Dean of Windsor, Randall Davidson, who later became Primate.

None of these four men approved the Founder's requirement that the College should be non-denominational. In the case of Benson and Davidson this was predictable, but the two laymen were equally disapproving. Sir Henry Thring told Ponsonby that he would have 'hesitated to advise her Majesty to sanction such a foundation', but 'as the Queen has undertaken to open the College I most certainly should not recommend any alteration of the plan, but should ignore altogether the deed of foundation and say nothing about it.'[41] Randall Davidson's comment was: 'The more I look at it [the Foundation Deed] the more unworkable does the scheme seem to me to be . . . But it is better than I had supposed . . . though I greatly regret that H. M. should have singled it as *the* place to receive the honour of a royal visit.'[42] However, he accepted to become a Governor, and his comment to The Revd John H. Ellison (who became a Governor in 1915) was: 'We must all do our best to make the thing work.'[43] Archbishop Benson wrote: 'I have heard that the whole scheme is one of non-religious education; but on the other hand I have heard also that it is purposed to alter that character . . .'[44] Once he had been assured that the College was not intended to be a 'Godless College' he consented to become a Governor, and under his influence the College was far more thoroughly permeated by Anglicanism than the Founder would have wished.

As a result of the reservations expressed by Thring, Davidson and Benson (and presumably by Prince Christian, though his first reactions have not been recorded) Ponsonby initiated an intrigue with the intention of securing a Board of Governors to which the Queen, as Head of the Church of England, could with propriety give her support. Since her own religious views were quite unorthodox, she would probably have been indifferent to this consideration, but Sir Henry Ponsonby manipulated her so skilfully that she was unaware of it. He informed her that 'Prince Christian, the Dean of Windsor and others are anxious that Mr Holloway [*sic*] should name the Governors before the opening day'.[45] He then wrote to the Archbishop that if the Queen and Benson himself were both to attend the opening of the College (as Martin-Holloway had requested), 'we must know who are to take charge of the College in the future . . . I would therefore ask whether, in answering his letter, you might say that you have written to me and find that I am not informed as to the Governors, and therefore you would like to know the constitution of the Governing body before answering his request.'[46]

As a result of these machinations, George Martin-Holloway was as worried as Ponsonby expected him to be. He had intended to make a preliminary quest for suitable Governors, but not to be pushed to rapid conclusions. He told Ponsonby quite frankly 'that he thought till the College was opened, that Governors would be a hindrance rather than an aid', but when Ponsonby bluntly informed him 'the Queen cannot open the College unless the Governors are appointed', he had no choice but to complete the selection as rapidly as possible, and to the satisfaction of the group which now controlled the Queen's approval. He told Ponsonby that Thomas Holloway had intended to appoint the Governors himself, but that death had supervened. Martin-Holloway and his co-trustees, Henry Driver-Holloway and David Chadwick were life-Governors.

'We have considered,' he wrote, 'that as the deed of Foundation provides for the filling up of vacancies amongst the Governors by certain corporate bodies that it would be in the best interest of the College to invite these corporations to exercise their privileges.'

Thomas Holloway had believed that to ensure the successful working of the College 'a certain business element' should be represented on the governing body, and, Martin-Holloway wrote, 'I feel that I should not be fulfilling my trust if I did not maintain ... the principles which guided him in this matter'. Four men had already consented to become Governors: Lord Granville, Samuel Morley MP, Mr Alderman Savory, 'a man of position and great energy of character', and Mr Walpole Greenwell who 'for many years was Mr Holloway's chief financial adviser'. In conclusion, he explained, 'There then remains to be nominated a Governor by the Lord President of the Council of the Education Department. One by the Chancellor and Senate of the University of London. One by the Corporation of Windsor and one by the Corporation of Reading. So that there will be little chance of any failure of efficient Governors.'[47]

The additional nominations, some of which were assisted by the good offices of Sir Henry Thring, satisfied the other interested parties. The complete list of the first Board of Governors was:

1.  George Martin-Holloway Esq. ⎱
2.  Henry Driver-Holloway Esq. ⎰ Trustees
3.  David Chadwick Esq. 
4.  HRH Prince Frederick Christian Charles Augustus of Schleswig-Holstein KG.
5.  The Rt Hon the Most Reverend Edward, Lord Archbishop of Canterbury.
6.  The Rt Hon Granville George, Earl Granville KG.
7.  Samuel Morley Esq.
8.  Lord Charles Frederick Brudenell Bruce.
9.  Sir Henry Thring KCB.
10. The Worshipful Richard Copley Christie, Chancellor of the Diocese of Manchester.
11. Joseph Savory Esq., an Alderman of the City of London.
12. Walpole Lloyd Greenwell Esq.[48]

George Martin-Holloway was intensely relieved that the matter was settled, and wholly unaware of the intrigue which had taken place in the background.

On 30 June 1886 Queen Victoria came to open Royal Holloway College, late on a hot summer afternoon. She recorded the occasion in her diary: 'The building is a unique and splendid one ... built and given by Mr Holloway. After he was presented to me, we drove round the whole College ... We then got out and were conducted to the Chapel by Mr Holloway (a very modest man) ...'

George Martin-Holloway, whom the Queen had obviously assumed to be the Founder, had composed an execrable *Ode* in honour of the occasion—

> God bless our Queen, Victoria the Great
> Whose mighty Empire owns an endless day,
> Strengthen her kingdoms and uphold each state
> In faithful unity beneath her sway ...

but sung to Sir George Elvey's setting it sounded splendid enough. The Queen was escorted to the Picture Gallery, of which she received only the vaguest impression, for she remembered having seen Frith's *Derby Day* and a picture by Landseer called *Palace Bears*![49] In the north quadrangle George Martin-Holloway presented to her a gold casket 'surmounted by a portrait model of Thomas Holloway seated in a classic chair', and containing an illuminated address. The Queen accepted it and requested Lord Kimberley to reply on her behalf and declare the College open. While this ceremony was taking place the local populace broke into the south quadrangle and devoured the sumptuous tea which had been set out there for the distinguished guests.[50] In the early evening the Queen drove home to dinner at Frogmore.

After all the excitement George Martin-Holloway developed laryngitis and was unable to speak for a week. No doubt he was suffering from a reaction to it all when he wrote to Ponsonby: 'I intended to ask you if the Queen was pleased with the casket and whether you found out how to open it. It would be gratifying for me to know that it gave her Majesty a moment's pleasure.'[51]

He received his reward the following year, when he was knighted by the Queen at Osborne. Count Gleichen did his best to obtain a baronetcy for him and, having failed, wrote to him: 'My dear Holloway . . . I dare not congratulate you . . . I am too disgusted', which must be unique among letters addressed to new-made knights![52] Sir George Martin-Holloway may have been disappointed, since his social ambitions had once led him to call himself Viscount d'Altenburg, but it is pleasant to record that he received some recognition for completing Thomas Holloway's labours. Thomas Holloway himself had cared nothing for honours, but he would have rejoiced that honour was shown to his work.

PART TWO


# THE EARLY YEARS OF THE COLLEGE
## 1887–1907

# 'ALL HAS BEEN EXPERIMENT'

## The Principalship of
## Miss M. E. Bishop
## 1887–97

> Where all has been experiment, there have necessarily
> been many difficulties and some mistakes; but in
> spite of them I thankfully believe that we have done
> something towards the fulfilment of the Founder's
> desire that the College should be ordered as a Chris-
> tian household . . .[1]

QUEEN VICTORIA'S approval of Royal Holloway College did not
disarm the opponents of higher education for women. A short
while after the official opening a paper appropriately named
*Moonshine* published a little scene which presented in drama-
tised form the effect which education at Royal Holloway College might
be expected to have on a middle-class girl. The scene is set a decade in
the future (ie 1896), when Mr and Mrs Dobbs are seated at breakfast,
enjoying coffee and bacon:

MRS DOBBS:    She is much improved, Samuel. She has grown slim
              and genteel. What a blessing to think there is such an
              institution in this country!

MR DOBBS:     Humph. I saw very little of her last night, but I can't say
              I was very favourably impressed.

*Enter Daisy Selina Dobbs. She makes a low curtsey, then sinks into her seat.*

MRS DOBBS:    How did you sleep, dear?

MISS DOBBS:   The somniferous influences generated by the prevalence
              of carbon in large centres of population is most provoca-

|                |                                                                                                                                                                                                                                                         |
|----------------|---------------------------------------------------------------------------------------------------------------------------------------------------------------------------------------------------------------------------------------------------------|
|                | tive of slumber, yet despite this, my wakefulness was quite too utterly remarkable.                                                                                                                                                                      |
| MR DOBBS:      | Humph.                                                                                                                                                                                                                                                   |
| MRS DOBBS:     | Will you have some coffee, dear?                                                                                                                                                                                                                         |
| MISS DOBBS:    | If your coffee is the unadulterated berry of Mocha, properly pulverized by the *moulin-à-deux-temps* method, I shall have no objection . . . but in no case add any lactael fluid, as that is apt to set up an action inimical . . . to the digestive functions. |
| MR DOBBS:      | That's worth knowing . . .                                                                                                                                                                                                                               |
| MRS DOBBS:     | Will you have some bacon, dear?                                                                                                                                                                                                                          |
| MISS DOBBS:    | No thanks, Ma; if you have any quail on toast, or a grilled kidney, I could regard such matters with complacence.                                                                                                                                        |
| MR DOBBS:      | Oh you could, could you? Now look here, Daisy Selina Dobbs, if you think you are going to come home to this establishment to give yourself airs and graces . . . you're mightily mistaken . . . Bacon's good enough for your mother and me, and bacon will have to be good enough for you . . .[2] |

Behind this laboured humour, in which education, in accordance with immemorial comic tradition, is represented as polysyllabic foolishness, lay genuine hostility and fear: hostility to the imagined luxury of Royal Holloway College, which might introduce a middle-class girl to upper-class standards of living, fear that a girl who received a better education than her parents might cease to respect them. The second consideration lay at the root of the prejudice against higher education for women. If girls left home and lived in women's colleges, and studied subjects beyond the domestic sphere, they might cease to be dutiful daughters who accepted a condition of subservience to their parents from which only marriage could release them or, if they remained unmarried, of perpetual servitude to the whole family. Independence for women, especially single women, was not envisaged as a blessing to a large sector of society, but as a threat to the integrity of family life. Emily Davies recognised the tyranny of the family when she wrote:

> I will try to be respecful to parents, but how is it possible to describe College life without showing how infinitely pleasanter it will be than home: it is a weak point which I am utterly at a loss to defend. I do not believe that our utmost efforts to poison the students' lives at College will make them half so miserable as they are at home.[3]

Fortunately not all Victorian middle-class homes were as miserable as Emily Davies supposed; nor were all parents inimical to women's education for, if they had been, the women's colleges would never have been founded. But if not inimical, they were suspicious, and needed to be persuaded of the advantages of educating their daughters. Economic independence for young women, though initially seen as a threat to the family, could be shown as an advantage if it were presented in appealing terms. An unmarried daughter might be an invaluable factotum, but still a burden to the family economy; a single salaried woman, so long as she continued to acknowledge her obligations to her family, could be a contributor to it.

Emily Davies refused to make concessions to parental prejudice, and modelled her College on the men's colleges, with the Mistress and her one assistant seated at High Table, their six students below, facing them in a self-conscious row. But other Founders and early Principals sought to reassure the parents of potential students, by persuading them that college life would not be so very different from family life, and so would not alienate the students from their parents or their home environment. Thomas Holloway, by stating in the Foundation Deed of his College that he wished its domestic life to be that of 'an orderly Christian household', had provided exactly the right kind of reassurance.

In December 1886 the Governors of Royal Holloway College advertised the post of Lady Principal, who in accordance with the Foundation Deed was to be a single lady, or a widow without issue, under forty years of age. Forty-six applications were received, but the Governors found none of them suitable, and accordingly applied to the Charity Commissioners for permission to remove the age restriction. The post was advertised again on 8 March 1887, and a further twenty-one applications arrived. Eight applicants were shortlisted, and four were interviewed at the Deanery, Windsor. 'They drove over to Englefield Green one by one,' wrote The Revd John H. Ellison. ' . . . I noticed that one in particular was an inch or two taller when she returned from the drive.'[4] The lady whose stature was increased by her appointment was Miss Matilda Ellen Bishop, the Headmistress of Oxford High School.[5]

Miss Bishop was born in 1842, the daughter of a scholarly clergyman who, throughout most of her early life, held the living of Martyr Worthy, near Winchester. He was considered a very conscientious incumbent, though he augmented his income by preparing young men for Oxford and the Army, and still found time to ride to hounds. He sent his daughter to a ladies' seminary in Brighton, where she was obliged to learn long passages of the Bible by heart, and given an excellent grounding in French by 'a gifted although very ill-tempered French lady'.[6] At the age of sixteen she was sent to Queen's College, Harley Street, where she fell deeply under the influence of The Revd F. D. Maurice, who lectured in History and Literature with a strong religious bias. Miss Bishop described him as 'the greatest man I have ever known, the strongest influence of my girlhood, intellectual and spiritual, with a mysterious power . . . too sacred for analysis'.[7] This near-idolatry characterised her attitude to the clergy of the Church of England, and was repeated with almost equal strength during her principalship of Royal Holloway College, when she idolised Archbishop Benson. A broken engagement and a period of housekeeping for her father, between his widowhood and second marriage, preceded her teaching career. At the time of her appointment as Principal of Royal Holloway College she had been Headmistress of Oxford High School since 1879 (in which post she had succeeded Miss Ada Benson, the Archbishop's sister).

Miss Bishop was a typical member of the first generation of Principals of women's colleges, who were cultivated women rather than intellectuals, for the institutions which would produce the woman intellectual did not yet exist, and were to be their creation. They were dedicated to pioneering the higher education of women, and in claiming women's equality with men as scholars they were very bold, for they pushed women students into the position of being obliged to justify themselves by their work. But having made this bold move they advanced no further. In other respects they accepted the most exacting social conventions of the period, above all the essential respectability of middle-class women, which required the strict chaperonage of young girls, and demanded unswerving virtue of the mature single woman. Professor Martha Vicinus in her recent study *Independent Women: Work and Community for Single Women 1850-1920* stresses the caution, bordering on pusillanimity, of the women Principals, and suggests that 'it locked women into a rigid mould of respectability when they might have gained more by daring more'.[8] But the Principals felt that they had no option to dare more, even had they sought it. Higher education for women had been introduced on sufferance, and deviation from social conventions would have been the death-knell of its acceptability. In some women's colleges respectability was supported by religiosity: Elizabeth Wordsworth ran Lady Margaret Hall as an Anglican family, and Constance Maynard set the Evangelical tone of Westfield (founded 1882).[9] Bedford combined a high moral tone with non-denominationalism, while Royal Holloway College was almost gathered into the Anglican fold. Miss Bishop, as the Anglican nominee of an Anglican Board of Governors, ensured the predominance of what she regarded as 'true religion' for a decade.

The intrigue of Sir Henry Ponsonby and Archbishop Benson to secure an Anglican Board of Governors was never revealed, but the sectarian character of the Board was obvious enough, and was increased when Samuel Morley, a strong advocate of non-denominational education, resigned on the grounds of ill health, and was succeeded by Mr A. J. Mundella, President of the Board of Trade, a keen supporter of higher education for women, and an Anglican. Nonconformist opinion was agitated by the composition of the Board of Governors and activated by the appointment of Miss Bishop. There was a mistimed protest in the Nonconformist Press at the beginning of 1888, when the College had already been open for a term. On 5 January *The Nonconformist and Independent* published a strongly worded editorial entitled 'A Sectarian Dodge', and on 10 February the Baptist periodical *The Freeman* followed with 'Perversion of the Royal Holloway College'. Both publications complained of the Anglican control of the governing body, the appointment of a 'High Church Lady' as Principal, and the prominent place given to Divinity in the curriculum. *The Nonconformist and Independent* admitted that Divinity was an optional subject, but concluded:

[ 73 ]

Our readers can estimate for themselves the chances that any hetero-dox student will have for obtaining the approval of the Principal for the omission of the subject of 'Divinity'. But even if the approval were given, it would only be after such expostulations, arguments and prudential warnings as would make the student a religious pariah . . . foul shapes of bigotry, priestcraft and spiritual chicanery are stalking abroad which we thought had been banished for ever.[10]

A question on the subject was asked in Parliament, and a disingenuous answer made on behalf of the Charity Commissioners that they did not know the religious views of the Governors, who had been appointed merely on the application of the Trustees.[11] *The Freeman* was correct in assuming that 'very little can now be done beyond learning a lesson and uttering a protest'.[12]

On her appointment Miss Bishop was fortunate in being given sole command of an institution which existed only as an empty building. Under Governors with whom she was in perfect accord she could develop it as she would. It was an opportunity and a challenge which succeeding Principals must have envied; her achievement was one they could only have admired.

Miss Bishop's first action was to suggest to the Governors the import-ance of providing scholarships, in order to secure students of ability whose work could set a high standard. Mr Walpole Greenwell accepted the task of approaching possible donors, and himself set an example by providing two scholarships of £50 per annum for three years. Miss Mary Ann Driver offered six scholarships for the same sum and duration, Henry Driver-Holloway offered two and Sir George Martin-Holloway two. External donors included Mr (later Sir) Henry Tate, founder of the Tate Gallery, and a total of fifteen scholarships of £50 for three years were provided.[13] As original fees were £90 per annum these were substantial benefits. The following year twelve Founder's Scholarships of £30 per annum for two years were established. Miss Driver offered the Driver Prizes of £5 in books, to be awarded annually for Latin, Greek, French, German, Music, Mathematics, Natural Science and English Essay (ie all the subjects in the curriculum except History, which was taught together with English, and Divinity). Mr Joseph Savory gave the Savory Divinity Prize. A few years later Sir George Martin-Holloway established the Martin-Holloway Prize for the most outstanding student, a paragon who was to excel in social responsibility and academic attainment.

In May 1887 the posts of resident lecturers in Classics, Mathematics, Natural Science, Modern Languages and History were advertised, and the applicants were interviewed by Miss Bishop at Oxford High School, where she was completing her final term in office. The original resident women staff, all of whom in accordance with the Founder's requirements were single, were appointed on Miss Bishop's recommendation. She was successful in bringing together the strong team needed to provide both standards and inspiration. With thumbnail sketches provided by later colleagues who remembered them, they were: Miss Thérèse Dabis (Lecturer in Classics 1887-9), 'surely the humanest of those who expound the humanities'; Miss Catherine Frost (Senior Staff Lecturer in Mathematics 1887-1907), 'demurely concealing a bagful of mirth and mimicry'; Miss Marie Péchinet (Lecturer in French 1887-1907), 'compelling, scintillating, penetrating, her tongue like a chameleon's, sure of aim'; Miss H. Neaves (Lecturer in History and English Literature 1887-9), 'a large lady of majestic mien', and Miss M. Seward (Lecturer in Natural Science 1887-91). Miss Ruth Mayhew, aged only twenty, was appointed to teach German for one term at a fee of £10, and at the beginning of the Lent term 1888 Miss A. G. Corry, 'exquisite, fastidious', took up the post of Lecturer in German, which she held till 1900. Surprisingly, in such a small faculty, a full-time teacher of Music was appointed. She was Miss Emily Daymond (1887-99), 'electrifying, Ellen Terry-like, yet her music all repose'.[14] She created a strong musical tradition at Royal Holloway College, and later became the first woman Doctor of Music; though her subject did not at first have academic status, she laid the foundations on which a distinguished department was established. The lecturers' salaries were £150 per annum, with the exception of Miss Péchinet and Miss Daymond, who received £100.[15]

They were joined, as non-residents by three male lecturers: Professor S. L. Loney (Lecturer in Mathematics 1887-1920), 'past master of the teacher's art, vivid, genial, yet wary withal'; Dr G. H. Fowler (Lecturer in Zoology 1887-91), and Mr J. H. Muirhead (Lecturer in Mental and Moral Science, 1887-97). Muirhead, a distinguished philosopher, also taught Classics until 1890, when the department was taken over by Professor E. H. Donkin, who remained at the College until 1918, living 'with his sister across the road [from the College], delightful and unworldly pair . . . with all the grace of perfect gentlehood'.

To the original subjects Physics was added in 1891, taught by Mr H. L. Callendar, who was soon succeeded by Professor W. R. Cassie (1893-1908). Chemistry was introduced under Miss E. E. Field (Head of Department 1893-1913), 'gracious Dresden china figure floating through our midst with unhurried urbanity'; and Botany was established under Dr M. J. Benson (1893-1922; Professor from 1912), 'a child of nature like the plants she handled, great in her ingenuous integrity'.[16] This is a courteous description of her lack of social tact and her unfortunate propensity for the *faux pas*.

The Principal gave a weekly class in Divinity which, as the Nonconformist Press had surmised, was morally obligatory though officially voluntary. During the first three years of the College she reported to the Governors that all the students attended her classes, with the exception of one, who was a Unitarian, though it is unlikely that she was made to feel a 'religious pariah'. Mr C. W. Carey (Curator of the Picture Gallery, 1887-1943) gave lessons in drawing and painting to those who desired them, and classes were also offered in cookery, hygiene, woodwork and dressmaking. The Gymnasium was in the charge of Miss Stuart Snell (1887-97) and 'gym' was attended by both staff and students. Miss Daymond's recollection of it is a delightful period piece:

I remember gym teas, when we all relaxed after the strain! Oil lamps were brought round . . . by a man called Strudwick whose other chief duty was to blow the organ. I can see now the rather shy look on his face when he brought the lamps on gym days. He would open the door of a study and find, within, several persons of the teaching staff whom he had been accustomed to look upon with respect, clad in gym tunics, sitting round the room. He always tried to put down the lamp on the dresser without raising his eyes to see a single person – wonderful![17]

[ 76 ]

Strudwick was one of a team of male college servants, which included Rogers, the head groundsman, who had been Clerk of the Works during the building of the College and claimed to have seen every brick of it laid; White, the gardener, who was also in charge of the pigs, which had been bought for the economic purpose of consuming the kitchen rubbish; and Mr Hornsby, the nightwatchman, the only man privileged to remain in the College at night, when he patrolled the corridors with his lantern and his dog. The female domestic staff, initially a dozen maids, were directed by the Lady Housekeeper, Miss Lethbridge. She was succeeded by Miss Knowles (1892-1918), a formidable autocrat, who was appointed on the strength of a single sentence in her letter of application: 'I have been accustomed to keep a liberal table.'[18] Miss Bishop, though herself abstemious, believed in keeping a liberal table for her staff and students.

The College community was completed by the arrival, on 4 October 1887, of the first twenty-eight students, a creditable total for the College opening but a small number to inhabit so large a building. All were lodged, with the resident lecturers, on West I and II.* The Founder's wish that the College should educate young women of the 'middle and upper middle class' was exactly fulfilled by the social background of the 'pioneers' or 'aborigines', as the first students called themselves. Eleven of the fifteen who had gained scholarships came from the High Schools founded by the GPDST. Of their fathers, three were gentlemen of independent means and nine were professional men: three solicitors, three clergymen, two surgeons and a physician. Others were connected with business and industry, and included an actuary, a bank manager, a chartered accountant, a civil engineer and a clay and iron merchant. Five women sent their daughters or wards to Royal Holloway College: two ladies of independent means, two clergymen's widows and one professional woman, a schoolmistress. One student, aged twenty-four, came of her own volition.[19] This type of social background remained fairly constant until the First World War, with solicitors, doctors and clergymen preponderating among the parents of students. Academics, schoolmasters, army officers, members of the diplomatic service and farmers followed, together with a small number of widows, doubtless determined

* The College corridors are numbered upwards: thus West I is the main floor, West II, III, IV above it. The same applies on East. The maids occupied the Vth floor rooms.

[ 77 ]

that their daughters should gain the means to become independent. Gradually a few students from lower middle-class or working-class backgrounds arrived: these included in 1898 the daughter of a private coachman, in 1907 the daughter of a dairyman and in 1912 the daughter of a blacksmith. The students were indoctrinated with respect for intellect, and while ladylike behaviour was inculcated, social snobbery was condemned. Indeed, the women's colleges in general were remarkably free of it.

From the beginning, education at Royal Holloway College proved its practical value in giving its students the means of independence. Of the pioneers one, Martha Whiteley (scholar, from South Kensington High School) became Assistant Professor of Chemistry at Imperial College, eight became headmistresses and four assistant teachers. Though the Founder had expressed the desire that the College should 'neither be considered nor conducted as a mere training college for teachers and governesses' a high proportion of the early students entered education, and this trend continued, for at the end of the nineteenth and the beginning of the twentieth century teaching provided almost the only career available to women graduates. Entrance to the medical profession was still only grudgingly permitted to women, and to the legal profession was not yet allowed. However, two alumnae of Royal Holloway College (M. H. Style, 1890-94 and Louisa Martindale, 1890-93) qualified as doctors before the end of the century, and one M. E. Sykes (1914-17) became a solicitor as soon as the Sex Disqualification (Removal) Act of 1918 permitted her to do so. Hilda Martindale, younger sister of Louisa (student 1893-5) entered the Civil Service and became an inspector of factories, before being appointed Director of Women's Establishments at the Treasury. E. Watts-Tobin (student 1914-17) was the first woman to qualify as a chartered accountant.[20] It is to be hoped that this high level of attainment would have satisfied the Founder's aspirations.


At the beginning of the academic year 1887/8 Miss Bishop had gathered a community which as yet lacked a social organisation. Her task was to create a society.

Part of this task falls within Professor Eric Hobsbawm's definition of 'invented traditions': ' . . . they are responses to novel situations which take the form of reference to old situations, or which establish their own past by quasi-obligatory repetition'.[21] Miss Bishop, for example, with reference to an old situation, took the model of the men's colleges in establishing a formal dinner in Hall every evening, where a High Table, at first omitted, was soon introduced. The whole community changed for dinner, the resident lecturers wearing the elaborate *toilettes* of the period, with trains and jewels if they possessed them, the students wearing simpler long frocks. The style of the occasion was reminiscent of a grand house party. Everyone assembled in the Library, where Miss Bishop chose a dinner partner from among the students. Thence they processed in pairs, through the Museum, which was unlit, along the dark and uninhabited East corridor, to the Dining Hall. Only a little time was required to make the dinner procession the most hallowed of College traditions. The original students established their own order of precedence by deciding that the scholars should lead them as seniors, and the commoners should follow as freshers.[22]

As student numbers grew the procession became more formalised, with the Principal sending a written invitation to the student of her choice (once a year to scholars, once in three years to commoners), the students inviting their lecturers as dinner partners, third- and second-year students otherwise inviting students in the years below them. A hierarchy of seniority was strictly observed. This degree of organisation required that dinner diaries should be filled in at the beginning of term. The maids waited at dinner, dressed in long black dresses and frilly white aprons and caps. Within a few years a butler was appointed, who directed proceedings with the precision of an orchestral conductor. Intelligent conversation at dinner was considered of the highest importance; shop-talk was eschewed, and staff were inclined to think poorly of students who did not prepare themselves with interesting subject matter. Since the community was isolated, in the days before the existence of mass media, both staff and students were grateful for the wide range of periodicals provided by the Governors, which kept them in touch with the outside world.[23]

The need for disciplined work, rather than the desire to establish traditions, led to the imposition of 'College Hours'. For the students the day began at 7.30 a.m., when the maids called them, bringing each a jug of hot water for washing. Chapel, which was compulsory, was at 8 a.m.

[ 79 ]

and was followed by breakfast. Lectures were continuous from 9 a.m. to 1 p.m., when half an hour was taken for lunch. The afternoon was given to games or gym, or for the non-sporting to walks or cycle rides, while the hard-worked scientists usually did their practical work. In the early days of the College the only game played was tennis. But in 1889 a newly appointed lecturer in English, Miss Lilian Faithfull (who later became a distinguished Headmistress of Cheltenham Ladies' College) suggested the introduction of hockey. At first it was played 'with a string ball and little bent ash sticks ... each side was divided into "forwards" and "backs", but the players followed the ball all over the field ... hacking at it and hitting it ahead in any manner that seemed good to them',[24] until in 1893 Miss Faithfull suggested that formal rules should be introduced, and then expert instruction was given, and hard balls and Slazenger sticks were bought. The days of happy amateurism were over, and intercollegiate matches were introduced. Cricket was also played during the 1890s, though with fluctuating enthusiasm, and in 1894 a swimming bath was constructed in the grounds.

Sports ended punctually at 4 p.m. when tea was served. For each student a College Roll – 'a nice, softish tapering oval, about four inches long with a maximum girth of eight inches'[25] – was provided, though students supplemented this allowance with extra bread, jam and cakes. Gym teas and hockey teas were the substantial feasts necessitated by exertion. Work was resumed from 4.45 to 6.45 (unless there were evening lectures); at 6.45 the dressing bell rang, and College prepared for the ritual of dinner. The novelist Ivy Compton Burnett (student 1902-07) satirically complained of the short time provided for doing her hair, 'an operation which Mother declares should occupy every lady at least half an hour'.[26] Students were forbidden to wear their hair loose; a mature coiffure was obligatory.

Until the First World War dinner at Royal Holloway College consisted of four courses, and included such home-grown delicacies as strawberries and asparagus, in season. The last course, served on a clean plate, was a single fancy biscuit. Even if the quail on toast requested by Miss Daisy Selina Dobbs did not appear on the menu, the catering at Royal Holloway College was far superior to that of the other women's colleges, which was generally characterised by the prunes and custard deplored by Virginia Woolf. After dinner members of staff invited their partner, with a small group of students, to coffee parties, which the guests were ·expected to leave promptly at 8.30 the senior guest breaking up the gathering. Work was resumed until 10 p.m., when the Principal read evening prayers in the Library. Thereafter the students were at leisure until a warning bell rang at 10.25. 10.30 was bedtime, after which complete silence was the rule until next morning.

Miss Marion Pick (student 1903-07 and Senior Staff Lecturer in Mathematics 1911-46) in an unpublished account of *Social Life at Royal Holloway College 1889-1939*, wrote: 'Most visitors noticed how quiet the College was during working hours. Anyone really roused by interruptions had the right to go and say to disturbers of the peace "May I remind you that it is College Hours and although you may not have work to do, others have".'[27] This was known as being 'jumped', and the correct response was a written apology before 9 a.m. the next morning. During the hours of darkness if the nightwatchman saw a light in a student's room he would knock on the door and say, 'Principal's instructions, Miss, that I ask you to go to your bed,' and students ordered to bed by Mr Hornsby, or his successor Turkentine, obeyed without question.

In imposing such a regimental discipline Miss Faithfull thought that the Principal had been too demanding:

> Noise was an agony to her, and order and neatness a passion, so there was naturally more sense of restraint than youth could quite bear. It was not easy for her to cease to be the schoolmistress and to realise that if the students were to be transformed from schoolgirls into women it was to be done by treating their immaturity as maturity . . .[28]

A general belief that Royal Holloway College had the ethos of a boarding school survived her day and proved hard to overcome.

Despite the discipline of College Hours, the students enjoyed some freedoms which would have been denied them at home. They were free from the trivial and intrusive demands of family life, and the constant obligation of helping in the house. Miss Pick, who came of a family which respected academic work, commented on her childhood: 'Although I was expected to be a scholar, doing something useful in the house was esteemed as worthier than studying more than just what my school required.'[29] Freedom to work was ensured at Royal Holloway by space and privacy which no Victorian daughter would have possessed at home. In place of a bedroom shared by two or three sisters, a student found herself possessed of a bedroom of her own, a private study, and the right to exclude unwanted visitors by hanging an 'Engaged' notice on the door. (A notice upside down rendered her study an inviolable sanctuary). In *A Room of One's Own*, in 1928, Virginia Woolf wrote that £500 a year and a room with a lock on the door were the prerequisites of creative work for women; the Royal Holloway student, with her fees paid and her 'Engaged' notice, was essentially enjoying these privileges forty years earlier. Then there was a freedom to choose leisure activities, which again would not have been available at home. The choice of sports and College societies was constantly widening as numbers increased, while for the less sociable there was the simple pleasure of wandering in the extensive grounds unchaperoned, or even entirely alone. At the turn of the century the grounds were probably at their most beautiful:

> . . . no one could forget the beauty of the gardens, the little copse carpetted with bluebells, opening out into buttercup meadows full of purple orchis, and, best of all . . . great slopes of flame coloured azaleas. The peculiar, pungent, intoxicating scent of azaleas will always bring back to a Holloway student sunny afternoons, when, though surrounded by many books, and full of good intentions, she dreamed rather than worked, gazing over a sea of orange to the blue hills beyond.[30]

Privacy, however, was fundamentally privacy to work, which was the *raison d'être* of the College, and hard work was demanded by the high academic standard which was set from the beginning. Miss Bishop professed herself willing to receive students who did not work for degree courses, but they were not permitted to distract their fellows by dilettantism. They followed courses of study approved by the Principal, for which from 1902 onwards a Special College Certificate was given for successful completion. Most students, however, read for Oxford or London degree courses, for which they received degrees from London, but from Oxford only notification of the class they had obtained. In the early years of the College the numbers of students choosing Oxford or London examinations were roughly equal; in 1891 they were exactly so, with twenty-three students sitting for each. Which they chose was probably a matter of the individual bent of the student.

In the Oxford examinations students could read the full specialist course in either Classics or Mathematics, the only options during the first decade of Royal Holloway College. Examinations for finals schools in English were introduced in 1897, and in Modern Languages in 1905. The London examinations were differently structured, and required a general foundation of academic knowledge. An Arts candidate was required to pass the Intermediate examination in Latin, Greek, French or German, English with History, and Pure Mathematics; in Finals she took Latin, Greek, a modern language, and either Pure or Mixed Mathematics, or Mental and Moral Science. A Science candidate was required to pass Intermediate in Inorganic Chemistry, Physics, Mathematics and Biology, and in Finals she had a choice of three subjects out of nine. Honours could be taken immediately after these examinations, in a chosen subject or subjects, but more papers were required in Classics, Mathematics and Mental and Moral Science. Despite the broad base of the London degrees, the influence of the older Oxford tradition made itself felt in that Classics and Mathematics were still regarded as 'genuine schools' and the others as 'soft options'.[31]

Miss Bishop had created the connection with Oxford, but she soon decided that the prestige of success in Oxford examinations was unsatisfactory so long as degrees were not granted to women. She began to favour the London examinations, especially when a closer relationship with London appeared possible.

The University of London had been founded in 1836, to conduct examinations and to confer degrees on the students of University College and King's College, and such other institutions as the Privy Council might approve. The governing body was the Senate, whose members were appointed by the Privy Council. The Charter of 1858 opened London University degrees (except those in medicine) to all students, whatever their place of education, and in 1878 this privilege was extended to women students. Later in the century a movement developed in favour of establishing a teaching university. Proposals were made to found a second university for the purpose, but two Royal Commissions, the Selborne Commission 1889-90 and the Gresham Commission 1891-4, were emphatic that there should be only one University of London. The

[ 83 ]

problem therefore became one of self-metamorphosis. In 1890 and again in 1895 Miss Bishop proposed to the Governors that Royal Holloway College should seek inclusion in the new teaching university when it should be founded.[32] The Gresham Commission recommended a federal constitution under which the member institutions should remain independent, but should be co-ordinated through the University. To seek membership as one of the 'constituent schools' seemed to Miss Bishop the most suitable future development for the College. The Governors took note of her views, but no action could be taken until the University had resolved its own affairs.

In the meantime, the question of religion once again came to the fore.

From the outset the religious arrangements had been in the hands of Miss Bishop. With the advice of Archbishop Benson she drew up a form of daily service which derived its structure from the Anglican Prayer Book, 'as any fixed form of service must necessarily do'.[33] The service was always sung, and Miss Bishop and Miss Daymond together compiled and arranged the College Psalter, in which the three-part settings for girls' voices gave 'a richness and depth to the singing unusual without a mixed choir'.[34] Each Sunday there was a sung Matins, and Holy Communion was celebrated once a month. On Sunday evenings a short service was read by the Principal, and the choir sang again. While Chapel attendance was compulsory for all students throughout the week, on Sunday morning Nonconformists were at liberty to attend their own Chapels, in which pews were reserved for them.

Though Nonconformist students accepted this arrangement without complaint, prominent Nonconformists outside the College continued to be dissatisfied with it. Several approaches were made to the Governors for the inclusion of Nonconformists on the Board as a matter of policy, and after initial resistance the Governors accepted the justice of these requests, and Nonconformists were appointed as honorary Governors. Two of these, The Revd Dr W. F. Moulton (Governor 1891-8) and Mr (later Sir) Evan Spicer (Governor 1893-1923) raised the question of Nonconformist worship in the College Chapel. That the institution of Nonconformist services would fulfil the requirements of the Founder more satisfactorily than the existing system was undeniable, but stronger resistance was shown by Miss Bishop than the Anglican Governors, even the churchmen.

Miss Bishop addressed to the Governors a reasoned objection, based chiefly on the contention that variety of worship would emphasise religious differences among the students:

> ... For it must be remembered that a large number of young women are Church-women or Nonconformists, not by conviction but by the accidents of birth and bringing up. They are practically indifferent, and are easily drawn away from the obligations of religious faith and practice. Serious harm must result from the constant presentation to them of competing religious services and teachings, among which they may take their choice, and from the atmosphere of aggressive controversy which must result therefrom; and this, just at the time when they are becoming more or less independent of home influences, and when new departures in thought and action have an almost irresistible attraction for them.[35]

Given the system and her own convictions it was not so much religious controversy that she feared as the lapsation of Anglicans under the influence of Nonconformist zeal. In a sense she was the victim of a change of policy, for she had faithfully carried out the wishes of the original Governors, and was now required to be the pliant instrument of a Board which represented different views. The Governors rejected her arguments and she tendered her resignation, which was accepted. The Governors resolved that under the new dispensation Anglican services should continue to be held each Sunday at 11.30 a.m., and Nonconformist services should be held on alternate Sundays at 10 a.m. The first was held on 8 May 1898, and the first Communion service for Nonconformists on 18 February 1900.

News of Miss Bishop's resignation was received with sorrow by past and present students. A letter of explanation from her was printed in the *College Letter*, which had been founded in 1890 for circulation to members of the Royal Holloway College Association (the alumnae society). Far from approving the new religious arrangements, many students, including Nonconformists, supported Miss Bishop. One hundred and thirty-four alumnae signed a letter of protest to the Governors deploring the

[ 85 ]

proposed innovations, and seventy-three of the one hundred and seven students in residence signed a separate letter to the same effect.[36] But progress, once initiated, showed its customary impetus; the changes, desirable if not desired, were inaugurated. Miss Bishop departed, to become in 1899 the Principal of St Gabriel's Church of England Training College for women teachers. In this congenial employment she died in 1913.

In the Chapel of Royal Holloway College Miss Bishop dedicated a stained glass window to commemorate its first decade of existence. The lower lights contained figures of St Alban and St Augustine, the latter a likeness of Archbishop Benson who had recently died. It was Miss Bishop's personal memorial to the man whose wishes, she said, had been her commands. Miss Bishop's portrait was painted for the College by J. J. (later Sir John) Shannon. It is a flattering likeness, in which the lines of her tense, gaunt face have been smoothed into an expression of tranquillity; in her right hand she holds a spray of pink roses, the College emblem which she had chosen.

In the autumn of 1897 the Principalship was advertised, and on 9 December the Governors appointed Miss Emily Penrose, who since 1893 had been Principal of Bedford.

---

$\cdot\!>\!\!:\!\!>$ 4 $\prec\!\!:\!\prec\cdot$

---

# THE LARGER LIFE OF A UNIVERSITY

## The Principalship of
## Miss Emily Penrose
## 1897–1907

> We think of her as the Principal who made it her work
> to introduce us to the larger life of a University. We
> remember, too, that as she grasped the significance
> of organic connection with a greater whole, she acted
> upon the conviction of the organic character of
> College within . . .[1]

F OLLOWING the controversy which had caused the resignation of
Miss Bishop, the Governors held a conference to discuss the
future of Royal Holloway College. During its first decade the
College had developed its own traditions and standards, and established
its position on the fringes of the academic world (the position occupied
by all the women's colleges) as an institution where good learning was
pursued for its own sake, and for the sake of the professional advancement
of women. It could develop no further without deciding the direction in
which its best interests lay.

The Governors felt that their first obligation was to consider the
wishes of Thomas Holloway, expressed in the Deed of Foundation: 'It
is the Founder's desire that power by Act of Parliament, Royal Charter,
or otherwise, should ultimately be sought, enabling the College to confer
degrees on its students after proper examination in the various subjects
of instruction . . .'

If this did not appear to be either practicable or desirable, then the
alternative courses were either that the College should seek to become
part of a larger university for women, or that it should seek inclusion in

the proposed teaching university of London, the course advocated by Miss Bishop.

In holding a conference of educationists to advise on these three possibilities the Governors were imitating the action of the Founder in 1875, and the vast increase in the range of expertise at their disposal was the measure of the advance which had been made in the higher education of women during the ensuing twenty-two years. The conference was held at the House of the Society of Arts on 4 December 1897, and was chaired by James Bryce MP (later Lord Bryce; Governor of RHC 1891-1907). It was attended by many men who interested themselves in women's education, including six representatives of Oxford University and six of Cambridge. The women educationists present included the Principals of several women's colleges: Mrs Henry Sidgwick, Principal of Newnham; Miss Welsh, Principal of Girton; Miss C. A. E. Moberley, Principal of St Hugh's Hall; Miss Constance Maynard, Mistress of Westfield, and Miss Faithfull who at this date was Vice-Principal of the Ladies' Department of King's College, London. Miss Bishop was present as Principal of Royal Holloway and Miss Penrose as Principal of Bedford, but the situation of both was somewhat delicate, as Miss Bishop's departure from Royal Holloway was imminent and Miss Penrose's application for the Principalship was under consideration. Neither, for obvious reasons, felt free to speak at the conference. The staff of the College were represented by Miss Dabis and Miss Field and Professors Loney and Donkin. Girls' schools, which had a vital interest in developments in higher education for women, were represented by Mrs Bryant, Headmistress of North London Collegiate, Miss H. M. Jones, President of the Association of Headmistresses, and Miss A. Hitchcock, Headmistress of Kensington High School, also representing the Association. Three of Thomas Holloway's advisers at the meeting of 1875 were also present to offer their riper judgement: Millicent Fawcett, Emily Davies and Sir Joshua Fitch.

The conference was opened by James Bryce, who outlined the three courses of action available to Royal Holloway College. He announced that each would be elaborated in a short paper by an individual speaker. Letters from 'persons competent to give their opinion but unable to be present' would then be read, and a general discussion would follow.

The case for seeking a separate charter for Royal Holloway College, enabling it to confer its own degrees, was presented by Dr R. D. Roberts (Governor 1894-1911), who in the spring had urged the desirability of implementing the Founder's wishes in this respect. He now expressed doubts that the College was either large enough or sufficiently well equipped 'to sustain with credit to itself and advantage to women's education the position of a separate university'.[2] So far as the alternative schemes were concerned, he expressed himself in favour of seeking inclusion in the proposed teaching university of London, which now appeared likely to come into being, as a result of the London University Bill, introduced by the Duke of Devonshire, Lord President of the Council, in the preceding parliamentary session.

The second speaker was Mr J. L. Strachan-Davidson of Balliol College, Oxford, who spoke eloquently in favour of the foundation of a women's university. 'The plan which I have the honour to lay before you', he said, 'was first developed as an incident in the struggle in which we were engaged last year over the question of granting the Oxford degrees to women. Though I was strongly opposed to that measure, I felt that it could not be satisfactorily met by a blank negative.'[3]

The struggle to which he referred had been precipitated by pressure from the women's colleges in both Oxford and Cambridge, and by their male supporters, for the admission of women to degrees. Both Universities, after bitter debate, had refused to admit them, and in July 1896 a conference of Oxford and Cambridge Committees, with all male membership, had advocated the foundation of a women's university, to be called 'The Queen's University'. The main objection of these committees was not to the higher education of women, but to their admission to full membership of the Universities through the granting of degrees, which would bring with it the right to participate in University policy-making and government. As Mr Strachan-Davidson developed his argument it became apparent that the present predicament of Royal Holloway College was seen by his party as the perfect means simultaneously of ridding Oxford and Cambridge of importunate women and of making handsome provision for them:

I hear it asked, What is to be the local seat of the new University? . . . It would be natural to look for a home in one or other of the Women's Colleges, and probably a suitable and dignified abode for the

[ 89 ]

University offices could more conveniently be found in the magnificent buildings of Holloway than in any of the other Colleges . . .[4]

This argument fell on deaf ears. The women educationists and the more committed of their male supporters were aware of the danger to the status of women's education inherent in measuring its standards by any criteria other than those accepted and recognised for men. In the third paper addressed to the conference, Mrs Bryant, of North London Collegiate, cogently presented the women educationists' viewpoint:

> Increasing numbers pass onward year by year from the schools to the Colleges, demanding a University education of the established type. It is too late to say that this type is or was, established for men only . . . There is no demand in the schools for a separate University for Women . . . Indeed, I have never met with a woman who for herself wanted a women's university . . . Cambridge, Oxford and London are in much demand. It is, to most persons, obvious that Colleges working for the Cambridge and Oxford courses should be at those places. Egham, on the other hand, is within easy reach of London, near enough to be included, when the University is converted into a Teaching University, in the list of Colleges whose teachers may be recognised as teachers of the University and whose students will be included as internal students of the University. In such a position the College would, I believe, enjoy the maximum of dignity, popularity, and educational use . . .[5]

These were the views accepted by the great majority of the audience, but before it had the opportunity to speak in support of them, James Bryce read aloud the letters from the interested absentees. Edward Caird, Master of Balliol, wrote in favour of the inclusion of Royal Holloway in London University, and Alexander Hill, Master of Downing College and Vice-Chancellor of Cambridge University, condemned the idea of founding a university for women which, he declared, 'would be to give up all the ground hitherto gained by the champions of equality'. Perhaps the most eloquent letter, concluding with a powerful image, was written by Maria Grey, now bedridden, who had been a dauntless fighter for women's education for almost half a century: ' . . . a Women's

University will always, because it is for women only, be held and very probably be inferior to . . . the Universities for men, and the value of any degrees conferred by it will never rank higher, in comparison to theirs, than a fancy medal to a standard coin of the realm.'[6]

In the open discussion which followed, these views were endorsed by a number of men and women educationists, whose different experiences had led them to the same conclusion. Millicent Fawcett described how she and her husband, Professor Henry Fawcett, had been among those consulted by Thomas Holloway in 1875, and had had the greatest admiration for his public spirit and his generosity. But she went on to express the belief that to adopt his plan of elevating Royal Holloway College to the status of a separate university 'would . . . amount almost to educational suicide'.[7] She was firmly in favour of the link with London University. Sir Joshua Fitch supported her views, and explained the American influences which had led Thomas Holloway to desire a development which now appeared to be profoundly mistaken. In America 487 educational bodies now possessed the power to graduate their students and give them academic titles:

> That was the vision that was before Mr Holloway. He thought nothing would be easier than to erect a College which should have, the moment he erected it, – as it would have done if he had been an American instead of an Englishman – the power to confer degrees upon its own students. I need hardly tell you that it is a proposal which would prove fatal to real learning.[8]

The impracticability of Royal Holloway's establishing itself as an independent university had already begun to seem sufficiently clear, but Sir Joshua Fitch's explanation of the Founder's attitude assisted in absolving the Governors from any obligation to pursue it further.

Emily Davies, the other survivor of Thomas Holloway's original advisers, made the point that American degrees had fallen into disrepute precisely because the power to confer them had been granted to too many institutions. She recommended the Governors of Royal Holloway to consider the success which Bedford College had achieved in preparing the students for London degrees (they already numbered 200 graduates). 'Another point about Bedford College,' she said, 'is that it has been accepted as one of the constituent Colleges of the proposed teaching University – the only women's college, I believe, to which that recognition has been accorded. These facts surely speak for themselves as regards what is likely to succeed and to command the public confidence . . . I would venture to urge upon the Governors of Holloway College to follow the example of Bedford College, and to make use of the courses and degrees of the University of London, with a view to its ultimately becoming a constituent College of the new University.'[9]

When James Bryce closed the discussion and summed up the proceedings, it was clear that the conference had not only directed the course of Royal Holloway's future but affected the whole development of higher education for women. While the Governors felt free of the obligation to follow Thomas Holloway's wishes regarding the pursuit of university status for the College, and supporters of 'The Queen's University' for women recognised that their plan was so generally condemned as to be non-viable. The conference dispersed without passing any resolutions, and the Governors of Royal Holloway later resolved to await the result of the London University Bill before taking any further action. This outcome would have satisfied both Miss Bishop and Miss Penrose, who must have found their self-imposed silence at the conference almost unbearable at times.

Five days after the conference, on 9 December 1897, Miss Penrose received notification of her appointment as Principal of Royal Holloway College.

The first generation of Principals of women's colleges had created the traditions of collegiate life for women; to the second generation fell the task of establishing the women's colleges as respected seats of learning. Miss Penrose typified the second generation and, through her achievements as a scholar, administrator and diplomatist, advanced the status of the three colleges of which she was successively Principal: Bedford, Royal Holloway and Somerville.

Emily Penrose, born in 1858, was the eldest daughter of Francis Cranmer Penrose, architect, archaeologist and astronomer, a nephew of Dr Arnold of Rugby, and a collateral descendant of Archbishop Cranmer (an ancestor of whom both Emily and her father were immensely proud).

After attending a private school in Wimbledon she studied modern languages in Versailles, Paris, Dresden and Berlin, after which she stayed in Athens with her father, while he was director of the British School (1886/7). In 1889 she entered Somerville, to read Literae Humaniores (Classics). She arrived knowing only some modern Greek, and three years later she was the first women to be listed in the first class in her subject. In 1893 she was appointed Principal of Bedford, where her success in forming close relations with London University had won the College the advantageous position it enjoyed when she was appointed Principal of Royal Holloway, the achievement which doubtless decided the Governors in her favour.

Miss Penrose's greatest strengths were the clarity of her mind and the certainty of her aims. Women's equality with men was not pursued but assumed by her; her ambition was its full recognition by the academic world. As Principal of Bedford and Royal Holloway she sought the admission of these Colleges to London University; as Principal of Somerville (1907-26) she was instrumental in gaining admission for women to Oxford degrees. The triumphal episode of her career was the degree ceremony in the Sheldonian Theatre in 1920, at which women took their places as full members of the University. In 1926 Oxford conferred on her an honorary DCL; her retirement was followed by a DBE.

Miss Penrose's unexpected weakness, well concealed from all but the most observant, was an excruciating shyness, which made her appear tense and forbidding even when she hoped to seem relaxed and friendly. She had, in fact, a sympathetic nature, and was desirous to help people in trouble and need: 'but even to them she appeared an intimidating woman, alarmingly suggestive of a tiger about to spring.'[10] Her physical grace, controlled energy and concentrated stare all contributed to her feline appearance, and like many feline people she detested cats. Perhaps it was not surprising that her shyness and tension found relief in acting; but it is extraordinary to imagine her impersonating Sir John Collier's portrait of T. H. Huxley, adorned with false whiskers and holding a skull![11] She was not the type of woman intellectual to neglect her appearance; her evening dresses were elaborate, her day clothes elegant. Possibly she was vain. Mr Carey photographed her in a variety of clothes and moods. While her mental ability was considered masculine, her accomplishments were those of a Victorian Lady: skating, embroidery and water-colour painting, in all of which she was expert. Her obituarist summed up her character in impressive words: 'For all her masculine powers and feminine accomplishments, her great qualities were neither masculine nor feminine, but simply those that belong to great persons.'[12]

Understandably, such a protean woman overawed her students. Marion Pick, on her arrival at Royal Holloway in 1903, as senior scholar of her year, was terrified by the ordeal of partnering Miss Penrose at dinner. 'On my first morning in College,' she wrote, 'there appeared on my door, stuck into the number-plate as was the custom, a small visiting card, on which, inscribed in copper-plate, was the summons "The Principal invites you to take her in to dinner to-night." I went through the ritual as if in a dream, really almost a nightmare. Miss Penrose was very tall; her stature and status alike made me feel like a pigmy. One may be able to amass marks in an examination, but conversationally I was an empty husk. I was finally left on the mat outside Miss Penrose's study barely animate.'[13]

A student of Somerville who knew Miss Penrose in later years explained the nature of the ordeal. Miss Penrose had no small-talk. She bolted her food and then fired a series of demanding questions at her partner, who, with the exigencies of answering intelligently, had difficulty in eating at all.[14] No doubt her conversational technique at Royal Holloway had been equally daunting.

Miss Penrose was unable to take up the principalship of Royal Holloway in the term following her appointment as this was the notice required by Bedford; fortunately the metamorphosis of the University did not progress too rapidly to suit her own timetable. During the Lent term 1898 Miss Neaves, one of the original members of staff, who had since retired, was requested to act as Principal. On arriving at College Miss Neaves, who did her best to conceal a kindly nature behind a majestic exterior, put up a notice inviting any students who felt tired or depressed to call on her that evening. Whether motivated by depression or curiosity, all 107 students in residence knocked at the door of the Principal's drawing room, and were entertained to an impromptu party.[15] Miss Neaves possessed a talent for telling ghost stories, so that her evening guests frequently scattered to their rooms in the still half-uninhabited College with the agreeable terror of the unendangered. Her term of office must have been a relaxing interlude between the high tone of Miss Bishop and the academic preoccupations of Miss Penrose.

At the beginning of the summer term Miss Penrose took up the reins of government with authority. She had already requested Randall Davidson, now Bishop of Winchester, to invite Anglican clergymen to officiate during the term, and had consulted Mr Evan Spicer on the choice of Nonconformist ministers. The new regime of Chapel services commenced with her principalship. Other changes were made, with the intention of eliminating the deplorable impression that Royal Holloway was more like a girls' boarding school than a women's college. On Commemoration Day the public distribution of the Driver Prizes, the reading of the Principal's report, the interminable speeches and uplifting sermon instituted by Miss Bishop were abolished in favour of a simpler Chapel service followed, if weather permitted, by a grand garden party, at which the band of the Royal Artillery played on the South Terrace. The Commemoration Garden Party, increasing in magnificence with the passage of years, and always characterised by mountains of strawberries, rivers of cream, military music and Ascot-like fashions, remained the outstanding social event of the College year until the Second World War brought its splendours to an end.

A less public but more significant innovation was the establishment of the Education Council, in addition to the Staff Meeting which hitherto had been responsible for College teaching but excluded from policy-making. Since the staff were not represented on the governing body, during the first decade there had been no official channel of communication between staff and governors. Under Miss Penrose the position of the staff was improved after the formation of the Education Council, which consisted of the Principal, three Governors and three members of staff, elected by their colleagues.[16] The Education Council was indeed the Trojan Horse which brought women into the policy-making of the College, though it was some years before they gained a place on the governing body.

A second link between staff and Governors was formed through the administration of the M. E. Bishop Loan Fund, of which the Principal was appointed Treasurer. The nucleus of the fund was a gift of £140, raised by subscription and given to Miss Bishop, which she presented to the Governors to be employed for advancing loans to students unable to meet their College expenses. The fund was augmented from time to time by gifts from the RHCA and private donors. Initially the loans were not to exceed £30 to any individual student, and were to be repaid at not less than £5 per annum interest free. Loans were to be arranged through application to the Principal, and subject to her recommendation.[17] With her status advanced by these innovations Miss Penrose prepared to negotiate the admission of Royal Holloway College to the University of London.

The teaching university was constituted by the University of London Act (1898) and, after consultation with the Education Council, the Governors empowered Miss Penrose to write to the London University Commissioners, requesting admission.[18] The initial response was disappointing. As Royal Holloway College lay outside the limits of the Administrative County of London, it could only be admitted as a constituent college of the University by means of a Private Bill amending the University of London Act. Miss Penrose was requested to seek an interview with the Duke of Devonshire to discuss the matter further. He must have been encouraging, for the Governors resolved to proceed, and Sir William Hart-Dyke Bt., MP (Governor 1891-1905) undertook to do all in his power towards getting a Bill passed.[19] The difficulty was thought to be that of finding a Member of Parliament of promising disposition and achieved good luck in the ballot. Hart-Dyke's contacts were clearly invaluable, as the Bill was sponsored by Sir John Gorst, Mr Balfour and the Attorney General. On 18 July 1899 Miss Penrose, 'holding her breath in the public gallery', witnessed its success, and heard the declaration that 'Section 8 of the University of London Act (1898) shall apply to the Royal Holloway College at Egham in like manner as it applies to the South Eastern Agricultural College at Wye' (which was likewise outside the County of London). On 9 August the University of London Act (1899) was passed, sanctioning the admission of Royal Holloway College to the University, and in 1900 it was named in the statutes of the University as one of its first schools in the Faculties of Arts and Science. Thirteen members of staff were immediately recognised as Teachers of the University,[20] and Miss Penrose was elected a member of Senate, as a representative of the Faculty of Arts.

Though the College forfeited its autonomy it gained in prestige, and its relations with the academic world were soon radically changed. The Oxford connection, though not immediately severed, was rapidly phased out; after 1903 only four students passed in Oxford schools.[21] The severence was facilitated by the fact that London degrees were now structured to provide either specialist honours courses or general pass degrees. For the students the paramount advantage was that the London syllabuses were drawn up by the Teachers of the University, so that students need never find themselves face to face with examination papers set on areas of their subjects of which they knew nothing, a perpetual hazard in the past. The number of non-examination students decreased, and though Miss Penrose introduced approved courses of study and Special College Certificates to encourage their work, her pursuit of academic standards appropriate to the new status of the College led her to give preference to entrants who had already matriculated and intended to read for London degrees. The supply of good students was assisted by the foundation of more scholarships funded by a bequest of £10,000 to the College by Miss Driver, who died in 1900. This bequest financed 'at least three' Driver Scholarships of £30 per annum, tenable for three years. In 1906 the Governors introduced Bursaries of £30 per annum for three years, to be awarded to promising candidates who did not gain scholarships but required financial assistance.

By 1899 the increasing responsibilities of the Principal, and the growing student numbers, necessitated the appointment of a Vice-Principal, Miss E. M. Guinness (student 1888-92), who already held the post of Librarian and was Lecturer in English from 1895 to 1898 and from 1901 to 1908. Miss Guinness was not only an efficient deputy, but also a perfect foil for Miss Penrose; she possessed the social graces and ease of manner which the Principal lacked. Admiring her without too much awe, and laughing at her wit without losing their respect, the students may have found her a more accessible model than Miss Penrose. Marion Pick's ambition was fired by the 'wonderful ensembles' and 'lovely jewellery' of Miss Guinness: 'Soon I had made up my mind to become a Lecturer here and waft along the Library in a real *toilette*.'[22] Miss Guinness was more than a gracious presence, she was a dedicated teacher and a dashing hockey player, in the dwindling time which her other commitments permitted. Her first love, however, was the Library, for which she purchased with a careful respect for the claims of all departments, and a determination that it should contain 'standard editions of great writers, such as a permanent College Library should aim at possessing in a reasonable degree of completeness'. From an initial grant of £400, and an annual grant of £150 from the Governors, by 1900 a total of 6,607 volumes had been collected.[23] Private donations had also contributed to it, not all sent from spare-room shelves; Miss Dabis, for example, was a systematic donor who presented the Library with many classical texts.[24]

At the turn of the century the College staff numbered eighteen, and included some notable appointments recommended by Miss Penrose. Some of them, as long-serving members, shared both the intellectual and social life of the College. Miss Margaret Taylor (Senior Staff Lecturer, Classics 1899-1934), nicknamed 'Cato', set rigorous standards of scholarship and conduct; according to a younger colleague her nickname was aptly bestowed, 'her standards were Roman'.[25] Miss K. S. Block, the highly respected head of the English Department (1899-1926), was described by another colleague as 'our intellectual conscience'. It was said that she destroyed every set of lectures after she had given them, in order to ensure a fresh approach.[26] In consequence she published little, but her surviving students count themselves privileged to have been taught by her. Miss M. Hayes-Robinson, appointed Lecturer in History when an honours course separate from English was established (Head of Department 1899-1911), 'must have been the best loved member of staff ever. She entered into everything, was a first class tennis player, and just radiated warmth and genial gaiety.'[27] Miss H. M. R. Murray (Germanic Philology 1899-1915; Senior Staff Lecturer from 1905) was the daughter of the great lexicographer Sir James Murray. Her skill as a lecturer enabled her to 'thrill' her students with an explanation of his work on the OED.[28] Miss E. M. Rowell (student 1895-9; Lecturer in Mathematics 1899-1937; Senior Staff Lecturer from 1907), who had been a young friend of Lewis Carroll, may have found it easier to entertain her students by explaining the relationships between Alice's adventures and Mathematics, including the Cheshire Cat's smile and vanishing lines at infinity.[29] While she was a student at Royal Holloway, Charles Dodgson ('Lewis Carroll') sent her the proofs of his *Symbolic Logic* to read and criticise. She was the author of a volume of philosophical essays entitled *Time and Time Again*.[30]

Some of these women and their older colleagues were portrayed in Ivy Compton Burnett's first novel *Dolores* (1911), which is set partly on a women's college modelled on Royal Holloway. Miss Block, for example, appears as Miss Cliff: 'She is a woman of forty, older at a glance; with a well-cut, dark skinned face, iron-grey hair whose waving is conquered by its drawing to the knot in the neck, and dark keen eyes under thick black brows.' Miss Péchinet is portrayed as Miss Lemaitre: 'a Frenchwoman, over fifty, with a sallow, clever face, and sad brown eyes which lighted with her smile; who had led a difficult life in the land of her forced adoption, and lived with its daughters, feeling that she owed it no gratitude.' The distinguished historian Dr Helen Cam (student 1904-07; Lecturer in History 1912-21) identified her tutors and colleagues among the characters of *Dolores*, and provided a key which readers of Ivy Compton Burnett can consult in the first volume of Hilary Spurling's biography of her, *Ivy When Young*.[31]

The eponymous heroine of *Dolores*, a country clergyman's daughter, a student and later a lecturer at her College, suffers profound unhappiness, repudiates love and marriage, and defers her career, as a result of a morbid sense of duty to her father. Though it was turgid and melodramatic, the novel had a topical theme, and the heroine's career bore some resemblance to that of Miss Bishop, of which Ivy Compton Burnett may have heard rumours. Dolores' College, though it compared very favourably with the dismal provincial society in which she had been brought up, was nonetheless characterised as 'a passionless ardent little world – a world of women's friendships; where there lived in a strange harmony the spirits of the medieval convent and modern growth.' One of Ivy Compton Burnett's fellow students was disappointed when she read *Dolores*, many years later. 'I'm surprised it wasn't more humorous,' she said. 'I should've thought there would've been more fun it it.'[32] The real Royal Holloway College was far from being a place without fun in it, but the conventional comparison also occurred to Miss Faithfull and Miss Pick, and derived naturally enough from College Hours and compulsory worship. The spirit of modern growth was seen in the pervasive feminism and dedication to attainment.

At the beginning of the twentieth century women academics conceived attainment almost exclusively in terms of successful teaching, for although women's colleges had passed beyond the stage of experiment to that of acceptability, they were still not institutions with which research would be generally associated. Their purpose was seen as being that of raising the standard of women's education, not that of producing original work.[33] This is not to say that no original work was done at Royal Holloway in the early years of the century, for 'the born scholar's urge to original research is ineradicable and infectious'.[34] For example Dr M. J. Benson, who had begun her research in palaeophytology at Newnham and University College, London, continued her work at Royal Holloway, and published papers in collaboration with her students E. Sanday (1896-1900, and 1901-02), E. M. Berridge (1894-8)* and Miss E. J. Welsford (College Botanical Gardener 1898-1910). Miss Hayes-Robinson laid the foundations of research in History at Royal Holloway, encouraging the work of M. L. Bazeley (1903-06) on the Forest of Dean, Helen Cam on Anglo-Saxon local government, and Fanny Street (1905-07) on the Borough of New Sarum.[35] However, opportunities for research were necessarily limited until funds should be allocated for the establishment of research studentships. In the meantime the only objective measure of achievement for many women academics at Royal Holloway was the good results obtained by their students, on which the reputation of the College was established.

Each year the College gained its crop of 'firsts', but the triumphal year of Miss Penrose's Principalship was 1907, the year of her departure to Somerville, when eight Royal Holloway students gained first-class honours in the London BA and B.Sc examinations, in English, French, History, Classics and Mathematics. Three of the eight later joined the staff of the College: Marion Pick, Helen Cam and Fanny Street (Lecturer in History, 1911-17; Governor 1933-47; Acting Principal 1944-5). Until 1924 Finals examinations were taken in the winter term following the students' third year, and as the results came out before the end of term, the 'firsts' could return to be honoured with the College's invented traditions. In 1907, after the eight 'firsts' had dined at High Table, they were escorted in a torchlight procession twice round the College.

* Dr E. M. Berridge (D.Sc 1914) was later engaged in bacteriological research at Imperial College, and was one of the first women Fellows of the Linnean Society.

The students of the various honours schools conducted their own representatives on trollies decorated with boughs; and torches, Chinese lanterns, and banners with appropriate mottoes were carried. A continuous chant of miscellaneous character was maintained, in which the Marsellaise, Rule Britannia, and Mandalay could be distinguished at intervals, whilst the Classical school shouted the Greek cry of Victory round their distinguished comrade.[36]

To the tune of 'Mandalay' was sung:

There's a College down in Surrey, south-west of London Town,
The best place in all England, where they wear the cap and gown,
For its emblem is a rose and mid roses fair it grows,
Set in leafy summer foliage, itself a red, red rose.

Then hurrah for RHC, for her future that's to be,
May she flourish now and ever for all the world to see
Sing hurrah for RHC, give a cheer with three times three,
For our Founder and our College, sing hurrah for RHC . . .[37]

The procession ended in the Founder's Quad, with more songs, cheers for the Founder and Jane Holloway, for Miss Penrose and the newly appointed Principal, Miss E. C. Higgins.

During the principalship of Miss Penrose the social life of the College developed organically as its numbers increased. Miss Penrose had aimed to bring student numbers up to 200, the community which the Founder had intended as the full complement, but this target had not been reached by the date of her resignation. However, between 1897 and 1907 the total of students had increased from 107 to 171, and Miss Penrose was congratulated by the Governors on her success in attracting applicants. With the rapid increase in numbers the College moved away from the ethos of an extended family to that of a collegiate life in which the members had a sense of corporate unity although they were no longer intimately acquainted with all their fellows.

In this situation the institution of the College Family came into being. When freshers arrived at College a small group, anything from three to ten in number, would coalesce into a Family. Its purpose was to act as a mutual support group, to ensure that nobody would be lonely or friendless. One of its most important functions was the making of tea at 4 p.m. and the acquisition of extra food from a common fund. Theoretically each member of the Family took her turn to make tea for the rest, an arrangement which was particularly beneficial to the scientists whose afternoons were occupied by practicals and who therefore usually relied on the good offices of the rest. Many Families became such close groups that they maintained contact throughout their lives. Some alumnae now in their eighties have told the author that these friendships from their College days have consoled them in what would otherwise have been intensely lonely old age. The disadvantage of the tradition, according to others, was that Families were formed in such early acquaintance that opportunities for close friendships with more congenial fellow students may have been lost. Families, though not in principle exclusive, tended to monopolise the social lives of their members.

College Hours and Family activities did not consume the entire work and leisure time of the students. There were numerous societies and clubs to occupy their apparently inexhaustible energy. During the early decades of the College most of the societies had staff presidents or committee members, and all had a high level of staff participation. With splendid dedication, the staff gave lectures to the societies, contributed papers, debated, danced, organised charities and played sports. 'Do the staff *live?*' queried a student, who wondered if they reserved any time for their private lives. The answer was that they did not; they were wholly absorbed in the academic and social life of the College.

Formed in the first term of the College's existence was the CHARD Society, its title being an anagram of Royal Holloway College Amateur Dramatic (later the anagram was taken to stand for Royal Holloway College Dramatic Association, and the word 'Society' was dropped). Miss Péchinet was CHARD's Stage Manager, or Director in modern terminology. Its first Treasurer was Constance Bicknell (student 1887-91) who played the part of Tony Lumpkin in *She Stoops to Conquer,* CHARD's first production. (After leaving College she qualified as a nurse, married Dr Auden, a general practitioner in York, and became the mother of the poet W. H. Auden.) CHARD's annual productions were great College events, but Miss Péchinet's direction was an ordeal for the actors, who winced from her proverbially sharp tongue. 'Pray, what emotion am I supposed to feel at *this?*' she would demand, giving a merciless imitation of the actor's efforts.[38] Miss Péchinet retired in 1909, in declining health, to die in 1911. At first no one could imagine how CHARD would flourish without her, but its direction was taken over first by Miss Honey (Lecturer in French 1905-43; Head of Department from 1910) and then Miss Rowell, until the First World War, when drama lapsed for the duration. Among CHARD's many enterprising productions in pre-war years were Lyly's *Love's Metamorphoses* and Gilbert Murray's translation of Aristophanes' *The Frogs.*

There were three musical societies: Choir, the Choral Society and Band, the College orchestra, in which both staff and students played. An early musical triumph was a joint performance by Choral and Band of Pergolesi's *Stabat Mater,* conducted by Miss Daymond. Choral and Band frequently worked together, and another notable joint achievement was their performance in 1905 of Mendelssohn's music to Sophocles' *Antigone,* produced by the Classics Department in the original Greek. Miss Phoebe Walters (Head of Department of Music 1904-15) adapted the music, which was originally written for a male voice chorus and a German translation of the text; she wrote with modest pride that the whole production turned out to be 'one of the permanently memorable occasions of life'.[39] In its early years Band was exclusively a string orchestra, and the exodus at the end of each summer term could reduce it to a small group of violins. Year after year Miss Walters appealed for new instruments and instrumentalists to enable Band to increase its repertoire; she was overjoyed when a viola was presented as a permanent gift, and when Professor P. V. Bevan (Head of Department of Physics 1908-13) joined Band as a cellist.

The departmental societies, with a few fluctuations, steadily increased in number. A representative selection in the early years of the century included the Science Discussion Society, the Botanical Society, the Literary Society, the History Society, French and German Reading Societies and the Classical Club. English societies proliferated, with Shakespeare, Dickens, Tennyson and Browning Societies, and a Browning Discussion Society. The Art History Society attracted members from all departments. It would be impossible to detail the support given by the staff to all these societies, but Miss Penrose herself set an example which the rest followed. In 1901 she brought her father to lecture to the Science Discussion Society on 'The Orientation of Temples and the Astronomy connected with It', and she herself lectured to the Classical Club on 'Greek Dress'. In 1903 she gave an open lecture to the College on the Parthenon, illustrated by 'lantern slides', and read a paper to the Art History Society on 'Greek Architecture'. The Literary Society was frequently invited to meet in her Drawing Room, where she also read aloud Ruskin's *The Stones of Venice* to a select audience on Sunday evenings. She advised on the Classicists' production of *Antigone*, and may have written the eloquent and informed appreciation of it in the *College Letter*.[40] But even Miss Penrose could unbend to entertain, and in 1904 she gave the College an amusing lecture on 'Athenian Life'. For all their serious intent, the departmental societies enjoyed entertaining themselves or the College with plays and competitions. The Botanical Society tried to spread enthusiasm for its subject with an annual Botany Tournament in which pairs of competitors were challenged to identify over a hundred plant specimens gathered in the College grounds.

The love of discussion and debate led to the founding of three societies. The Political Society was organised as a shadow Parliament 'complete with parties, front and back benches, Speaker, and the forms and titles of the House of Commons'.[41] Conservatives and Liberals took office turn and turn about, at the beginning of each session, but the 'government' could fall on a division. The Royal Holloway College Parliament debated the issues currently preoccupying the Parliament at Westminster, though frequently with very different results. Regardless of which party was in office, the House was generally reformist in temper: before the end of the nineteenth century it had granted women the vote, restored the Elgin Marbles to Greece and abolished the House of Lords! The Debating Society concerned itself with the type of moral problem which often commends itself to such societies; for example, 'That a lawyer is utterly unjustified in defending a client whom he believes to be in the wrong' (a motion which was lost). When the debates were concluded, the society adjourned to the Picture Gallery and ended the evening with a dance. The Sharp Practice Society specialised in impromptu debates, with speeches limited to 3½ minutes, on less serious topics, such as 'Babies generally receive more attention than they deserve'.

The earliest of the College charitable societies was the Waif and Stray

Society, which adopted a 'College Waif', destined for domestic service, and with the aid of the Chapel Offertory collections maintained her in a children's home. A needlework group, which met at teatime, made clothes for her. In 1898 the President, Miss Daymond, reported that the Society had made for the current 'College Waif', Ellen Pooley, 'a present of a long cloak (her particular ambition)'.[42] In 1891 a branch was formed of the Lambeth Association, to help the Club for Factory Girls, later known as the Daisy Club. In the same year a society was formed to support the Women's University Settlement in Southwark. Both these societies performed fund-raising entertainments, and invited parties from the Club and the Settlement to spend the day at College. A children's Christmas party was organised every year in Southwark.

The first religious society to be founded in College was a branch of the Society of the Annunciation, which originated as a guild of Anglican women students in the Oxford colleges, formed in 1893 by Bishop Gore. It was based on the belief that women in higher education 'had special gifts to be consecrated, temptations to meet and services to render'.[43] The particular service which it rendered at Royal Holloway was to encourage the spiritual life of the maids by helping to prepare them for Confirmation and holding joint meetings for devotional study with them. In 1906 this work was extended by the formation of St Mary's Guild for communicants, which comprised equal numbers of maids and members of the Society of the Annunciation, under the presidency of Miss Hayes-Robinson. The meetings of the Guild cannot have been altogether easy, for under other circumstances the students were strongly discouraged from social intercourse with the maids. Both the SA and the Guild lapsed after the First World War. In 1900 a College branch of the Christian Union was founded, which in 1905 became a branch of the Student Christian Movement. Besides organising prayer meetings and Bible Circles, SCM formed a Foreign Missionary Branch, which soon absorbed an already existing Foreign Missionary Society. In 1903 a branch of the Missionary Settlement for University Women in Bombay was founded, and in 1906 a branch of the Universities' Mission to Central Africa. The Amritsar Society founded in 1911 helped to support pupils at the Alexandra High School, Amritsar.

In an attempt to reduce the conflicting claims of societies as far as possible, the Principal apportioned the weekly evenings among them:

[ 105 ]

Monday was for Band, German Reading and Art History; Tuesday for Choral; Wednesday for meetings devoted to Arts subjects; Thursday for Open Meetings; Friday for Science subjects; Saturday was 'a cheerful free-for-all'. Obviously this arrangement did not eliminate all dilemmas, but most students must have felt that the primary obligation was to belong to their own departmental societies and that other enthusiasms had to be accommodated in so far as work permitted. In order to avoid the temptation of joining too many societies, Marion Pick and her friends formed a private group, 'The Second Year Systematic Study Society', which in the next year became 'The Third Year Tenacious Toiling Troupe'.[44] She at least was rewarded by gaining a first.

The sports societies, which could claim the afternoons, did not clash with the rest, which was fortunate since sport preoccupied its enthusiasts to an extent incomprehensible to the non-sporting. 'Hockey was all embracing,' wrote Marion Pick. ' . . . it stuns one now to realise how hardly the games cult pressed on us.'[45] Royal Holloway College, with its excellent on-site facilities for sport, produced strong teams which were frequently successful in inter-collegiate matches and contests with local clubs. The Tennis Club dated from the earliest days of the College, and its first outside match was a victory over Somerville on 30 October 1890. The following summer Royal Holloway lost to Westfield and beat Girton. These three Colleges became regular opponents, with varying fortunes. The Hockey Club, founded under the presidency of Miss Faithfull, began to hold outside matches after the adoption of official rules in 1893, when the first opponent was Wimbledon High School, which was defeated. Matches with Somerville, Lady Margaret Hall, and local ladies' hockey clubs soon followed. The Hockey Club sensibly elected some non-playing members whose function was to prepare the huge teas which the players' appetites demanded. The club won the approval of sporting and non-sporting students alike with its annual Hockey Entertainment, a good-humoured satire on College life, which paid particular attention to the foibles of the staff. For example, a student who impersonated Miss Taylor ('Cato') brought the house down with the lines:

Of College conscience I've the key,
They'd have no morals but for me.[46]

[ 106 ]

While hockey was 'all embracing' other games had their periods of popularity: cricket, lacrosse, badminton, netball and croquet clubs came and went. In 1905 a Boat Club was formed, and thenceforward boating, which was non-competitive, became a favourite College recreation. No student was permitted to go on the river until she could swim three lengths of the College swimming bath fully dressed; though the swimming bath was small the test was demanding, for the clothes, kept specially for the purpose, comprised a long-sleeved blouse, a long skirt, petticoats and a corset. A boat's crew was four: a Captain, an Efficient, a Moderate and a Beginner, or a combination of these categories of expertise, so long as the Beginner was in a minority of one. Qualified staff acted as judges of the categories, and sometimes as Captains. The members of the Boat Club walked or cycled, in their spotless whites and straw hats, down to Nichole's boatyard near Runnymede, and hired a boat or a punt, taking a picnic if time permitted. Some departmental societies organised a river picnic as an annual celebration. Members of staff enjoyed the privilege of boating alone.

'To me the greatest joy', wrote Miss W. E. Delp (Head of Department of German, 1908-44), 'was occasionally to take my tea roll . . . in a single sculler, and tie up under the great chestnuts opposite Runnymede, or better still, to slip right in among a bed of rushes a little further up. There I could lie and watch the reed-warblers and the water creatures . . . for an hour or so of perfect peace . . .'[47] In the years before 1914 the sweet Thames ran softly, without much traffic on the water, or many habitations along its banks.

Back at the College the peace of College Hours or the business of a well-ordered society was broken from time to time by the noisy activities of the Fire Brigade, the only extra-curricular organisation of which membership was compulsory, for first-year students. The brigade had been formed in 1889 at the instigation of Miss Bishop, and had received instruction from Egham Fire Brigade. Its weekly fire practices with pumps, buckets and hoses, but no water, were brisk and efficient, while its 'wet drill' in the summer term tended to chaos. The fire risk in College appeared to be high, for the long corridors had no fire doors and their wooden floors were impregnated with beeswax polish; in the study of every student and lecturer there was a coal fire, and in every bedroom there were candles, for electric light was provided only in the studies. However, the risk may have been greater in appearance than in reality, for supplies of coal were small (one scuttle per day per person) and the quality of the coal was such that the fires were notoriously difficult to light. A member of staff spoke for everyone in a poem on her perennial struggle with her study fire:

> My little fire, my humorous friend,
> Why do you always let me spend
> More time than I can really spare,
> More labour than is just and fair
> In urging you to make a start
> And play at once your natural part? . . .
> For though it may be good and bold
> To sit up writing in the cold
> Like many a Renaissance student,
> One might as well be duly prudent,
> Since on a dull November night
> A good fire keeps the spirits bright
> And stirs the brain. So, let us try
> Which is the master, you or I! . . .[48]

Miss Penrose, however, was taking no chances. In 1903 she acquired a canvas escape chute, and thenceforward a new and terrifying element in College fire practices was the obligatory descent by the chute from second floor windows. Miss Penrose and Miss Guinness inaugurated the chute by making exemplary descents. Thereafter some students found the chute practice exhilarating, but for the fearful its very real hazards remained obvious: for the small and thin a rapid descent could result in friction burns and a hard landing; for the plump there was the claustrophobic terror of getting stuck. Fortunately the efficiency of the Fire Brigade was never seriously tested, nor was the real emergency value of the chute.

Miss Penrose's gesture in descending it epitomised her attitude to all College activities: her belief in the importance of participation. While she was Principal of Bedford Miss Penrose had urged her students to make the best of College life:

[ 108 ]

Miss Penrose impressed upon us that the present was the golden opportunity for making experiments with ourselves, for expanding and developing our individuality, for acquiring convictions . . .

After touching on the priceless opportunity College life affords for forming lifelong friendships . . . Miss Penrose summed up the reasons for joining in College life under three heads: 1) for the sake of the College itself; 2) for the important training in business details and committee organisation, and 3) for the harmonious development of the whole being, according to the Greek ideal of physical and moral perfection.[49]

It is the second reason, seemingly the most mundane, which gives the clue to Miss Penrose's deepest conviction. To her, the development of women's individuality through university education, and the acknowledgement of women as the equals of men in the universities were not ends in themselves. The ultimate purpose of higher education, in freeing women from the imprisonment of domesticity and social triviality, was to prepare them for active citizenship and a life of service to society. The students of Royal Holloway College accepted these ideals.

'A new world was being created,' wrote Marion Pick, 'and I remember the zest with which we all carried on our daily affairs. Our way of life was intended to be a training in virtue; we all looked forward to "Doing good" somehow, somewhere.'[50] For the students, Miss Penrose's greatest achievement was to have made the College a place where these aspirations seemed capable of realisation.

[ 109 ]

PART THREE

# YEARS OF CONSOLIDATION
# 1907–35

----------- :>:> 5 <:<: -----------

# 'THE COLLEGE *IS* MISS HIGGINS'

## The Principalship of
## Miss E. C. Higgins
## Part One: 1907–18

> . . . more and more I seem to see that the College *is*
> Miss Higgins and Miss Higgins the College . . . The
> sense of duty, of playing the game, the lack of pose
> or pretentiousness, the tolerance and kindliness and
> hospitality, the straight-forward, simple outlook of our
> students are I think a direct reflection of Miss Higgins'
> own fine attitude, they are her*self*.[1]

'THE INVASION OF THE HUNS' was the name given to the unprecedentedly large intake of thirty-two students in 1890, which
matched the number in residence and brought the student
community up to sixty-four. There was nothing barbarian about the
'Huns' except the impression that there was a horde of them; indeed,
they brought distinction to the College. Twenty-one of them gained
degrees, or were awarded classes in the Oxford examinations.[2] Five
became headmistresses and five assistant mistresses; two became doctors
and one a university lecturer. One became Principal of the College: the
redoubtable Miss E. C. Higgins.

Ellen Charlotte Higgins was born in London in 1871, of Scottish
parents who sent her to school in Scotland. She came to Royal Holloway
College with an Entrance Scholarship from Edinburgh Ladies' College.
She won a Founder's Scholarship in 1892 and Driver Prizes in 1893
and 1894. These achievements were sufficiently impressive, but in 1894
she also gained the unique distinction of being placed in the first classes
in Final Honours Mathematics at Oxford and BA (Honours) English,
with the Gilchrist Prize, in London. She was a brilliant student to whom

success came easily, but she enjoyed hard work and sought relaxation from it in an almost hoydenish enjoyment of sport. She excelled at both hockey and cricket, and joined the Unicycle Club, whose members 'drove big wooden hoops round the terraces in cold weather to warm themselves up before first lecture . . . E. C. Higgins preferred a noisy iron hoop which rattled on the concrete.'[3] She was also musical. In Band she played the violin and the viola, and during her years as Principal she performed on the cello and the double bass. In later life she took up the clarinet, and had lessons with Frederick Thurston. Friends who met her during her retirement heard her playing the flute in a remote cottage in Scotland, on a quiet evening during the Second World War, a detail which illustrates that throughout her life she never lost the desire to learn. A portrait photograph taken in Edinburgh, at the end of her student days, shows her as a thoughtful, sensitive girl, with a fresh prettiness which she would soon lose.

From Royal Holloway Miss Higgins went to teach Mathematics at Cheltenham Ladies' College, where she remained twelve years and became Head of Department. In 1907 she was appointed Principal of Royal Holloway College, at the age of thirty-six.

Miss Higgins believed that she had no dress sense, and accordingly she consulted Worth on a suitable style of dress for a College Principal.[4] Worth designed for her a suit with a jacket of masculine cut and a long skirt, a severe fashion affected by many women intellectuals of the period. Miss Higgins was satisfied, and never saw any reason to change her style. Her tailored suits, of worsted in winter and heavy silk in summer, were replaced year in year out, until her retirement in 1935, by which time they were unfashionably quaint. With the passage of years her appearance grew increasingly masculine, the effect enhanced by her close-cropped hair, stiff-collared shirt and tie, cufflinks and heavy gold wristwatch.

'She fought a battle for women's education,' wrote a man who knew and respected her. 'She believed in it as a right and not as a concession or favour. She fought against men – asked no favour and gave no quarter . . . Her struggle for the rights of women, perhaps, made her accentuate the masculine, as though she would fight the battle on equal and level terms.'[5]

Though the impression she created was undeniably odd she was far too formidable to be ludicrous. Her powerful personality inevitably inspired a wide variety of responses: 'You might not like her, but you could not forget her'[6]; 'She was apt to shatter the hypersensitive'[7]; 'Even those who were afraid of her found a friend.'[8] The students soon nicknamed her 'Chief'; to an admirer she was 'our incomparable Chief'. Dr M. F. Richey (Lecturer in German 1918-48; Head of Department from 1944; Reader from 1945), in a little book of verses entitled *Collegiate Causeries*, described her as

> The Scottish Chief
> Of manly mien, of words directly fired
> In sentence brief,
> Whose rule was famed for steadfast
> strength of mind,
> Resolved yet reasonable, firm but kind.[9]

Her kindness, which showed itself in many generous actions, and the geniality which shone through her brusque manner endeared her to those students who were not too overwhelmed to respond. 'I loved dinner nights with her,' wrote the past student who contributed to her obituary. 'I was very shy, but she had the power to make me able to talk naturally.'[10] When she led the dinner procession Miss Higgins' appearance was changed almost beyond recognition, for she donned one of her 'magnificent but fashion-defying evening dresses'[11], sombre in colour and rich in material, often worn with a splendid necklace of cornelians and diamonds.[12]

Despite her aura of power, Miss Higgins' students found her genuine warmth a welcome contrast to the all-terrifying personality of Miss Penrose. But there was a greater contrast between Miss Higgins and her predecessor than that of personality. The principalship of Royal Holloway College had been an episode in the career of Miss Penrose; Miss Higgins made the College her life. Miss Penrose, in a formative decade, set the College on the path which it would follow successfully; Miss Higgins, in a principalship almost three times as long, continued to build the character of the College and consolidate its success. At the end of this long tenure of office, Miss Rowell, who had known her throughout, summed up her achievement in the words, 'The College *is* Miss Higgins and Miss Higgins the College.'

Miss Higgins followed Miss Penrose in her determination that Royal Holloway College should be an active and integral part of London University, but it soon appeared that the status of the College in relation to the University might be called in question again.

The teaching university established by the University of London Act (1898) and the Statutes of 1900 had proved too scattered and amorphous to be easily administered. Its Schools, with the exceptions of University College and King's College, were excluded from the Senate on the grounds that institutional representation would be disruptive. The University possessed certain powers of inspection and visitation of its constituent Schools; it controlled syllabuses and degrees and could influence senior academic appointments. But it possessed no direct authority and no financial control over the Schools, and it had no financial resources to offer them. Without more control over its Schools the University was still not a teaching university in the sense of one which taught its own students.

Slowly London University progressed towards becoming such an institution: in 1905 University College became incorporated in the University, losing its separate legal existence and submitting to the control of a committee appointed by the Senate; King's College followed the same course in 1908 (except for its Theological Department, which became a separate School of the University). Thus the University gained educational and financial control over its two main teaching centres, while the other Schools remained in the same relationship to it as before. It soon became clear that a university which was neither fully incorporated nor fully federal would remain an unwieldly organisation. In 1907 Imperial College received its Charter, and the question was raised whether it should become a technological university in its own right, or if not, what its relationship with the University of London should be. The time was opportune to examine and reconsider the whole structure and constitution of the University. For this purpose the Royal Commission on the University of London was appointed under Lord Haldane in 1909.

The inspection of Royal Holloway College for the information of the Haldane Commission took place on 22 and 23 November 1909, and the resulting report gives an objective view of the achievements and limitations of the College at this date.[13] The work of all the Departments in both Faculties for the most part received warm praise, though in several instances the need, or impending need, for additional teachers was stressed. There was a considerable imbalance between the two Faculties, with fifteen staff and 128 students in the Faculty of Arts and eight staff and thirty-seven students in the Faculty of Science (with five Arts students taking one Science subject). Three members of staff taught Mathematics in both Faculties. The Inspectors noted that the Heads of Department were styled 'Professor' when they were men and 'Senior Staff Lecturer' when they were women, and that this local usage would require revision if University Professorships were established at Royal Holloway College. (The first was the Chair of Botany, to which a woman, Dr Benson, was appointed in 1912).

In the Faculty of Arts the Department of Classics was under the joint headship of Professor Donkin and Miss Taylor, who divided the teaching 'according to a scheme settled by them from time to time'.[14] They were assisted by a visiting lecturer, Mr T. W. Allen (1893-1918), and Miss E. B. Mitchell (1907-09) who taught Ancient History. With ten Honours students their work was considered heavy, 'and some further assistance will be required before long'.[15]

In the Department of English the teaching 'which appears to be conducted with great efficiency' was shared by Miss Block and Miss Murray, assisted by Miss A. H. Davies (student 1897-1901; staff 1906-11; Governor 1919-33). They had five students reading for Intermediate and fourteen for Honours, with one external Honours student and one of the last reading for the Oxford examinations. The Inspectors expressed the hope that the opportunity of reading for an MA might soon be introduced.

The Department of French had just lost Miss Péchinet and acquired Miss Honey as its head. M. Louis Brandin was visiting lecturer from 1905 to 1909, and there was an *Assistante*, Mlle M. C. Brachet, who 'according to an excellent arrangement which has long been customary in the College . . . aids the students in obtaining a command of French for the purposes of conversation'.[16] Seven students were preparing for

[ 117 ]

Intermediate and five for Honours. The Inspectors noted with approval the existence of the French Reading Society and a 'language table' in Hall.

The Department of German was run by a single Lecturer, the universally beloved Miss Wilhelmina Delp. German by birth and British by naturalisation, who lived for the College and its students, and on the outbreak of the First World War made it her 'duty and pleasure to overlay the propagandist view of the wicked Germans given in the lower type of newspaper by that of the Germany of Goethe and other poets, musicians and artists'.[17] Miss Murray of the English Department also taught Germanic Philology to the students of German, of whom there were two reading for Intermediate and three for final Honours, besides ten for Intermediate and three for final Pass. Miss Delp also taught German to a Science class which required a sufficient knowledge to read 'scientific works in that tongue'.

The Department of History was designated 'Modern History', though it included Medieval (Ancient History was the province of the Department of Classics). Miss Hayes-Robinson, the Head of Department, was assisted by a visiting lecturer, Mr Carlyle (1907-21), and a part-time lecturer, Miss Bazeley (1908-11). Five students were reading for Intermediate and twelve for Honours. The presence of one advanced student and the promise of another offered hope that the Department might progress to advanced work on a permanent basis. The Inspectors suggested the establishment of a Historical Research Scholarship.

Passing to the Faculty of Science, the Inspectors were quite shocked to discover that the Head of the Department of Physics, Professor P. V. Bevan (1908-13) was 'in the unsatisfactory position of not having a regular teaching Assistant'. He had nine students reading for Intermediate and seven for the Pass B.Sc. 'including one who may go in for Honours'. No research was being done by students, 'but the Professor is at present engaged in a spectroscopic investigation'. Professor Bevan's difficulties were increased by the fact that 'the work of this Department is carried on in a series of some 15 small rooms situated at the end of a corridor on the ground floor at the east side of the College . . . The provision for lectures is probably sufficient for the small number of students attending at any one time, but the difficulties are considerable of keeping in touch with members of Practical Classes necessarily working in small separate rooms . . .'[18]

The Head of the Department of Chemistry was Miss Field, and her Assistant Lecturer and Demonstrator was Miss Boyle (1903-33). Their facilities were far more satisfactory than those provided for Physics, as the Chemistry Department was housed in a detached building in the grounds, which contained a lecture room, a general laboratory capable of accommodating about thirty students, 'a separate balance room and two smaller well-arranged laboratories for advanced research work'. The resources of the Department were not stretched, for there were only nineteen students, eight preparing for Intermediate, ten for Pass B.Sc. and one for Honours. No research was being done by students, 'but an important investigation of the iodobenzenesulphonic acids has been recently completed by the Demonstrator as a Thesis for the Doctorate of the University'[19] (which she obtained in 1910).

The Head of the Department of Botany was Dr Benson, with Miss A. Williams as her Assistant Lecturer and Demonstrator, and Miss Welsford as Botanical Gardener. The Department had rooms in the College and a laboratory and greenhouse adjoining the Chemistry Building, in addition to its garden; while the College grounds, Windsor Great Park, and the environs of Virginia Water provided varied opportunities for fieldwork. Botany, always a popular Science subject for women, had attracted twenty-two students, six of whom were reading for Honours. The Inspectors acknowledged that the number of published papers emanating from the Department, including three in 1909, proved that 'original investigation is being carried on with enthusiasm'.[20] Zoology was taught as a subsidiary subject to Botany, by a part-time lecturer, Miss Buchanan (1889-93 and 1899-1921).

The Department of Mathematics, in both Faculties, was headed by Professor Loney and Miss Rowell as Senior Staff Lecturer, with Miss E. Williams as Lecturer (1908-10). It was she who was succeeded in 1911 by Miss Marion Pick, who had discovered as a student that the College offered 'good learning, a good life and a mannerly tradition'[21], and for thirty-five years on the staff contributed to all three. The Department had fifty-six students, thirty-five in Arts and twenty-one in Science, of whom eighteen were Honours students. Miss Higgins, not wishing to lose touch with Mathematics, took 'an active share in teaching certain Pass classes every

[ 119 ]

year'.[22] The 'highly competent Mathematical staff' impressed on the Inspectors that 'if they were to undertake advanced work, or research in Applied Mathematics', an increase in their numbers would be needed.

All in all, the Inspectors admired the vigour of these small Departments, and acknowledged that the College was outstandingly successful in turning out teachers.[23] But they deplored the fact that certain subjects were not taught at Royal Holloway College at all. 'No instruction is at present given in the College in Philosophy . . . We regard this . . . as regrettable in the interests of the educational system of the College at large.'[24] (The Mental and Moral Science course – described as 'Mental and Moral Philosophy' in the Governors' Report of 1890–91 – had by now been dropped, and a Department of Philosophy has never been established). Among the Science subjects unrepresented were 'Geology, including Physical Geography [and] Animal Physiology.'[25] However, the strongest criticisms were reserved for organisational and administrative defects. The Inspectors deplored the exclusion of women and members of staff from the governing body (both in accordance with the Foundation Deed) and the lack of a staff pension scheme, and they criticised the method of co-ordinating the teaching through the Education Council and the Staff Meeting. They described the College as plentifully supplied with undergraduate scholarships, but in need of financial provision for postgraduate and research students. They commented adversely on the very small number of students who attended inter-collegiate lectures in London, and on the fact that no students from London Colleges ever attended lectures at Royal Holloway, though they noted with approval that two Royal Holloway students, one from each Faculty, were members of the Students' Representative Council, and attended its London meetings once or twice a term.

Details concerning the social organisation of student life tended to convey an impression of self-sufficiency within the College: 'The students of the College as a body hold meetings and pass resolutions which are communicated to the Principal by the Senior Student. The Senior Student who is thus the recognised intermediary between the College and its authorities, is nominated by the Principal from among students of the fourth and fifth years and elected by the whole body of students.'[26]

The position of the Senior Student was in fact a difficult one, and her role as the Principal's mouthpiece in disciplinary matters was not always conducive of popularity with her fellow students. The Senior Student's characteristic self-importance was rather amusingly satirised in a Hockey Entertainment song:

> Propping up the College,
>   Altering its tone,
> Keeping law and order,
>   Making First Years groan.
> Activities unbounded,
>   My position always clear,
> You really ought to know me
>   I'm the Senior Student here . . .[27]

The current Senior Student gave the Inspectors a 'very clear and satisfactory account of the social arrangements of the College'; they were obviously surprised at the liveliness and sheer number of the College societies. Music, which did not fall within the purview of their survey of departments, they regarded as among the most valuable of the College's social amenities; they did not report that the high standards of Choral, Choir and Band owed much to an exacting annual appraisal by a musician of national prominence.

They concluded their report:

Altogether, the social conditions of the College seem to be exceptionally satisfactory; as to its brightness there can be no doubt whatever, and to spend two days in the College is sufficient to show how well-ordered it is in every respect, and how pleasant and stimulating must be its everyday life.[28]

The impression they received was of civilised life on an island far removed from the archipelago of the University. In Royal Holloway's distance from the main group of Colleges lay the danger to its future status.

In response to the Report, the Governors of Royal Holloway College made a number of innovations.

[ 121 ]

When the Report was received a controversy over the admission of women to the governing body had been going on for some time. The Foundation Deed of the College had contained the provision that no woman might be a Governor of the College, and that no change might be made in the constitution for twenty-one years. In 1907, as that period approached its end, at the Annual Meeting of the RHCA, one of the 'pioneer' students of the College, Miss S. C. N. Gurney (1887-92) proposed that a committee be appointed to request the Governors to alter the Foundation Deed so that women might be admitted to the governing body, and to appoint as Governors the Principal, one or more representatives of the RHCA, and one or more representatives of the staff.[29]

The RHCA proposals inevitably encountered stiff opposition from an all-male governing body, entrenched in its powers and defensive of its privileges. The most strenuous opposition came from Henry Driver-Holloway, who declared that to amend the Foundation Deed in favour of women Governors would be 'in direct opposition to the strongly held and frequently expressed opinions of the Founder'[30], a view which was supported by Sir Joseph Savory and Sir Walpole Greenwell (both created baronets), who were the only surviving members of the original Board of Governors to have been nominated by Thomas Holloway himself. However, the RHCA Committee found a strong supporter in Lord Cozens-Hardy, Master of the Rolls (Governor of RHC 1900-18), who persuaded a majority of the Governors to seek a High Court judgement on the issue, and in November 1909 Mr Justice Swinfen-Eady gave judgement in favour of the competence of three-fourths of the Governors 'so to alter the rules and regulations as to enable a woman to be a Governor or Honorary Governor'.[31]

There was some delay in implementing this decision while its supporters lobbied for a three-fourths majority, which was at last obtained when, Henry Driver-Holloway having died, Sir Joseph Savory and Sir Walpole Greenwell reluctantly waived their objection. In 1912 the Governors executed a Deed Poll, which provided that two of the co-optative Governors henceforth should be women; but as though to counterbalance feminine influence, they resolved at the same time that two extra male Governors should be co-opted. The first women Governors were the Hon Mrs John Bailey (1912-19) and Mrs Creighton

(1912-27). The other proposals of the RHCA were not conceded, but the Principal was already present at the Governors' meetings by invitation, and after 1912 two members of staff were also invited, the first pair being Professor Loney and Miss Block.

In 1915 the RHCA Committee again requested the representation of the Association on the governing body, and the following year the Governors conceded that on the first vacancy for a woman Governor occurring, the RHCA should be invited to submit three names for consideration. In 1919, at the conclusion of the Hon Mrs John Bailey's term of office, Miss A. H. Davies became the RHCA's first representative Governor. She served for two seven-year terms (1919-33), and was succeeded by Miss Fanny Street. In the meantime the Foundation Deed had again been amended in 1920, to provide for the appointment of the Principal as a Governor ex officio, and of two staff Governors, the first being those already familiar to the Board through their invited presence: Miss Block (Governor 1921-4) and Professor Loney (Governor and Trustee, 1920-38). The impression that women were appointed on sufferance was entirely obliterated when Princess Alice, Countess of Athlone, became Chairman of the Governors in 1936.

The other innovations suggested by the 1909 Report were much less controversial, and were made more speedily. The first research studentships were founded in 1910, the Staff Meeting was metamorphosed into the Academic Board in 1912, and in the same year a contributory pension scheme for both administrative and academic staff was established. Less easy to overcome was the problem of isolation from London.

The Haldane Commission reported in 1913, and summed up its conclusions with the words: 'We are convinced that it is not possible to organise a great University merely by giving a number of independent institutions with different aims and different standards a formal connection with a central degree-giving body which has practically no control beyond the approval of syllabuses for degree courses, the recognition of individual teachers and the conduct of degree examinations.'[32]

The limited power of the University over its Schools showed itself above all in the lack of financial control. 'The power of the purse is indeed the most important means of control which the University should possess if it is to organise the teaching with which it is concerned.'[33]

The President of the Board of Education appointed a Departmental Committee to consider the steps by which effect might be given to the Commission's Report, and it set itself the objective of reproducing in London the pattern of a unified city university, with central control of finance and educational policy, and with a physical concentration of teaching activities in a centralised university quarter, which was to be a site close to University College, in Bloomsbury. Under such a scheme there was no place for the independence of the individual governing bodies, and the overlapping of departments, which had resulted from the organic growth of the University in the nineteenth and early twentieth centuries. It was not surprising that the proposed reforms met with strong opposition from many Colleges, and not least from Royal Holloway. If all the Colleges of the University were to be incorporated Royal Holloway desired to be among them, yet the Governors did not wish to lose their financial independence. These aims were in themselves incompatible, but a greater problem was the proposed centralisation. Once again the administrative County of London was proposed as the limit within which the University sites should be located; once again Royal Holloway College was threatened with ineligibility, as it had been when its first proposal to join the University had been made. But should Royal Holloway be excluded from the centralised University proposed by the Haldane Commission, it would be seriously disadvantaged, for the Oxford connection which had been strong in its earlier years was by now almost severed. The Principal and Governors protested strongly, and cited the achievements of the College, which compared favourably with those of any other, as evidence of its worthiness to become an incorporated College.[34]

The Students' Representative Council as a whole upheld the Haldane Report. It had provided evidence for the Commission, and was to be granted two seats on the University Court which the Commission recommended to be established. This offer of direct influence in policy-making, together with the proposed establishment of a university quarter, had obvious appeal to the students, especially those of the predominantly non-residential London Colleges. When the SRC announced a General Meeting to pronounce its approval of the Report, Miss Higgins was quick to take counter measures. She addressed the students of Royal Holloway on the danger to their College inherent in such an approval, and despatched a party of sixty to oppose the resolution. As a result of their vigorous action the SRC meeting was adjourned. However, in December 1913 the adjourned meeting sat again and passed its supporting resolution, in spite of the opposition of a Royal Holloway contingent of 102 students.[35]

The crisis in University affairs resulting from the Haldane Report was unresolved when the outbreak of the First World War obliged the Departmental Committee to abandon its task. Miss Higgins was accustomed to write an occasional contribution entitled 'University News' in the *College Letter*. In 1914 she commented with dry satisfaction:

... it seems to be highly probable that the Senate in its present form may now look forward to several years of strenuous work, with a Constitution neither undermined by its past labours nor shattered by the application of drastic reforms.[36]

Miss Higgins' mobilisation of the students to resist the majority of the SRC proved that the remoteness of Royal Holloway College did not make its students invincibly apathetic to larger issues.

In the years immediately preceding the First World War the issue which aroused their spontaneous enthusiasm was votes for women. In 1908 the Royal Holloway College Women's Suffrage Society was founded, with a membership of forty-nine students and eleven staff, and was affiliated to the National Union of Women's Suffrage Societies.[37] 'One of its most successful meetings was addressed by Miss Gladys Pott, a leading anti-suffragist, whose exposition of her creed brought many recruits to the suffrage cause.'[38]

On 25 May 1911, the Society reported in the *College Letter*: 'Mrs Cather, a member of the Women's Social and Political Union . . . gave us an extremely inspiring address on the "Militant Methods" of the Suffragettes. This was the first time that this particular aspect of the women's movement had been dealt with by a speaker at an open meeting . . .'[39]

Later in the year, as militancy developed outside the College and found sympathisers within, the Society was disaffiliated from the NUWSS, to avoid the possibility that a splinter group might seek affiliation with the WSPU. In this instance the College authorities may have been thankful for its remoteness from London, which made it difficult for students who sympathised with militant methods to join in suffragette demonstrations. It is easy to imagine the shock wave which must have run through the College in 1913 when one of its alumnae, Emily Wilding Davison (student 1892-3, Hons English Class I, Oxford 1895), threw herself in front of the King's horse in the Derby and, whether or not she intended suicide, attained the status of a martyr for women's rights. A contingent of the RHCA walked in her funeral procession.

However, the temptation of lotus-eating in a beautiful locality probably calmed and disarmed many a potential suffragette. Frances Stevenson (student 1907-10) was perhaps an example, for in her autobiography she described her enthusiasm for women's suffrage but gave more space to the 'attraction of Englefield Green . . . its proximity to Windsor Park and the town of Windsor', where seclusion blended with glimpses of the great world:

> The distance on a bicycle through the Park to Windsor was a trifling one, and the students made regular excursions in that direction. We must have looked very prim in our long skirts, our stiff collars and our boaters, but there was no primness in our hearts. Innocence there was, for our College life was a conventional one, and most of us were content to have it so. One afternoon as we were bicycling through the Park we came suddenly upon King Edward VII and the Kaiser in a clearing. They were resting during a shoot, and dismounting from our bicycles we looked on at the little party a few yards away – a stout gentleman who was the King of England, and the German Emperor, an arrogant handsome figure in a flowing green cloak and Tyrolean hat. We saw him again during my last year at College (1910) when he came to Windsor for the funeral of King Edward, and we went over to Windsor to see the procession. He looked even more majestic in his white cape and gilded helmet, and even a shade more arrogant, I thought.[40]

A surviving student contemporary of Frances Stevenson recalls: 'When I went to College Lloyd George had fallen in love with a girl in the Third Year. She was very clever and quite lovely – I didn't blame him.'[41] From Royal Holloway Frances Stevenson went immediately to become his private secretary, and for many years accepted the half-life of an unofficial consort until he was free to marry her almost at the end of his life. Of her happy College days Frances Stevenson recollected tennis parties at a local rectory, 'when God-like young men . . . met the lovely maidens of the neighbourhood. It was a glorious, golden, top-heavy world, soon to be destroyed for ever.'[42]

There was an instant in the summer of 1914 when its impending destruction was recognised, which is encapsulated in a memoir by Miss Delp:

It was on a summer evening . . . that Miss Field and her cousin Florence took me on the river for supper. We had read that morning of the assassination of the Archduke and Archduchess of Austria, and we could think of little else. I remember Fieldie giving me a long look. 'That will mean war,' she said. It did; and the last carefree epoch for the country and the College came to an untimely end.[43]

When College reassembled in October 1914, everyone shared a sense that darkness had descended, and a certainty that 'nothing would ever be quite the same again'.[44]

The shadow of war fell upon the College as it fell upon the whole of society. Here as elsewhere there were few women who did not have a male relative in the theatre of war or, if they had none of their own, did not fear for the husbands, brothers and kinsmen of their friends. The arrival of telegrams was dreaded, lest they should bring news of death in action. Yet in this time of anxiety, morale remained high. Miss Block, who was 'almost fiercely British, inclined to recoil from everything foreign . . .' according to the unimpeachable testimony of Miss Delp, 'never let an anti-German remark go unchallenged, if it seemed to her unfair. It was a case of *noblesse oblige*.'[45]

The first acknowledgement that wartime conditions enjoined austerity was the abridgement of dinner by the abandonment of the biscuit course, 'to the regret of all those British souls who value tradition at its true worth'.[46] In 1916, when a potato shortage was threatened, Miss Higgins and some members of the staff made themselves responsible for cultivat-

[ 127 ]

ing a 'potato patch', a newly established croquet lawn being sacrificed for the purpose.[47] With 94 acres to choose from it seems bizarre to have selected the croquet lawn. The fact that it was a quarter of an acre in extent, and flat, though not as yet satisfactorily smooth for the game, may have been the explanation. Or perhaps the sacrifice of a piece of ground set aside for a purpose which seemed frivolous in wartime may have made its utilisation seem appropriate.

Enthusiasm to participate in the war effort first showed itself in a positive epidemic of knitting:

The whole College population in its leisure hours is given up to one pursuit. Business meetings, debates, coffee parties, four o'clock teas, unholy eleven o'clock repasts, midnight cocoa orgies and netball 'scrums' are alike graced by a certain glittering weapon – the knitting needle.[48]

Knitting comforts for the armed forces was an easy way of participating in patriotic fervour, and the emotional impetus of the activity was captured in a verse written by a past student, D. T. Stephenson (1903-06), which was published in the *Westminster Gazette*, and reprinted in the *College Letter*:

Plain and purl, plain and purl,
   List to the murmur of woman and girl;
Purl and plain, purl and plain,
   With steel and ivory, hank and skein.
Jack is watching the North Sea wild;
   Wind for him, knit for him, mother and child.

Click and frown, click and frown
   (Things for the Tommies must all be brown).
Frown and click, frown and click,
   (Blue for the Navy, and wanted quick).
Frosts fall deep, on the trenches piled;
   Knit for him, wind for him, mother and child . . .[49]

[ 128 ]

Miss Emily Daymond,
Head of Department of Music,
1887–1899.

Miss C. Frost,
Senior Staff Lecturer,
Department of Mathematics, 1887–1907.

Miss T. Dabis,
Lecturer in Classics,
1887–1899.

Miss E.C. Higgins,
the future Principal,
at the end of her student days.

Students in the Dining Hall:
centre left, Miss Penrose at High Table.

A Family has tea in a study.

A Family has tea out of doors.

Royal Holloway College students boating on the Thames.

Royal Holloway College Cricket Team, 1890s.

An early game of hockey: figure in centre foreground is
Miss E.C. Higgins, the future Principal.

Band, conductor Miss Emily Daymond.

ΛΕΥΣΣΕΤΕ ΟΙΑ ΠΡΟΣ ΟΙΩΝ ΑΝΔΡΩΝ ΠΑΣΧΩ ΤΗΝ ΕΥΣΕΒΙΑΝ ΣΕΕ

The Classics Departm■
production of *Antigon*■
1905.

Royal Holloway Colle■
the Library, 1937.

Miss E.C. Higgins, Principal of Royal Holloway College, 1907–1935.

The interior of Royal Holloway College Chapel.

By such efforts and emotions, or by hearing the occasional 'throb of a patrolling aeroplane overhead', the students of Royal Holloway College, together with the rest of the civilian population, imagined that they were glimpsing 'the meaning of war', a supposition bitterly castigated by more than one soldier-poet who endured the horror of the trenches.

In 1915 war work was organised on a more efficient basis. At the beginning of the academic year two College work rooms were established on West III. Miss Higgins provided a sewing machine on permanent loan, and other machines were loaned according to demand. During the first week of term registration forms were sent to every member of the College, and 128, or 73 per cent of the total, were returned. At first the total number of hours offered was 265, an average of two hours a week by each person who returned a form. Further offers, perhaps from those originally reluctant, followed; soon the work rooms were in use for 300 hours a week. Miss Knowles, the Lady Housekeeper, directed the work of making hospital clothing, such as 'day shirts', 'operating shirts' and 'helpless case shirts', for the Princess Christian British Red Cross Military Hospital, Englefield Green.[50] A few weeks later another work room was opened, in which bandages were rolled on hand-operated machines; during the term 520 bandages were sent to the Kensington War Hospital Supply Depot.[51]

Despite the anxiety of wartime the College could still cast the potent spell of happiness which it had cast upon the pre-war students. A student who came up in 1915 wrote in retrospective self-reproach:

I had no business to be so happy. Both my brothers were at the front . . . and nearly all my new found friends were in similar case. Sometimes I took myself to task for being so irresponsible, but how readily I assured myself that I could do no good by worrying, and sped upon my thoughtless happy way.[52]

The obvious outlet for high spirits was in sport. In the absence of the College gardeners at the front, the students willingly took upon themselves the task of maintaining the grass courts and hockey pitches. During the war the Tennis Club continued to organise inter-collegiate matches within the University of London Athletic Union; but the Hockey Club, faced with the problem of transporting larger teams, abandoned away matches for the duration of the war. However, there was plenty of available talent within the College, and in 1915 someone had the idea of organising a Beauty versus Brains Hockey Match. Miss Pick accepted the invidious task of selecting the teams. The match was a great success:

> During the first half Beauty seemed all-conquering, for when the half-time whistle sounded she led by four goals to nil. In the second half we had a veritable moral sermon on the transitoriness of Beauty and the solid endurance and sustaining energy of Brains; for, in spite of the brave stand made by Beauty, the final score was four all. It seems that the lesson of this match was that in the ideal woman, beauty and brains conmingle in equal proportions.[53]

Such events were the highlights on a generally sombre picture. Each year of the war a few students dropped out of College: in the academic year 1914–15 the total number of students fell from 163 to 156; in 1915–16 from 154 to 149; in 1916–17 from 148 to 144. The next year a total of 155 was maintained.[54] Explanations may be that these students left to take up the wider opportunities for war work now available to women (such as joining the VAD), or returned home to support a bereaved mother; but without individual histories these explanations remain conjectural. For the most part the students were convinced that higher education for women was of greater value than ever before. 'We know that we are facing a future in which every resource, whether of brain or soul or training, will be needed to build up a purer society on the ruins of the past.'[55] Alas, this idealism was one of the most tragic casualities of the war.

Members of the RHCA undertook a wider range of war work, such as nursing in military hospitals at home and abroad, work for Government Departments, welfare work, canteen work and child care. Many reported their experiences in the *College Letter*, encouraging Royal Holloway students to follow in their footsteps when they had completed their courses. Constance Beaumont (student 1909-12), private secretary to Sylvia Pankhurst, contributed to the *College Letter* an impassioned plea to graduates not to become 'lady munitioneers', a form of war work which might appear to be the highest patriotism, but was in fact the highest egotism, since it wasted intellect in unskilled labour, and took work from less educated women who could perform it efficiently.[56] The most intellectually distinguished of the 'pioneer' students, Dr Martha Whiteley, gave the following account of her work at Imperial College during the First World War:

> Those were very exciting days, for our laboratories were requisitioned by the Ministry of Munitions who kept us busy analysing and reporting on small samples collected from the battlefields or from bombed areas at home. These included flares, explosives and poison gases. It was my privilege to examine the first sample of a new gas, used to such effect on the front that our troops had to evacuate Armentières as it was reputed to cause blisters; it was called Mustard Gas. I naturally tested this property by applying a tiny smear to my arm and for nearly three months suffered great discomfort from the widespread open wound it caused in the bend of the elbow, and of which I still carry the scar. Incidentally, when shortly afterwards we were carrying on a research for a method of manufacturing the gas, my arm was always in requisition for the final test.[57]

Throughout the war Royal Holloway College students past and present 'did their bit' in the parlance of the period, and in November 1918 shared in the rejoicings which followed the Armistice 'with bonfires and revels'.[58] But rejoicing was brief. The great influenza epidemic which followed the war struck the College the week after the Armistice, and enforced its closure three weeks before the end of the winter term. Nationwide the epidemic claimed a high death toll, but the College was fortunate in losing no lives. On this muted note of thankfulness the members of the College scattered to their homes. Society began to count the cost of the Great War, and those who had presciently observed that 'nothing would ever be quite the same again' soon saw how right they had been.

---

## :>:> 6 <:<:

# TRADITION VERSUS INNOVATION

## The Principalship of
## Miss E. C. Higgins
## Part Two: 1918–35

> Throughout old Europe the war years had thrown
> many outworn conventions from their pedestals, and
> the new generation was impatient of the old . . . the
> post-war students strained at the leash . . . and a
> vigorous 'junior staff' arose, at least as restive as the
> students . . .[1]

D
URING the early years of the College the important post of
Secretary to the Governors was held by Mr J. L. Clifford-Smith
(1887-98). On his death they decided that henceforth this
appointment should be filled by a woman, a spontaneous decision which
contrasts surprisingly with their determined rearguard action on the
question of women Governors. A series of women Secretaries occupied
the post for a few years each, none long enough to develop its potential
as a position of power and influence.[2] The situation was reversed after
the First World War, for in the ensuing sixty-five years the secretaryship
was held successively by four immensely influential individuals: Miss
U. R. Dolling (1918-35); Mrs M. R. Akehurst (1935-48); Miss Dorothy
Hustler MBE (1948-64); Mr Richard Hardy (1964-85).*

In 1918 the Governors appointed Miss Ulrica Dolling, an imposing
Northern Irishwoman, whose formidable efficiency was sugared with a
pleasant wit: ' . . . her stories, alas unrecorded, of life in Northern Ireland
at the turn of the century, were pure Somerville and Ross.'[3] With the
characteristic versatility of a liberated Victorian lady, she was an expert

---

* Since the merger of Royal Holloway College and Bedford College in 1985,
Mr Hardy has continued in office as Secretary of Royal Holloway and Bedford New
College.

[ 132 ]

mountaineer, 'an accomplished needlewoman and superb cook', and she later became a terrifying driver of a succession of small cars. She was 'a large person, great-hearted, wide-minded and physically impressive with her red hair, erect carriage and alert, outward-looking personality.' Her obituarist, in the *Journal of the Ladies' Alpine Club*, admired her mastery of a range of responsibilities at Royal Holloway College, 'from adminis- tration and finance to drainage, the welfare of pigs, and the maintenance of the fabric of the buildings, including all those serac-like pinnacles.'[4]* She soon became as much a part of the College as any of its architectural features: 'One remembers her clothes, nearly always in the shades of brown and gold that went well with the red gold of her hair; or the imposing sight of her and Miss Pick [who was also large and red-haired] playing their double basses in orchestra . . .'[5]

From their first encounter at her appointment, Miss Dolling and Miss Higgins became inseparable companions, working together on College affairs, travelling and mountaineering together in the vacations, and living together after their retirement in 1935. During the decades following the First World War they seemed to succeeding generations of Royal Holloway students to be the twin embodiments of the College traditions of good living, good manners and strict discipline: grand, exacting and anachronistic.

The ethos of the College was profoundly changed after the First World War. 'In 1918 we breathed once more,' wrote an anonymous member of staff, 'and together with renewed hope we found new problems. Throughout old Europe the war years had thrown many outworn conventions from their pedestals, and the new generation was impatient of the old.'[6]

This was inevitable, for the war had changed the condition of women throughout society. Women who had worked in military hospitals or munition factories, or undertaken traditionally masculine jobs in the absence of men, were contemptuous of the conventions which had trammelled them in pre-war days, and were not prepared to submit to them again. The students who came to College immediately after the war soon showed that they had been affected by the spirit of the age.

---

* 'One of the castellated masses into which a glacier is divided at steep points by the crossing of crevasses.' *Concise Oxford Dictionary*.

But for them more decisive still was the fact that from the combined allied forces over 5,000,000 men had been killed, and many thousands more had subsequently died of wounds, or having been listed as missing disappeared without trace. In Britain alone there were approximately 1,000,000 women regarded as 'surplus'. There was little point in chaperoning young girls to preserve their chastity for hypothetical marriages which were unlikely to take place. The independence which their mothers' generation had struggled to win was theirs by necessity, for most of them would have to earn their own living.

Miss Muriel Glyn-Jones, daughter of a Member of Parliament, who entered Royal Holloway College after the war described the clarity with which this situation was recognised in her family:

My father decided to discuss my future with me. He said he would like to see me happily married, but after what had gone on in Flanders for the past four years that could only be doubtful. He would never be able to leave enough money for me to live on, but he was prepared to spend any money I could use for my education. It was later decided I should go to Royal Holloway College . . . [7]

Not all fathers would have been so honest with their daughters, or so forward-looking, but many young women understood their situation for themselves. 'Most of my generation of students,' wrote one who came to College in 1918, ' . . . did not expect to marry . . . because our opposite numbers had all been killed . . . teaching was the obvious activity for which most of us studied.'[8]

Contrary to their expectations, of the eighty-one students who came up in 1918, twenty-nine ultimately married; but thirteen of these had already taken up independent careers, in most instances, teaching.[9] The author of the previous quotation, Mrs Kathleen Lathbury, (student 1918-22), who married in 1930, was an exception, for she became a research chemist in industry, a career in which she found that promotion for women was discouraged by constant injustices and petty humiliations. It is pleasant to record that in later life she had a second career as a successful portrait painter.[10] It is not surprising that these young women who had ambition thrust upon them were less submissive to convention

[ 134 ]

than their Victorian and Edwardian predecessors; what is surprising is that they did not demand even larger liberties.

The time for demanding sexual freedom was not yet, since the opportunity to indulge it was lacking. However, any student who had a male visitor other than her father or her brother was now permitted to invite him to tea without also inviting a member of staff as chaperone, a new concession in acknowledgement that times had changed. It might have been supposed that with expectations of contacts with the opposite sex at a low ebb, lesbian relationships would have become commonplace in a large and fairly isolated community of young women. Close friendships dating from student days, and later shared lives, were common among women of this generation, but sexual relationships between them were probably far rarer than a more permissive generation imagines. Disapproval of lesbianism was so extreme as to render it completely unmentionable, so that ignorance of its existence was not uncommon in the young. The relationship of Miss Higgins and Miss Dolling was not perceived in these terms at all, as it might have been in later years. As late as the 1940s ignorance of homosexuality was still possible, as a student of that period recalls with astonishment: 'I remember [my friend] Lucy saying "Do you think X and Y are – you know?", "I don't know" I replied, and was enlightened – my first acquaintance with lesbianism, at that age!'[11]

Innocent and earnest, the post-First World War students came to College determined to prepare themselves for their careers. They worked extremely hard, and enjoyed the same relaxations as their predecessors: tennis, hockey, boating, and eating huge teas with their College Families. The importance of tea supplies found its way into a Hockey Entertainment operetta, *College Life* (1929). To the tune of 'There is a Tavern in the Town', one student sends another shopping to Englefield Green:

> Oh, are you going to the Green?
> You are? I was afraid that you had been.
> I want some cakes
> The kind that Dallen makes,
> You know the sort of thing I mean . . .[12]

[ 135 ]

There were two bread and cake shops in Englefield Green, Bindle's and Dallen's. Their names gave rise to two verbs: 'to bindle meant to hurry round as speedily as possible, and to dallen, to take one's time and go the longest way.'[13]

The perennial preoccupation with the acquisition and consumption of extra food was not an implicit criticism of College catering, even though Miss Pick lamented that 'After the Versailles Peace Treaty had been signed and the wartime rigours had vanished . . . I do not think that our cuisine ever fully recovered.'[14] In fact, if the College cuisine suffered permanently, it was probably not the consequence of the war, but of the retirement of the Lady Housekeeper, Miss Knowles, in 1918. Her successor, Miss Simpson (1919-31) may not have prided herself on 'keeping a liberal table' as Miss Knowles had done, but she still provided meals of Edwardian profusion, which during the summer term included the home-grown asparagus which was the delight of the College. On Sundays, to give the maids a rest, she served cold chicken and a very alcoholic trifle which were left in readiness for a buffet supper. The trifle was much appreciated by Professor Benson who was a strict teetotaller, but 'nobody had the heart to tell her why . . . [it] . . . tasted so particularly nice.'[15]

So far as food was concerned the post-First World War students had nothing to complain about, but the students of the 1920s were not much given to complaint. They do not even appear to have thought College Hours irksome, a grumble of the following decade. They showed their new spirit of independence chiefly in wanting to control more areas of their social lives than before. While most clubs and societies had been founded by members of staff, and had continued to be controlled or guided by them up to the First World War, after the war control of most of them passed into the hands of the students. The changing character of the political clubs under their control mirrored the new spirit. The Political Society, the College's shadow Parliament, which had seemed such a lively gathering during the first two decades of Royal Holloway's existence, began to seem like a charade during the sombre days of the First World War, and it came to a faltering conclusion. The Royal Holloway College Suffrage Society saw its main purpose achieved with the passing of the Sex Discrimination (Removal) Act (1918), which granted the vote to women over thirty. Its place was taken by an affiliated

[ 136 ]

branch of the National Union of Societies for Equal Citizenship, which in turn thought its purpose achieved with the removal of an age discrimination between male and female voters in 1928.[16] In 1919 a Socialist Society was founded, at first affiliated to the University Socialist Federation, but later to the Fabian Society. In 1920 the society was addressed by George Bernard Shaw on the subject of 'University Socialism'. A sub-branch of the League of Nations was founded in 1921, which flourished during the next two decades. The Left Book Club, founded in 1938, changed its name to the Political Discussion Group, and in 1939 became the Politico-Economic Club. In the Lent term of 1942 some of its members broke away to form the Left Club.[17]

In spite of these activities, Royal Holloway College between the wars had the reputation of being politically apathetic. Some students from the 1920s have expressed retrospective astonishment at how little interest the General Strike of 1926 aroused in College; while students from the 1930s have expressed equal surprise at their lack of concern with the Depression, even though it endangered their prospects of employment. The novelist Rosemary Manning (student 1930-33) told the author:

> 1933 was a very bad year for anyone to come out in the world . . . it was just coming into the Slump . . . Our politics came to us after we'd left College, when we were forced to see, of course, what unemployment really was which we hadn't even thought about at College . . . I don't think it impinged on Holloway at all . . . Getting a job was a struggle and suddenly our middle-class eyes were opened to the fact that even being middle-class didn't get you a job. Therefore I would blame the College very seriously for giving us a very rude awakening when we got out into the world. I suppose the ostrich-like quality was rather emphasised at Holloway College because we were cut off from the University.[18]

However, the politically active minority, the organisers and members of the political clubs, came away with an entirely contrasting impression. Lady Linstead, née Marjorie Walters (student 1933-6; MA 1938; Member of Council 1969-84) wrote:

The world outside *did* break in. William Beveridge came to lecture. He referred to the *structurally unemployed* a phrase which I remembered ever after and have recognised in recent years as a description of those ... who must of necessity (perhaps) be numerically redundant to the needs of society, a waking nightmare of a concept. Harold Lasky came and many others, from many walks of life ... RHC ... created an attention to the world and its ways in which the poor ... had a role and a place.[19]

Not long after the First World War the staff-dominated College Meeting began to seem anachronistic: 'the staff began to find itself in an exclusive minority against the students; the situation became untenable and they withdrew.'[20] In 1923 the Students' Meeting reformed itself as the Royal Holloway College Union Society, and became affiliated to the National Union of Students. The staff decided that the business hitherto conducted by the College Meeting could be discharged henceforward by the Union, and the College Meeting formally disbanded itself in 1925. At this date it could be said that the student community came of age.

Not all the innovations in College life resulted from student initiative. After the war retirements and new appointments changed the character of the academic community. New members of staff were not willing to yield to the total immersion in College life which had been expected of the older generation; they wanted to reserve some time and space for their private lives. As student numbers grew the traditional obligation for everybody to know everybody began to approach the limits of the possible. There were 200 students by 1920, a total which fluctuated only slightly during the decade. This was the student community which the Founder had envisaged, on the basis of two rooms for each student, but it was a number which made dining in Hall, for example, an exhausting experience, no longer the house party-like ritual of old. 'To one returning to College after dinner had begun,' wrote Miss Pick, 'from under the North Tower the sound was that of a rough sea breaking on rocks, from outside the Hall door the noise was that of an avalanche.'[21]

The staff introduced for themselves the respite of dining in turn, once or twice a week according to seniority, in Retreat, a small dining room, West I 32, in which eight women at a time could enjoy a quiet dinner. But some staff found that Retreat was an insuffficient remedy for the noise and for the galling fact that students were reluctant to invite new staff to be their dinner partners, and were inclined to invite the old and familiar members, who discovered to their amusement that they were nicknamed 'Greybeards'. In 1932 the general dinner partner system was abandoned, and the staff dined at the High and Staff Tables, leaving the students to select their dinner partners among themselves. The students, however, did not abandon the time-honoured hierarchy of seniority. At this period the custom of the 'Slave Market' was introduced; at the beginning of the academic year freshers were lined up in the Picture Gallery in front of *The Babylonian Marriage Market*, for their elders, in order of seniority, to select their dinner partners, a ritual which must have imposed a great deal of misery and embarrassment to the shy, though most alumnae now remember it with amusement. Miss Higgins continued to invite student partners to the High Table as a means of knowing them personally, an invitation which was either appreciated or dreaded according to the social capacity of the student. A student from the 1930s described her own solution to the problem of talking to Miss Higgins:

I knew that she had been abroad in the summer holidays, so naturally asked her about it. She was well and truly launched when she suddenly stopped and said, 'But, Miss Griffiths, *you* are supposed to be entertaining *me*' – to which I replied 'But, Miss Higgins, some people have to be listeners!' She was quite amused.[22]

Some older members of staff regretted the opportunity of conversing with the students at dinner, and extended their invitations to coffee, in imitation of Miss Block who had long kept a Sunday morning salon at which acceptance was a highly valued privilege.

From 1921 onwards the Governors decided that four senior women members of staff should be permitted simultaneously to be non-resident.[23] This decision followed the creation of a University Chair of History at Royal Holloway College, and the appointment of Professor Hilda Johnstone (1921-42), who claimed the right of non-residence as a professional prerogative. Up to 1939 only four members of staff had availed themselves of the privilege, so that it was scarcely 'significant of a certain disintegration' as an anonymous member of staff lamented.[24]

The privilege of non-residence may have represented a valuable principle, but there were obvious reasons why it was not much pursued in practice. Residence was financially advantageous, for the non-residence allowance was initially £150 per annum, which would not have provided a standard of living equal to that in College, besides which freedom from domestic responsibility was too great a convenience lightly to be abandoned. Miss Pick confessed that there were days 'when residence made one feel crushed'.[25] For her, a period of solitude with an 'Engaged' notice on the door, a trip to London, or half an hour in the bird sanctuary which she established in the College grounds, were usually enough to make residence seem bearable again. For those in need of a longer rest, the Marie Péchinet Memorial Fund had been set up immediately before the First World War, to provide a sabbatical term for a resident of not less than six years' standing. After a tour of the sites of ancient civilisations in the Near and Middle East financed by this fund in 1928, Miss Pick, who had dallied with the idea of non-residence, decided to remain in College after all. She probably expressed the thoughts of many other devoted Hollowegians when she wrote, 'I know I should have gloomed at nights and felt I had been shut out of Paradise whenever I looked at the lights of the College.'[26]


Miss Pick was discreet in mentioning no names when she wrote of traditionalists and innovators, but details of staff changes between the two World Wars provide the dramatis personae of a period of some social conflict and much academic achievement.

Around the time of the First World War many members of staff appointed in the nineteenth century either reached retiring age or decided to move on. Miss E. E. Field, Head of the Department of Chemistry since 1893, retired in 1913, to be succeeded by Professor George Barger, who was appointed to the newly established University Chair of Chemistry tenable at Royal Holloway College; but he resigned only one year later, on being appointed Research Chemist under the Medical Research Committee.[27] In 1915 Miss H. M. R. Murray, Lecturer in Germanic Philology since 1899 (Senior Staff Lecturer since 1905) left Royal Holloway to become Director of Studies in English, Historical and Comparative Philology at Girton.[28] Professor Donkin of

Classics, appointed in 1890, retired in 1918. He and his sister Miss Donkin had a special place in the social life of the College, for their custom was to perform little plays or 'dramatic interludes' written by Miss Donkin, at fund-raising entertainments for College charities. Their simplicity and kindness had made them much beloved.

Professor Loney, Head of the Department of Mathematics since the first year of the College's existence, retired in 1920. He was a great teacher, whose name was familiar to generations of mathematics students as the author of a famous series of textbooks; as a practical man of affairs he was a valued business adviser to the first three Principals of the College. In the University he was Chairman of Convocation and a member of the Senate, and after his retirement he found time to accept the office of Mayor of Richmond. Professor Loney's retirement from teaching did not diminish his influence on Royal Holloway, for he remained a Governor and Trustee of the College, and was Chairman of the Finance Committee from 1921 to 1937. In the autumn of 1938, a few months before his death, he attended a dinner in Hall to celebrate his half-century of association with the College. His appearance, with fierce dark eyes and pointed white beard, was that of an eminent Victorian. It is not surprising to read in his obituary:

> To the eager progressive he seemed an inveterate reactionary. But much of his dislike of change sprang from sentiment for tradition, and even those who differed from him in matters of policy recognised and admired his devotion to the College and its interests.[29]

After 1920 only four full-time members of staff appointed in the Victorian period remained: Professor Benson, Miss Taylor, Miss Block and Miss Rowell. These surviving Victorians, together with the slightly younger group of staff appointed in the early years of the twentieth century, represented the forces of tradition, opposed to the innovations of the 1920s and 30s, but not always unfriendly to the innovators as individuals.

The Faculty of Arts contained some of the oldest and most vigorous of the traditionalists. In the Department of Classics Miss Taylor, Senior Staff Lecturer since 1899, and for many years acknowledged as the College's guardian of morals and arbiter of manners, remained in office until 1934. Her antique austerity was combined with a progressive commitment to the rights of women, including their right to ordination as priests in the Church of England, an issue which is likely to remain controversial for many years to come.

In 1920 Professor J. H. Sleeman was appointed Head of Department (Professor of the University of London 1922-46). He was described as 'a devoted, patient and accurate teacher of every type of pupil, from the weakling to the good honours student', and he was enthusiastic in extending the postgraduate work of the Department. His special interest was in Neo-Platonic philosophy, especially the works of Plotinus. He spent his retirement working on the Index of Plotinus, which was completed but unpublished when he died in 1963.[30] Miss Avery Woodward joined the Department in 1928, as Lecturer in Classics, became Senior Lecturer in 1936 and Reader in 1947. She retired in 1953, as a far more genial woman than the reserved young scholar the College had first known. Miss Woodward's socialist politics had first distanced her from some of her colleagues, most of whom were Conservatives and could not imagine 'a lady' holding views left of liberal!

Miss Block headed the Department of English from 1899 to 1926. In her early years, when the College was severing its connection with Oxford and establishing its position as a constituent school of London University, Miss Block 'threw all the weight of her energy and personality into securing, as far as her *own* subject was concerned, that the College should fill this place worthily and strenuously. This meant hard labour as Examiner and on committees; in particular it fell to her as Chairman to steer the untried Board of Studies in English through an important phase of its early life after the break-up of the old composite Board of Modern Languages.'[31] One of her early students remembered her determination to show 'that English was no soft option, but that it afforded scope for the strenuous mental discipline rightly associated with the Classics'.[32]

In 1915 she was joined by Miss G. D. Willcock (student 1908-13; staff 1915-55: Head of Department from 1926; Reader from 1938; Professor from 1946; Governor 1936-9; Member of Council 1951-3 and 1954-5). Professor Willcock's teaching was characterised by her 'resolutely enforcing Block's Law that the school of English requires a tough academic discipline'.[33] Her dry wit led her to declare at the end of her teaching career that for each of forty years she had been 'peeling off yet another choice word, ironic play or lively reference (especially Biblical) in her effort to keep in constant touch with the current student's possibly ready-to-be-filled but more probably all-too-vacant mind'![34] Yet her postgraduate students and later her younger colleagues felt that 'one always worked *with* Professor Willcock, never *under* her'.[35]

Miss Block and Miss Murray had edited texts for the Early English Text Society, and some of their pupils had worked on Linguistic and Medieval Studies. Under Professor Willcock postgraduate work in English 'tended to focus itself on Renaissance Literature, especially the mid-Tudor and Elizabethan'.[36] Together with her colleague and former student Dr Alice Walker (student 1919-23; Ph.D. 1926; Staff: Department of English 1928-31; Librarian 1939-41; Principal's Secretary and Registrar 1941-4), she edited Puttenham's *The Arte of English Poesie* and planned a study of the Elizabethan critical mind, which she was never able to undertake. 'In her days,' wrote her obituarist, 'the best energies of the few women who attained high scholastic rank went into their teaching, and this, because of circumstances now completely unfamiliar, had a large domestic resonance.'[37]

Professor Willcock's power to inspire her students, not only with her delight in her favourite period of Elizabethan literature but also in the more austere pleasures of Early English, is amusingly illustrated by a pastiche Anglo-Saxon poem, 'To the Flower of the Willcockingas', written by a second-year student to encourage the third years taking their finals:

> You have started your struggle, stout-hearted sitters,
> Gathered in gallery, grim under gown;
> Pen-pushers panting o'er pulsating paper,
> Vitally vigorous, victory-sure . . .
> You will emerge, by evil unscathed
> Away from woe, we shall have wished it;
> Out of the horn-gabled hall of your hardship
> Stiffly but splendidly. So should men do.[38]

The English Department gained two long-serving members during the inter-war years: Miss H. A. C. Green (1928-67) and Dr J. M. S. Tompkins (1934-65). Miss Green was appointed to teach English

Language and her own specialist study, which was Old Icelandic. She belonged to the tradition which gave everything to teaching, and resisted the growing pressure on academics to publish. Her greatest pleasure was to encourage students who wanted to study the Norse languages and to read the Icelandic Sagas, which she particularly loved, in their original forms. Believing that 'once one had committed oneself to a society . . . it should have one's wholehearted support'[39], she lived for the College as exclusively as any of its founding members had done. Dr Tompkins came to Royal Holloway from Bedford, in the hope that the smaller College would provide her with better opportunities to pursue her own work.

'When I got to Holloway,' she told the author, 'I desperately wanted to write a book . . . I was well in my thirties, a fact which the College never took in at all.' She believed that she had found the rural peace which she sought: 'When I went down to be interviewed by Professor Gladys Willcock, I walked round the grounds with her, and a snake crossed our path.'[40] During her years at Royal Holloway Dr Tompkins produced a much acclaimed book, *The Art of Rudyard Kipling* (1959), and completed *The Poetry of William Morris* after her retirement. But far from avoiding College social life, she participated with zest in every aspect of it, including fencing and productions by CHARD.

The Head of the Department of French, Miss M. E. D. Honey, had been appointed under Miss Péchinet in 1905, and succeeded her in headship which she retained until her retirement in 1943. Miss N. McWilliam, appointed Assistant Lecturer in 1915, also retired in 1943, having acted as Principal's Deputy during the two preceding years. Neither Miss Honey nor Miss McWilliam was a Recognised Teacher of the University, as Miss Péchinet had been, which inevitably placed the Department at a disadvantage during this period, even though its efficiency was never in doubt. Dr Constance West, appointed to the Department in 1928, left the College for a brief period from 1932 to 1935, and then returned to remain as Senior Lecturer until her retirement in 1965. In 1938 she published *Courtoisie in Anglo-Norman Literature*, but her later research on nineteenth-century literature and especially on Flaubert did not lead to any publications, probably because of her increasing involvement in administration. From 1946 to 1950 she was

[ 144 ]

Vice-Principal of the College, an office which had been in abeyance since the resignation of Miss Guinness in 1908.

Dr W. E. Delp, Head of the Department of German from 1908 to 1944, taught the whole range of German Literature unaided until the appointment of Dr M. F. Richey (1918-48; Reader and Head of Department from 1944). Dr Richey, educated by her father, a country parson in County Tyrone, took her first degree through a correspondence course and entered University College as a postgraduate student of Professor Robert Priebsch, a beloved and revered teacher who introduced her to the world of Medieval German Courtly Poetry. Her love of it, especially the work of Wolfram von Eschenbach, was passed on to her own students in vivid lectures and imaginative translations, and in her own verses:

> '*Ein wiser man von Eschenbach*', 'tis he
> More than all others who has proved the human
> Throb in the living heart of man or woman
> Of that strange noble world of chivalry
> He knew, and clothed with colours that survive,
> As though the hand that blent them were alive.[41]

Her studies in Medieval German Literature at Royal Holloway culminated in the publication in 1935 of *The Story of Parzival and the Graal*. Her first book of verses, *Collegiate Causeries*, in which she celebrated College customs and paid tribute to some of her colleagues, was followed by a second collection, *Herzeloyde in Paradise* (1953), which took its title from a poem on the arrival in Heaven of Parzival's mother. During her retirement she also wrote *Studies in Wolfram von Eschenbach* (1958).

Dr Delp's long tenure of the headship of the German Department might have been a few years longer had she not chosen to take early retirement, in order to permit Dr Richey to have a reasonable period of headship in her turn and so gain the Readership to which her distinguished research entitled her. German studies attracted few students during these years, for political reasons, but those who chose to read German at Royal Holloway College found a lively and inspiring department.

The Department of History had been established as a single honours school in 1899, under Miss Hayes-Robinson, who in 1911 resigned to become a tutor at Somerville. She was succeeded by Miss Fanny Street (Senior Staff Lecturer 1911-17). The following year Miss Helen Cam, one of the most distinguished past students of the College, was appointed Assistant Lecturer. Helen Cam's First Class Honours of 1907 had been followed by a Fellowship at Bryn Mawr College in the United States. After a short period of teaching at Cheltenham Ladies' College, Helen Cam was Lecturer in History at Royal Holloway from 1912 to 1921, when she moved to Girton, where she was successively Research Fellow, Lecturer and Director of Studies in History and Law, and Vice-Mistress. From 1948 to 1954 she was Samuel Zemurray Professor of History at Harvard, the first woman appointed to a professorship in that University.

> Her work began and maintained its roots in the local communities of hundred and shire, which were the basis of the larger national representative institution of Parliament, and her own interest in politics followed the same lines. She was a devoted worker for the Cambridge Labour Party, and ... believed also in encouraging her pupils at Girton to take a practical interest in local government.[42]

No doubt these interests had already manifested themselves during her years at Royal Holloway, at the end of which she published *Studies in the Hundred Rolls* (1921). Later books were *Liberties and Communities* (1944), *England before Elizabeth* (1950) and *Law Finders and Law Makers in Medieval England* (1962).

History was already a strong department when Professor Hilda Johnstone was appointed to the University Chair of History tenable at Royal Holloway College in 1921. She had been a student of the great Medievalist Professor T. F. Tout, but during the First World War she had worked for the Board of Trade, detecting and blacklisting firms which traded with the enemy. Her arrival at Royal Holloway coincided with the opening of the Institute of Historical Research, which was a great stimulus to advanced work at the College: 'Students from elsewhere could be registered as non-resident students of RHC working at the Institute under Professor Johnstone, and students from RHC could work there at seminars under scholars of other Colleges.'[43]

Professor Johnstone's own work was chiefly on the administrative history of England in the fourteenth century, as in *The Wardrobe and Household of Henry, son of Edward I*, and *The Letters of Edward II as Prince of Wales* (1931). In 1936 she prepared the second edition of Tout's *Place of Edward II in English History*. Her students for the most part worked on allied subjects, and a strong school of historical research was developed under her guidance.

Miss I. G. Powell (Lecturer in History 1922-55) specialised in Early Stuart Naval History. Her own publications were quite exiguous, though she was an admirable supervisor of the students' seventeenth-century studies. One of them described her to the author as 'a witty woman, when you could hear what she said'. Her chief love was for the College itself, and the memorial of her devotion is her bequest of the Powell Gates, the wrought iron gates in the North Tower entrance, which in 1958 replaced the original wooden doors. Miss Powell typified the new staff of the inter-war years, who came to identify themselves with Royal Holloway College and remained to become the 'Greybeards' of a later epoch.

In the Faculty of Science two of the three departments were headed by men, which in the instance of the Department of Physics had been so from the beginning. The Department had been founded in 1891 under Professor H. L. Callendar, an expert in his time on the thermal capacity of water, whose specific heat measurements were accepted as standard for many years. Callendar was succeeded by Professor W. R. Cassie (1893-1908) whose chief interest was in spectroscopic instrumentation; and his successor, Professor P. V. Bevan (1908-13) was another spectroscopist. After Bevan's sudden death, following an operation, Professor Frank Horton was appointed to the newly established University Chair of Physics, which he held from 1913 to 1945. During his early years at Royal Holloway Professor Horton researched in the field of thermionic emission and in the study of gaseous ions, to which he contributed some important papers.[44] Possibly he was first deflected from research by his determination that a new Physics Laboratory should be built at the College, which was achieved after a considerable struggle over finance with the Governors. The new building, shared with Botany, was opened in 1927, and is now incorporated in the Tolansky Laboratory. From this time forward Professor Horton was increasingly occupied in administration. In 1939 he was elected Vice-Chancellor of London

University, and held this office throughout the Second World War, until his retirement in 1946.

The Department of Chemistry had been founded under Miss M. W. Robertson (1891-3) who was succeeded by Miss Field (1893-1913), on whose retirement the RHCA put in a strong plea for the appointment of a woman to the new Chair of Chemistry which was about to be established. However, the appointment of Professor George Barger was accepted with a good grace, and no similar agitation preceded the appointment of his successor, Professor T. S. Moore (1914-46). During the First World War Professor Moore supervised work on the electrolytic oxidation of ethylene to acetic acid and on the removal of arsenic from sulphuric acid, in addition to promoting work on explosives. From 1928 to 1933 Professor Moore was Secretary of the Chemical Society. In that year he was joined in the department by Dr Millicent Plant (1933-47) who took over the teaching of Organic Chemistry, while Professor Moore taught the inorganic and physical courses. These two constituted the entire permanent staff of the department until the end of the Second World War, during which, in spite of difficult conditions, several of Dr Plant's students performed research, with an emphasis on bio-chemistry.[45]

The Department of Botany, established in 1893, continued under the headship of Dr Margaret Benson until 1922. The Botanical Garden was established in 1896, and Dr Benson also developed the area between the South Terrace and the ornamental lake as a wild garden for ferns and shade plants, an enterprise in which she was advised by Sir Joseph Hooker, formerly Director of the Royal Botanic Gardens, Kew, who during his retirement lived not far from the College, at Sunningdale. Her appointment as University Professor and her research in palaeophytology have been mentioned in a previous chapter. In 1917, with the assistance of her students, Professor Benson began a study of an area in Windsor Great Park in which the trees had been felled. The account of the resulting recolonisation was published jointly by Professor Benson and her successor Miss E. M. Blackwell, as 'Observations on a Lumbered Area in Surrey' (*Journal of Ecology*, vol 16, 1926).[46] As the dates of this work imply, Professor Benson did not sever her connection with the College after her retirement. She was present when the new Physics and Botany building was opened in 1927, when she made a speech memorable for a colossal *faux pas*, which fortunately was received with good humoured hilarity: 'She . . . said that each of her botanical assistants had been better than the one before. It so happened that Dame Helen Gwynne-Vaughan, who was in the chair, had been the first.'[47] (As Miss Fraser, Dame Helen had been Assistant Lecturer and Demonstrator in Botany at Royal Holloway from 1905 to 1907. She was appointed Head of Department at Birkbeck College in 1909, and Professor in 1921. During the First World War she was Chief Controller of QM AAC British Armies in France, and during the Second World War she was Director of the ATS from 1939 to 1941. She retired from Birkbeck in 1944.)

Miss E. M. Blackwell, Head of the Botany Department at Royal Holloway from 1922 to 1949, over a long period conducted research on the pathogenic fungus *Phytophthora*, and in particular its reproductive organs. In 1942, as President of the British Mycological Society, Miss Blackwell delivered the Presidential address 'On Germinating the Oospores of *Phytophthora*' (*Transactions of the British Mycological Society* vol 15, 1943). One of her collaborators in this research was Dr Grace Waterhouse (student 1924-8), with whom she published 'Spores and Spore Germination of the Genus *Phytophthora*' (Ibid., vol 15, 1931). Dr Waterhouse herself became President of the British Mycological Society in 1961, an honour accorded to only ten women since its foundation in 1896.[48]

In the Department of Mathematics in both Faculties, the traditionalism of Professor Loney was maintained by Miss Rowell (1899-1937) and Miss Pick (1911-46). Their student Dr Ida Busbridge (student RHC 1926-9; Lecturer, Fellow and Tutor, St Hugh's College, Oxford, 1936-70; Member of RHC Council 1969-82) has paid tribute to their teaching:

[Miss Rowell] did not push us; she was too ladylike! I thank God for Marion Pick! She drove us! . . . From [Miss Rowell] I learnt the elegance of pure mathematics. After a very elegant solution to a problem she would say 'That is so, is it not? Yes!' . . . Marion Pick . . . said to me 'You must criticise your own work and tear up any solutions to problems which take up more than a page.' This is the best piece of advice which I have ever received and I have passed it on to my own pupils.'[49]

On Professor Loney's retirement in 1920, Professor A. E. Joliffe was appointed to the Chair of Mathematics which he held only from 1920 to 1924, when he moved on to King's College, London. According to the appreciation written after his resignation, 'His students regarded him almost as a magician in Mathematics, so much did his brilliance impress, while his untiring expenditure of time and energy on their behalf won their gratitude and affection.'[50]

He was succeeded by Professor Bevan Baker, who occupied the Chair of Mathematics at Royal Holloway for twenty years (1924-44) and was a Governor from 1928 to 1934. 'Much appreciated by students both for his work and his unfailing kindness and consideration, he was highly successful with undergraduate pupils, and it was a disappointment to him that, owing to the war [ie the Second World War], the College was unable to change to a more modern syllabus and develop a postgraduate school.'[51]

Professor Bevan Baker enjoyed the social life of the College, especially its music. As 'a gifted performer on several instruments' he was a valuable asset to Band, and equally valued as a male voice in operatic productions.

Music, since the earliest years of the College, had suffered from its ambiguous status: its connection with Chapel raised it above the status of a social amenity; its non-academic status placed it below the level of a degree subject. Rosemary Manning (student 1930-33) remembered bitterly how musical enthusiasm had had to be sacrificed to expediency: 'My Classics tutors came down on me like a ton of bricks, "Oh, you mustn't learn the viola, Miss Manning. It isn't going to improve your Greek proses, is it?" And of course . . . it meant that I gave up the viola.'[52]

This was an extreme example of the conflict which the claims of Music imposed so long as it remained a non-academic subject. Yet, remarkably, College Music continued to recruit students and enhance its standards, until it achieved the status of a full Department and developed into a distinguished Faculty of Music. The foundations had been laid by Dr Emily Daymond (1887-99), Miss Crawford (1899-1904) and Miss Phoebe Walters (1904-15), and their part-time, non-resident helpers, notable amongst whom was Miss Glazebrook, 'grande dame in more than one sense'[53], who taught singing and voice production from 1893 to 1923. Miss S. M. Barker (1915-41) wrote:

When I first came to College in 1915, my most vivid impression was that of entering upon a great inheritance. The musical traditions had been so wisely and firmly established by Dr Daymond, and carried on by Miss Crawford and Miss Walters, that all that was required of their successor appeared to be a carrying on of the traditions, in so far as she was able. The Chapel Services, Choral, Band and Choir Practices ... a fund for the purchase of music so that no expense need be incurred by the students, free voice production and harmony classes, and a general feeling that Music should be given a fair chance: all this was part of the College customs and was being made the best use of by all members who were musically inclined.[54]

Aspiring soloists could perform at Sunday Music, an informal weekly recital given by College musicians to a College audience. Sunday Music, encouraged and developed by Miss Higgins, remained popular until greater student mobility during the 1960s led to a large exodus from the College at the weekend, which depleted both performers and audience.

Of great assistance in establishing high musical standards was the visit of an external examiner, each summer term. 'The purpose of the visit was twofold: to examine candidates for the Driver Prize in Music, and to report to the Governors on the health of Music in the College ... The examiners were normally appointed for three years; they were always of considerable status in the musical world – music fellows at Oxford and Cambridge, composers, university professors and principals of the London conservatories.'[55]

The first examiner, in 1889, was Sir Hubert Parry, whose pupil and protégée Dr Emily Daymond had been. In the inter-war period the examiners were Sir Walter Alcock, Dr Daymond herself, Stewart Macpherson, Thomas Dunhill, Dr Harold Darke and Sir William Harris. Most of the examiners were impressed by the high standards of College Music. Harold Darke, in 1933, wrote in his report: 'Considering that the music making is chiefly voluntary, I think the results are quite wonderful.'[56] That the standards of Choral were consistently higher than those of Band was frequently remarked upon, and the perennial explanation was clearly expressed by Dr P. A. Browne, in 1949: 'Most undergraduates have voices of sorts and a stimulating choir trainer can make them into a choir. But only a few come up able to play an orchestral

[ 151 ]

instrument, and the conductor of the orchestra has to make what she can of these . . .' He went on to lament the dearth of wind players, and the shortage of instruments: 'If the College possessed a set of wind instruments, it is more likely that various students would take them up and thus add considerably to the orchestral resources.'[57] As late as 1951 there were only two oboists: 'but, alas, they shared a single oboe.'[58]

When the College celebrated its Jubilee in 1937, Miss Barker reported:

A recent development on the academic side has been that Harmony and Counterpoint may now be taken as ordinary subjects in Intermediate and General Arts. There have been candidates in the former for the last four years, but none so far in the General.[59]

This was the first indication that Music at Royal Holloway College was seeking official recognition, and would in time achieve full academic status.

A few years after the First World War the reorganisation of the University of London, which had been interrupted by the outbreak of war, was resumed again. It now appeared necessary to reconsider the work of the Departmental Committee which had been appointed to implement the recommendations of the Haldane Report; for this purpose a new Departmental Committee – the Hilton Young Committee – was appointed in 1924.

The Hilton Young Report, published in 1926, set aside the recommendations of the Haldane Report, which were now out of date, for in the intervening years conditions within the University had considerably changed. The constituent Schools of the University had all increased in size, and the effect of the war years had been to increase the independence of all of them, apart from the two incorporated Colleges, University College and King's. Even the incorporated Colleges had not proved as subservient to the control of the University, either educationally or financially, as the Haldane Commission had anticipated. After the war, the foundation of the University Grants Committee in 1919 had provided state funding for the Schools, and this had had the effect of enhancing their independence, because the grants had been made on an individual basis, and not out of a block grant to the University to be subdivided subsequently. (Royal Holloway College received its first grant of £3,000, for the session 1920–21 following a direct application by the Governors).[60]

In these circumstances the Hilton Young Report dismissed the recommendations of the Haldane Report as no longer applicable.

We are convinced that with the lapse of time and material change of circumstances some of the main recommendations of the Haldane Report have lost their force, and that the ground for attempting to impose such an entirely new constitution on the University as the Report proposed no longer exists.

A practical scheme of reform and reorganisation must, in our opinion, be evolutionary rather than revolutionary.[61]

Accordingly the principle of complete centralisation, and the incorporation of all the Schools, was rejected as undesirable. Instead it was recommended that the University 'be considered as an organic association of institutions actively engaged in university work and forgoing some measure of full autonomy in order to share in, and contribute to, the life of the University as a whole'. So far no statutory provisions had been made for the representation of these institutions, other than University College and King's College, on the governing body of the University, but the Hilton Young Committee declared that 'in our view the University cannot hope to realise its full possibilities unless the constituent units take their full share in its government'. The Report therefore recommended collegiate representation on the Senate, and on a Standing Committee to be called the Collegiate Council.[62]

On finance, the Hilton Young Report recommended that there be a University budget 'related to a coherent university policy and formulated by the University; and that there must be in the University a body so constituted as to qualify it to negotiate with grant-giving bodies, to engage them in a discussion of the University budget, and to allocate the resulting grants among the schools.' The Report suggested the creation of a new body, to be called the Council, to control and allocate the funds.[63]

The reorganised constitution of the University was to consist of (i) the

[ 153 ]

Council (which became the University Court); (ii) the Senate; (iii) three Standing Committees of the Senate, which were to be (a) the Academic Council; (b) the Council for External Students; (c) the Collegiate Council. The Schools represented on the Senate were to be University College, King's College, Imperial College, the London School of Economics, Bedford College, East London College (which later became Queen Mary College) and Birkbeck College. Two representatives of Schools not granted direct representation might be co-opted. On the Collegiate Council, likewise, representation of Schools other than those named rested upon the Senate's decision.

The Hilton Young Report caused great dismay in Royal Holloway College, for even though the main recommendations of the Haldane Report had been set aside the College had not benefited, since it was still to be excluded from the policy-making bodies of the University. The Principal and Governors made a strong protest that the arguments offered for the inclusion of the College in the centralised University envisaged in the Haldane Report had not been given due consideration before the war, and that these arguments still retained their force for its inclusion under the newly proposed constitution.

In 1926, following the Hilton Young Report, a new University of London Act was passed, which empowered a body of Commissioners to draw up new statutes for the University, under the chairmanship of Mr Justice Tomlin (later Lord Tomlin). A deputation from Royal Holloway College, consisting of Lord Askwith (Chairman of the Governors 1925-36), Professor J. W. Mackail (Governor 1920-38), Miss Higgins and Miss Dolling, appeared before the Commissioners on 10 February 1927 and presented a memorandum stating the College's claims to inclusion, which no doubt they argued eloquently at the same time.[64] The Commissioners were receptive, and in the new Draft Statutes of the University prepared before the end of the year Royal Holloway College was granted direct representation on the Senate and the Collegiate Council. The Principal became an ex officio member of both bodies. Thus, after years of uncertainty, the status of Royal Holloway College within the University was secured. Miss Higgins, who throughout her principalship championed the cause of the College in the University, had been a member of Senate since 1911 as representative of Convocation, and in her new capacity she retained her membership until her retirement in 1935.

The evidence of Miss Higgins' active role in University politics contrasts surprisingly with the view of Dr Edith Batho (Principal of RHC 1946-62): 'I don't think that she took her duties as Principal very seriously.'[65] Dr J. M. S. Tompkins implied the same when she recalled, 'She said to Miss Woodward that when she was at Cheltenham she worked in the morning, watched games in the afternoon, and read novels in the evening – a blameless life, but not appropriate to a College Principal.'[66]

The probable explanation of these views is that both women knew Miss Higgins during the later years of her principalship, when the battle for the status of the College had been won and her vigilance in matters of University politics could be relaxed. Her chief interest during these years was to regulate the social life of the College in accordance with the traditions which she had inherited and developed. With these pre-occupations it might indeed have appeared that her duties were not very demanding.

Miss Higgins, silenced by death, cannot protest, but it seems likely that she would have regarded her last years at Royal Holloway as fully occupied by her rearguard action against the forces of change, of which she could not approve. She herself was not incapable of moving with the times. After the First World War she learnt to drive a car, at least as badly and as alarmingly as Miss Dolling. Though for years she forbade smoking in College, when the scent of illicit cigarettes began to pervade the corridors after dinner, she capitulated, and permitted students to smoke in their studies. Odd behaviour which had the merit of being traditional she could accept with good humour. For example, Miss Kathleen Vinall (student 1923-6) recalls a revival of an old tradition called 'ventilating', which required first-year students to climb through the transom windows above their study doors. Miss Higgins, encountering one struggling to emerge, paused to remark, 'In my day we used to do it feet first.'[67] She could even overlook a genuine peccadillo, if it amused her and did not endanger the reputation of the College. According to Miss Doreen Urwick (student 1923-6):

One summer a College Family was inspired by the Ascot Week traffic past the gates to go on a secret spree to the Races. Without either elegant invitations or suitable apparel, it seemed a good idea to dress

[ 155 ]

down rather than up. So they left College as themselves, but emerged from Englefield Green as 'Mum' (a dowdy hat, rusty black and a bulging picnic bag) with three daughters in acting box jumble. Almost on arrival they walked slap into a grey-toppered party of 'Mum's' relations, who looked right through them. Much encouraged, they were soon tightly wedged in the crowd against the rails where they saw Steve Donoghue come in seventeenth. 'Cor,' said Mum's neighbour, with a nudge in the ribs, 'the bloody twister!' 'Not arf' she agreed. This was indeed Seeing Life. Not sure afterwards how it would be received, they said little about their very happy afternoon. Then how did 'Chief' manage to regale 'Mum's' father with a lively version of the story at a College Garden Party?[68]

'Chief' saw everything, and could show her disapproval with severity. Though her own hair was cropped, she disliked seeing students with bobbed or shingled hair, though she recognised that this was not a matter of discipline. Hats, however, were. Her determination to enforce the old rule that hats should be worn on all excursions outside the College gates became a cause of resentment. The easing of conventions in the inter-war years would have given most middle-class girls considerable freedom of movement while they lived at home; the College rules which had seemed liberal at the end of the nineteenth century had undergone less change, and now began to seem oppressive. Miss E. B. Leggett (student 1929-32) recalls:

> One student of my own year, Una Robertson, began the questioning of old rules. At student meetings she would fairly regularly rise to state her '*Delenda est Carthago*' that students should not have to sign for late passes when going no further than 'Egham, Staines and Windsor' (a fine rhythm that appealed to me).[69]

Miss Higgins would not yield where she considered a principle was involved. College Hours were immutable. When she herself was bidding goodnight to some noisy guests and a student called out of a window the time-honoured challenge, 'Don't you know it's College Hours?', she overwhelmed the offended party with confusion by calling on her to apologise before 9 a.m. the next morning. She was probably delighted

[ 156 ]

to honour a tradition which she was trying to defend against the mounting complaints of a grumbling majority.

Compulsory Chapel was another cause of complaint. After the First World War church attendance had dropped throughout the country; the College would have followed suit had it been permitted. But Miss Higgins, who was a strong churchwoman, refused to relax the College rule, and discontent grew. Miss Higgins had been a student at Royal Holloway in the principalship of Miss Bishop, and it was the earliest traditions of the College which were dearest to her. Her own authoritarian rule belonged to the tradition of Miss Bishop and Miss Penrose, a style which was anachronistic in the 1930s. 'Miss Higgins was a strong believer in a committee of one,' was Miss Pick's dry comment. Miss Higgins had been accustomed to consult the Governors but not the staff, and this, she realised too late, had been an error.[70]

In 1935 she tendered her resignation, one year prematurely, generously suggesting that it would be appropriate for an incoming Principal to celebrate the approaching Jubilee of the College, and to be established in authority when the celebration took place. The Jubilee would inaugurate a period of innovation, over which Miss Higgins had no wish to preside. An era ended with her retirement, and she and Miss Dolling retired together, apotheosised by respect and affection, with all causes of complaint forgotten. Their vigour was undiminished, for a few years later they climbed the Matterhorn.

PART FOUR

# YEARS OF WAR AND PEACE
## 1935–62

—————————————— :>:> 7 <:<: ——————————————

# 'CAPAX IMPERII NISI IMPERASSET'

## The Principalship of
## Miss J. R. Bacon
## 1935–44

> In the five years between her appointment and the
> War breaking out she was very well thought of in the
> University . . . '*Capax imperii nisi imperasset*', she said
> of herself.[1]

MISS JANET BACON was the unanimous choice of the Governors of Royal Holloway College as the successor to Miss Higgins. The daughter of a barrister, Janet Ruth Bacon was born in Oxford in 1891 and educated at Oxford High School, from which she went to Cambridge to read Classics at Girton. After teaching at King Edward VI's High School, Birmingham, during the First World War, she returned to Girton as Lecturer in Classics, and was Director of Studies in Classics from 1925 to 1935. In 1925 she published *The Voyage of the Argonauts*, which was acknowledged the standard work on the subject. Her conclusion that the voyage of Jason was a real quest for real gold recently encouraged Mr Tim Severin to re-enact the voyage in a replica galley, without modern navigational aids, which twenty men rowed from Volos in Northern Greece to Soviet Georgia, the modern location of Colchis. There he learned that staking out a sheepskin in a riverbed had been until recently a local method of panning for gold, so that a genuine 'Golden Fleece' was lifted from the water.[2] Miss Bacon would have been delighted to learn about his practical application of her research, but unfortunately she had died over a decade too early, in 1965. Admirers of her style and scholarship were disappointed that her later publications were limited to articles in classical periodicals. However, the same qualities were brought to the weekly open lectures

[ 161 ]

which she gave at Royal Holloway, recalled after her retirement in a verse by Dr Richey:

> One hour henceforth must be
> Lost in our calendar,
> An hour of Arcady
> Bestowed on us by her
> Whose love of gracious things,
> Whose wit and charm,
> Hellenic mastery of living form,
> And spacious warmth of clear Hellenic light
> With fair imaginings
> Made our thoughts bright.[3]

Wit and charm were Miss Bacon's pre-eminent qualities. Her weakness, an amiable one, but disadvantageous in a person in authority, was a desire to be universally liked. However, on her appointment as Principal of Royal Holloway College, everyone was disposed to like her, and to welcome her as a mediatrix between traditionalists and innovators. As a non-home-bred Principal it seemed unlikely that she would show the close attachment to tradition which had made Miss Higgins' rule begin to seem inflexible; as a representative of a civilised discipline and an old university, it also seemed unlikely that she would offend traditionalists with brash innovations. It soon appeared that this estimate was correct, for she had a pleasant and easy way of dealing with causes of grievance. The disciplinary concept of College Hours was quietly allowed to lapse, and the idea that it was good manners not to be noisy at times when other people might wish to work was substituted.[4] The grievance of compulsory Chapel was a little more difficult to handle, but Miss Bacon found a way of dealing with it. While she made no pronouncement on the subject, since to end it might have upset the traditionalists, she overlooked absenteeism unless it were brought forcibly to her notice. For example, when an officious person felt obliged to inform her that a certain student had attended Chapel only once in the term, Miss Bacon sent for the student, outlined the situation, and then asked, 'What led you go to on *that* day?'[5]

Miss Bacon did not attempt to change the supportive rituals of College life. Each evening the dinner procession made its way through the

Library and Museum to Hall, with one student partnering Miss Bacon, enchanted or terrified by her easy flow of *bons mots*. There was by now a postgraduate table below the High, and woe betide any unwary student who mistakenly took a place at it; to do so was as reckless as to walk into a lions' den. The butler, Mr Frank Pyne (1921-65), rather enjoyed his famous resemblance to the portrait of Miss Bishop, beneath which he took his stance during dinner. He and his two assistants, Seeley and Cottrell, would carve 'seven or eight legs of lamb' for dinner, and take their nights off on Tuesday and Friday when fish was served.[6] The impression of good living at Royal Holloway was enhanced when Miss Bacon provided wine at dinner on Saturdays and sherry at the High Table on Sunday lunch.

Miss Bacon has been described as 'a large, solid lady, who walked majestically about the corridors ... [and] ... spoke with a leisurely drawl.'[7] She had a handsome, aquiline face, and wore her dark hair in a loose knot at the nape of her neck, a style unfashionable in the 1930s. She had one eye slightly smaller than the other, which gave her a permanently quizzical look. Inevitably she was nicknamed 'Ham', and a student whose father, assuming this to be her real name, wrote to her as 'Dear Miss Hamm', was filled with consternation, and intensely relieved that Miss Bacon was amused, not offended. 'She was extremely nice to us,' Miss A. D. Thompson (student 1937-40) recalled. 'Her wit is the thing that stands out.'[8] She had a sparkling talent for writing light verses which entertained staff and students alike. A delightful example was 'Genius Loci', an acrostic poem of which the first letters of each line spelt ROYAL HOLLOWAY COLLEGE, and the names of members of the staff were amusingly worked into the verse:

> Roseate as early dawn its walls are seen
> Outspread upon a wide expanse of GREEN
> You gaze in awe upon the massy Pile;
> Around – east WEST and south – see Nature smile.
> Look WOODWARD: sweeter spot what man could want?
> How soft the MOSS! how verdant every PLANT!
> Or where the HONEY-laden buds grow thick
> Look, if you will, but do not rashly PICK.
> Lo, mark yon Rabbit; scare him not I beg,

THE HISTORY OF ROYAL HOLLOWAY COLLEGE

Or he WILLCOCK his ears and show a LEGGE.
Within what comfort, what enjoyment! Here
Albeit not FAIRWEATHER there is Cheer.
Yonder lie ready on a Table laid
Crisp products of the BAKER's useful Trade;
Or, on chill mornings, to delight your souls
List to the BACON sizzling o'er the COLES.
Learning doth here display its RICHEYst Treasure
Expended in no parsimonious Measure.
Go, take your fill of that unstinted store:
Every enjoy, and ever ask for MOORE.[9]

'Genius Loci' was published in the 1939 edition of *Erinna*, an annual literary magazine founded in 1938 to which both staff and students contributed. It took its title from H. S. Leifchild's statue *Erinna*, which occupied the Picture Gallery, at once an object of affection and an encumbrance. During the inter-war period when College Dances were inaugurated in the Picture Gallery, with dancing partners invited *en bloc* from Sandhurst, *Erinna* was festooned with young men's coats and scarves. Her functional period ended when Miss Bacon's successor Dr Edith Batho banished her to an outdoor site near the tennis courts. In the meantime she was herself somewhat whimsically regarded as a kind of *genius loci*, hence the title of the magazine.

1936, the year following Miss Bacon's appointment, was the fiftieth anniversary of the opening of the College by Queen Victoria, and the year in which Miss Higgins, in offering her early resignation, had assumed that the College Jubilee would be celebrated. However, it proved impossible to arrange a royal visit in 1936, for this was the year of the death of King George V and the ensuing crisis caused by the abdication of Edward VIII. Accordingly it was decided to celebrate the Jubilee as the fiftieth anniversary of the opening of the College as a teaching institution in October 1887. At the annual RHCA reunion at Whitsuntide a historical pageant 'RHC Cavalcade 1887-1937' was performed in the Picture Gallery. On 12 October 1937 Queen Mary visited the College accompanied by Princess Alice, Countess of Athlone, who the previous year had been appointed Chairman of the Governors. Queen Mary planted an oak tree to commemorate the occasion, and the royal guests toured the College and the Botany and Physics laboratories, heard a recital of songs by the Choral Society, and watched a display by the Fencing Club. This was the most recently formed of the College's sporting clubs, founded with the encouragement of Miss Bacon and the active participation of Dr J. M. S. Tompkins. Miss E. M. Tanner (student 1934-7), who arranged a guard of honour for Queen Mary, had captained the London University Women's Foil Team.[10]

Celebrations continued with a Jubilee Dinner held at the Savoy Hotel on 16 October, attended by Princess Alice and some 450 guests, including many members of the RHCA. They heard a speech by Professor J. W. Mackail (Governor 1920-38) which included the words 'Something has been said in condemnation of Royal Holloway College as architecture,' (in 1937 the reputation of Victorian architecture was at its nadir) but 'fifty years hence, when it comes to celebrate its centenary ... it will be recognised not as a relic of defunct Victorianism, but as one of the architectural treasures of the nation,'[11] a prophecy which has proved correct, for Royal Holloway College is one of the few Victorian buildings to be listed as Grade I. A service of thanksgiving for fifty years' achievement was also held, for which Miss Bacon requested The Revd J. H. Ellison (Governor 1915-44) to compose a special prayer for her to offer. His first draft included the words, with reference to the staff, 'that they may strive together more abundantly'; but she begged him to alter these words, saying that she found the staff strove together quite enough without her praying in public for more![12]

All these celebrations were appropriate, but a more lasting commemoration of the Jubilee was the endowment of the Jubilee Reasearch Fellowship by the RHCA. The Fellowship, tenable for two years, was 'intended to promote research work by women in subjects which fall within the purview of the Faculty of Arts or the Faculty of Science of the University of London, but preferably in those subjects in which University courses are provided at the College'.[13]

Miss Bacon enjoyed organising celebrations. In the spring of 1939 she was delighted to be host to the Classical Association which held its Annual General Meeting and Annual Dinner at the College. She decided to entertain the Association with a play after dinner, and produced the *Mostellaria* of Plautus in her own translation, for which she also designed the sets and costumes. The play was received with immense enthusiasm, and a second performance was given for the whole College at the beginning of the following term. One may imagine this play inspiring the last free and easy laughter which echoed round the College for a long time to come.

The summer term passed, dominated for the Third Years by their Finals, for the rest of the students by their usual preoccupations: boating, tennis, trips to Dallen's, essay crises, Chapel or Chapel avoidance. But even the least politically-minded student must have been aware that this was not a summer term like any other. The Munich Crisis had passed, the fleeting hope of peace had given way to the certainty that for the second time in half a century Europe was about to be plunged in total war. On 3 September 1939 the Second World War was declared.

On the outbreak of war, Miss Bacon reported in the *College Letter*, 'our relations with the University became unprecedentedly intimate'.[14] The new Senate House, the University's headquarters in Bloomsbury, was taken over by the Ministry of Information, and the administrative staff of the University moved thence to Royal Holloway College. For office use they were given the Picture Gallery, the Governors' Board Room, the Governors' Dining Room and the Queen's Room (a small room specially furnished for the reception of Queen Victoria in 1886). For residence they had most of the rooms on West I and some on West II. There were forty members of University staff working at Royal Holloway, of whom three-quarters were resident in College while the remainder came in daily. They were easily accommodated because student numbers had fallen in recent years: from the peak of 208 students in the academic year 1929/30 the total had dropped to 168 in 1939/40.[15] While financially and academically this was a cause of anxiety, there was at least some advantage when the College was faced with the obligation of housing an alien community.

In fact, the visitors soon ceased to seem like aliens, and adapted to life in College. One of the University staff, Mr David Kennard, wrote:

At mealtimes we occupied two cross-tables in the Dining Hall reserved for our own exclusive use, so there was little mixing with the students, but after a while various personal contacts were made and coffees were drunk in students' rooms and vice versa. I was once reprimanded by a patrolling staff member (whose name I forget) for being in a student's room after 10.30 p.m. In view of my ignorance of the rules I thought at the time she could have put it more politely.[16]

This was the College's first experience of male residents, and no doubt the staff felt obliged to be vigilant even over the most innocent social contacts.

At the beginning of the Lent term 1940 the University staff entertained the College with two one-act plays, *Refund* by Fritz Karinthy and *The Man in the Bowler Hat* by A. A. Milne, which gave great pleasure. '*Refund* is the tale of a man who learned nothing during his schooldays and returns years later demanding his money back. The teaching staff examine him in history, geography, physics and mathematics . . . and by intricate and ingenious reasoning prove his answers right and his claim false.' This highly appropriate piece of fun was followed by A. A. Milne's melodrama, in which Mr Kennard, playing one of the villains, 'looked exceedingly "tough" '.[17] So the College staff took their visitors to their hearts, and Miss Bacon wrote:

We can feel nothing but admiration and gratitude for the spirit with which they have adapted themselves to cramped quarters and, to them, strange ways of living . . . were it not for its occasion we could wish their stay might be a long one.[18]

But an unpleasant shock was in store. During the Easter vacation of 1941 the War Office announced its intention of establishing an Officer Cadets' Training Unit of the ATS at Royal Holloway College, the original intention being to take over the whole College. A reconnaissance was made by Sir Edward Grigg MP and Dame Helen Gwynne-Vaughan, and the latter certainly thought that the interests of the ATS, her own creation, took precedence over those of her old College. They recommended the building as suitable accommodation for between 500 and 600 cadets.[19]

'The summer of 1941 will live in the College memory as a time of mental and physical disturbance,' the Principal reported. 'We made great efforts to avert the incursion of the ATS, in which we were strongly supported by the Member of Parliament for the University (Sir Ernest Graham-Little) and by the Association of Headmistresses, whose President, Miss de Zouche, did yeoman service in writing protests to the Press and to high authorities; the University Grants Committee helped to prevent the requisitioning of the Dining Hall and Kitchen. After many long, baffling and largely vain negotiations it was almost a relief to turn to the practical problems of the *fait accompli*, multitudinous and gigantic as they seemed.'[20]

These negotiations should have been described as 'partly vain' rather than as 'largely vain', for whatever inconvenience the College was obliged to endure, at least it was not forced to evacuate. The ATS took over the East side of the College, together with the Music Rooms and the Picture Gallery, accomodation for an OCTU less than a quarter the size of that originally envisaged. To the regret of the College the University administrative staff were obliged to leave, and at the end of August 1941 they took up residence at Richmond Theological College. During the summer vacation Royal Holloway grappled with the logistical problem of fitting the entire community into the West side of the building. The greatest change was a temporary expedient which became permanent: the students ceased to have two rooms each, and every bedroom and study became a study/bedroom. By this means, and aided by a mass purchase of divan beds, the whole student population could be accommodated on West, even when numbers jumped from the lowest total since 1918 of 158 at the end of 1942 to 170 at the beginning of the next academic year. The increase was absorbed by making some of the largest rooms – those with 'bulges' – into double study/bedrooms, Miss Bacon freed more space on West I by moving into the second floor flat in the South Tower; the first floor was occupied by the Governors' Secretary, Mrs Akehurst, who had succeeded Miss Dolling in 1935. The erstwhile Principal's Drawing Room became the Staff Common Room.[21]

The East side of College required adaptation to be made suitable for the purposes of the ATS. The Picture Gallery was to be used as a Lecture Hall, and accordingly some of the pictures were removed to the College strong room, while those which remained were fitted with protective screens. The partitions dividing the Music Rooms were removed to make space for a Mess Hall, and adjoining kitchens were also installed. Extra bathrooms and lavatories were required on both sides of the building, but fortunately the original ones had been approached through large empty vestibules in which extra plumbing could be installed, 'a masterpiece of clever contrivance by the plumbers; the foreman of their work party was a man who had worked on the original plumbing.[22] In the autumn of 1941 the College was ready to accommodate two strictly segregated communities, academic and military.

On 29 October the first training unit of a hundred cadets arrived to occupy the College, which to them was No. 2 ATS OCTU, headed by Chief Commander Mary Baxter-Ellis. According to the *Official History of the ATS*:

The object of the training of an officer cadet was to develop her powers of leadership, to inculcate a sense of responsibility and to give her basic administrative knowledge . . . the copious précis and notes which she took away with her provided a book of reference to help in the initial stages of her career as an officer, but the administrative training was always subordinated to the wider aspects of an officer's job.[23]

Each course lasted six weeks, and an officer cadet who attended the second course wrote an account of it which was published in *Erinna*. A cadet's day might not have seemed uncongenial to a College student, had they changed places.

A typical day in a Cadet's life started at 7 with Reveille. Breakfast was at 8, and before first lecture at 9 o'clock was a very busy time when rooms were swept, dusted and tidied, and buttons and shoes cleaned. Three lectures and one period for drill occupied the morning until dinner at 1.15. We were free most afternoons, and some played hockey, netball, tennis or squash on grounds lent to us by the College, while others worked at their notes, wrote letters or went for walks. Tea was at 4.15 and from 5 to 7 we had two more lectures, or sometimes a Test – rather unpopular at that time of day. Supper was at 7.30, after which we amused ourselves until Lights Out at 11 o'clock.[24]

[ 169 ]

As a result of 'certain administrative difficulties' No. 2 ATS OCTU left Royal Holloway College in the spring of 1942 and moved to the Imperial Services College, Windsor, where it remained until the end of the War. Its place at Royal Holloway was taken by an ATS Junior Officers' School, for the instruction of officers up to and including the rank of Junior Commander. Once again a hundred ATS personnel were accommodated on each course, which was of three and a half weeks duration. 'The instruction was divided into four main subject groups, administration, discipline, training and welfare. It was both theoretical and practical, and lecturers from the War Office came and talked on their own departments in relation to the ATS.'[25] The Junior Officers' School remained at Royal Holloway until July 1945. Throughout this period the College authorities continued to resent the presence of their unwanted guests, and coexistence was probably made easier by the policy of segregation pursued by both communities.

The College adapted itself as best it could to cramped quarters and wartime conditions. The sudden rise in the number of student applications for the academic year 1942/3 followed the extension of the call-up regulations to women, which obliged them to perform National Service at the age of twenty. This meant that only students who were under eighteen at the beginning of the academic year in which they entered College (reckoned from 1 October) could complete a three-year course. Consequently many girls who normally would have stayed at school for another year hastily applied to the universities. From 1942 students who entered College over the age of eighteen were obliged to complete their degree courses in two years, or else to secure permission from the University to take part of the course, with the possibility of returning to complete it after their demobilisation from National Service. By the end of 1944 twenty-three second-year students had taken final examinations.[26]

At the beginning of 1942/3 the College managed to accommodate an intake of seventy-three students by the introduction of shared study/bedrooms and the conversion of the bungalow in the College grounds for use as a reading room, common room and study. This bungalow, which lies a few yards to the east of the College, had been occupied by W. H. Crossland while the building was in progress, and up to the outbreak of the Second World War it had been used as an isolation hospital for students suffering from infectious diseases. Most of its occupants had been sufferers from measles or other such relatively minor ailments, but Miss Frieda Winter (student 1920-23) had lain there close to death for many weeks, and believed that she owed her recovery from typhoid to the care of Miss Higgins, who summoned Lord Dawson of Penn to her bedside, and with characteristic generosity bore the cost of most of her medical treatment.[27] During the war isolation was impossible, and students who fell ill were nursed in their own rooms by Sister M. G. Moss (Sister-in-Charge 1935-65), who commented: 'Happily the health of the students generally was very good in wartime . . . as somehow when they were hard pressed, taking degrees in two years instead of three, they kept fit and well.'[28]

The social life of the College was far more profoundly disrupted by the Second World War than it had been by the First.

The most obvious sign of wartime conditions was necessitated by the Black-Out Regulations. Thousands of yards of black-out material were purchased, and it was a nightly preoccupation that not one of the College's multiplicity of windows displayed so much as a chink of light. Fire-Watch Regulations obliged all women between the ages of twenty and forty-five to register for this duty, and rosters were made up which included staff, students and maids. Volunteers from among them continued to do Fire Watch during the vacations, except for a week at Easter and a short period of closure during the summer vacation, when Fire Watch was taken over by the remaining male employees of the College, assisted by Professor Baker and members of the Home Guard.

The service tunnel underneath the College was given a new use as an air-raid shelter, though many students would have preferred to take their chance above ground rather than face the easily imagined horror of being entombed beneath thousands of tons of masonry. With the danger of air-raids it seemed prudent to abandon the ritual of dinner, which gathered the whole community into the Dining Hall, and in the event of a direct hit on the College could have cost the lives of all. An informal supper, taken in two sessions, was substituted. Food shortage may also have played a part in the decision to dispense with formal dinner, for it would have been dismal to sit in grandeur at tables so much less opulently supplied than in the past. According to Miss Philippa Moeller (student

[ 171 ]

1942-5), 'there was always plenty of soup, so our normal procedure was to grab and wolf our first course, grab and wolf our pudding, and fill up on soup. This was deplored by the Principal.'[29] Miss Bacon endeavoured to derive some entertainment from the austerity of wartime conditions, and when Lord Woolton, the Minister of Food, appealed to the public to eat less meat and fill up on potatoes, she assumed his voice and wrote a verse entitled 'Food Flash':

> Now England on her own Roast Beef
> Can not be wholly fed
> Our meals must be supplied, *très vif,*
> From something in its stead;
> So, need constraining us to tread
> The frugal path of Cato,
> Eschew the meat when it is red
> And plump for the Potato . . .
>
> Nothing is here for sighs or grief:
> Let no salt tear be shed.
> Think of that lovely verdant leaf
> To precious tuber wed!
> So fancy in our garden-bed
> The Perfect State of Plato
> With me, Lord Woolton, at its head
> To plump for the Potato . . .[30]

Miss Bacon's advice was soon enforced when stringent food rationing was introduced. The College asparagus was dug up, and the huge beds were turned over to growing potatoes. This now appears, like the sacrifice of the croquet lawn in the First World War, an act of unnecessary vandalism; but at the time the substitution of a necessity for a luxury was regarded as a positive act of patriotism and, with labour in short supply, it would have been easier to convert the asparagus beds than to break new ground.

A War Work Committee was set up, with the Principal as Chairman and Miss Powell as Treasurer. Staff and students undertook knitting, salvage (ie waste paper collection), sewing and book collecting. Funds were raised to present a mobile canteen to the YWCA, and subscriptions were paid to the Red Cross to provide comforts for prisoners of war. Donations were sent to innumerable charities for the benefit of members of the armed forces, and for the victims of war. As in the First World War, the students helped to maintain the College grounds, and when the call-up reduced the domestic staff they also assisted with the washing up. In the vacations many of them did agricultural work, which was propagandised as 'Digging for Victory'.

Overcrowding, austerity and anxiety imposed severe strains on staff and students alike, and the stresses of College life were exacerbated by the curtailment of external activities. With the evacuation of the London Colleges, inter-collegiate lectures ceased for the duration of the war, as did sporting fixtures, and the University of London Union was closed. The dangers of wartime London and the difficulties of travel severed the students of Royal Holloway from the cultural life of the capital. A student who came up in 1940, forbidden to travel through London by her anxious parents, arrived from Luton driven cross-country in a taxi.[31]

The staff had little leisure for excursions to London, even had they had the inclination to face the difficulties. Dr Mary Bradburn (student 1935-8; M.Sc., Maths 1940; Lecturer in Mathematics 1945-80) described the effect of the tensions imposed by isolation:

There can be no doubt that the College staff suffered from the strains of the war. Pre-war there had been theatres, exhibitions and foreign travel to act as distractions and to provide interesting High Table conversations. Of course they let off steam from time to time and had flaming rows, but this happens in families and they got over rifts as families do, and remained friends and supporters of one another in crises. The war cut them off from their customary intellectual diversions, they were short staffed and had to teach contracted courses, and some of them were past retirement age and not resilient. I sense that the staff divided up into factions . . . and that all sorts of trifles added to the divisions.[32]

An authoritative Principal might have prevented disharmony, but Miss Bacon had never been authoritative. With her amiability and her desire to be liked, she lacked the force of character to reimpose a sense of unity on a society in disarray. She retreated from her difficulties by becoming increasingly reliant on her closest friend Dr Alice Walker, whom she appointed Principal's Secretary and Registrar, and excluding from her confidence those colleagues whose views or personalities she found unsympathetic. Increasing strife and bitterness were the inevitable results of her failure to maintain impartiality in her relations with her staff: those who continued to like and respect her found a convenient scapegoat for her failings in Dr Walker, while those who turned against her formed an increasingly hostile opposition. In these unhappy circumstances her health broke down, and the administrative staff were left to carry out her responsibilities as best they might.

'I think that Miss Bacon's position became untenable,' was Dr Bradburn's conclusion. 'She was tired and run down and conscious that she would never be able to heal these rifts . . . I do not think that she had a breakdown in the sense that her mind went. I think she remained supremely intelligent and with her logical classical training saw that a smooth and prosperous future would only be possible if she removed herself and left the healing of the wounds in an impartial person's hands.'[33]

The grounds of ill-health on which she tendered her resignation in 1944 were both dignified and sufficient, but her sense of failure was made plain by the harsh judgement of herself which she uttered in conversation with Dr J. M. S. Tompkins: '*Capax imperii nisi imperasset.*'


Miss Bacon's last active part in College affairs was her membership of the Post-War Policy Committee, which was appointed by the Governors early in 1943, on the recommendation of Professor Horton, to offer advice on the future development of the College, and especially to discuss the revolutionary suggestion that the College might break with its past and become coeducational.

Sir William Marris (Governor 1938-46) was appointed Chairman of the Committee, and its original members were Miss Bacon, Mr M. L. Jacks (Governor and Member of Council 1937-61), Professor Margaret Deanesly (Department of History 1936-50; Professor and Head of Department from 1942; Governor 1945-8) and Professor Moore. Dr Alice Walker acted as secretary to the Committee. It was at first proposed that Professor Horton should be a member, but he declined on the grounds that as Vice-Chancellor of the University it would be improper for him to sit on a Committee which was concerned with the affairs of an individual College. He was, however, consulted as one of a select body of expert witnesses. Among the other witnesses were Sir Walter Moberly, Chairman of the University Grants Committee; Professor A. D. Laurie, Secretary of the Association of University Teachers; Sir Fred Clarke, Director of the Institute of Education, University of London; the Principals of a number of Colleges and the headmasters and head-mistresses of several prominent schools, including Cheltenham Ladies' College, with which Royal Holloway had many personal links, and Bedales, which had a particular relevance since coeducation was to be discussed. Representatives of the Academic Board, the staff, the Students' Union and the RHCA were also consulted.

The Post-War Policy Committee held eighteen meetings, between 16 March and 11 December 1943, before issuing its Interim Report. This first series of meetings was dominated by the discussion of a possible coeducational future for the College. The Committee reported:

On the most difficult question which has come before them the Committee regret that they have not been able to reach a unanimous conclusion. The majority think that the prospects are not good of maintaining in vigorous life after the war an isolated residential College of moderate size for women only; and for these reasons they would seek powers to admit men students . . .'

The Report went on to explain:

Our main reason . . . is our belief that whatever may be the case up to the school age limit, segregation at the University stage is now becoming out of date; and that its disadvantages are markedly en-hanced in a residential College which, unlike women's colleges at Oxford and Cambridge, and to a lesser extent women's colleges in London, is not in close touch with male society.

. . . we find strong support for our view in the growth of mixed colleges in provincial universities, in the notable and beneficial inter-mingling of young men and women in all kinds of activities which the

[ 175 ]

war has brought about, and in such personal opinions as some of us have formed about the outlook of young women towards the questions of freer intermingling and the sharing of their pursuits with men.[34]

A majority of the Committee agreed that 'lack of educational and social contacts with a wider society may have a detrimental effect upon keener intelligences among the students and even more upon the staff', and accordingly recommended 'that the policy of converting the Royal Holloway College into a mixed College after the war be definitely adopted, subject to the necessary amendment of the Deed of Foundation.[35]

The dissentient voice was that of Miss Bacon, who argued strongly that Royal Holloway should remain a women's college. Initially this seems surprising, for her relationship with the College had not been long enough for her to become sentimentally attached to its traditions, and her principalship had been in general characterised by a policy of moderate innovation. Wartime conditions had forced innovations which she would have preferred to avoid, but the discussions of the Post-War Policy Committee revealed the limits of her willingness to change. On the issue of coeducation she recorded a 'Minute of Dissent' which was appended to the Interim Report. It was a closely argued essay which explained her preference for segregated education for women and her doubts that coeducation would bring Royal Holloway College the advantages envisaged by the other members of the Committee.

> First and foremost, I think it wrong to tamper with the fundamental provisions of the Deed of Foundation unless there is grave cause to think that these are ... so much in conflict with contemporary or predictable future opinion as to hamper the College's working or jeopardise its position ... in the absence of such conviction I strongly feel that the Trust Deed should be regarded as immutable in this respect ...

She went on to point out that among girls making applications to Colleges the established order of preference was (i) Oxford or Cambridge, (ii) a segregated London College (Royal Holloway, Bedford or Westfield), (iii) a mixed London College, (iv) a provincial University. If Royal Holloway sacrificed the characteristic which it had in common with

[ 176 ]

Girton, Newnham, Somerville, Lady Margaret Hall, it would not thereby rise to the position of a first choice but sink to that of a third.

... My own opinion is that RHC in its pre-war spaciousness was more truly civilising to a large proportion of its students than Girton, in whose favour I was naturally biased. I believe that this civilising power rested largely in the essential equality of all students here and in the freedom of everyone to develop her latent capacities undisturbed by emotional distractions.

Coeducation does not seem to offer advantages so cogent as to make it imperative ... it has not seriously challenged 'monastic' traditions. Bedales has not undermined the position of Eton; mixed London Colleges are not serious rivals of Balliol or Christ Church in Oxford, Trinity or St John's in Cambridge ...

Another fact to be reckoned with is the College's isolation ... Englefield Green will not become Oxford or Cambridge, no matter what we do, and it is not a suitable environment for a coeducational experiment with the adolescent ... The obvious danger of scandal could be guarded against by rules ... but no regulations could prevent the unbalanced state of mind that might be induced by the jealousies ... to be apprehended in a close society not all of whom could be equally attractive to the other sex. Given that the absence of men breeds frustration in some women, I believe that their presence would breed more, and of a far more dangerous kind ...

Finally we must recognise that answering any possible demand for more opportunities for men might amount to refusing opportunities for women, who are still far from having equal chances with men of a university education. To the priority of women's claims we are bound by our whole history, by the terms of our Foundation, and by the wisdom of not sacrificing the demonstrable benefits we enjoy by snapping at the shadow of an advantage that is, at the best estimate, very doubtful indeed.[36]

Some of the points of Miss Bacon's argument have become obsolete but others retain their force. In the few women's colleges which have not converted to coeducation the debate continues, so that Miss Bacon's eloquent plea for segregation had not become a mere historical curiosity.

[ 177 ]

But no doubt her disagreement with the majority of the Post-War Policy Committee and her failure to convince her colleagues added to her sense that she had failed as Principal of the College, and contributed to her decision to resign. The Interim Report was presented to the Governors on 27 January 1944 and Miss Bacon's resignation was tendered on 7 March.[37]

Between 20 May and 19 December the Committee held a further eight meetings before presenting its Final Report early in 1945. In the second series of meetings Miss Bacon again found herself in disagreement with her colleagues, this time on the subject of the picture collection. The majority of the Committee, in accordance with mid-twentieth-century taste, despised Victorian painting:

> The pictures are, in fact, of an unusually bad period of British art . . . The majority of the Committee would get rid of quite a large proportion of the present pictures . . . even without exchanges *it might be wise to give away*.[38]*

In her 'Note of Dissent' to this suggestion Miss Bacon confessed 'a reluctance to see resolved into pieces . . . a collection which as a whole has few equals as a representative sample of nineteenth-century British painting. Granted that the period was not a good one, it may still be useful that a comprehensive view of it should be available.' Her concluding objection deserves the College's respect and gratitude: ' . . . the history of art . . . collections abounds in instances of objects discarded by succeeding generations which appreciated in value with the passage of time and whose loss was bitterly regretted when it was too late. I should wish to take warning by these and not incur the same regrets. Two hundred years hence Victorian art will be in perspective and our collection may be a powerful factor in its assessment.'[39]

The reassessment has progressed more rapidly than Miss Bacon foresaw, and fortunately the College still possesses the valuable collection which might have been dismembered almost for nothing. The meeting on 30 September 1944 was the last which Miss Bacon attended before her resignation took effect. Her place on the Committee was taken by

* Author's italics.

Miss Fanny Street, who had been appointed Acting Principal of the College while a new Principal was sought. Dr Alice Walker had resigned with Miss Bacon, and on her departure the newly appointed Registrar, Miss J. I. Beale, became secretary to the Post-War Policy Committee.

On the remaining wide range of topics discussed the Committee was unanimous in its recommendations. The appointment of Miss Beale as Registrar (1944-8) was made in accordance with the recommendations concerning College organisation. The stress of wartime conditions, and Miss Bacon's personal difficulties, had made it appear that 'the Principal has to bear an excessive burden, and the emphasis on her duties as "head of the household" has inevitably left her inadequate time for her more important duties as a scholar, as head of an academic institution, and as that representative of the College in the counsels of the University and in the academic world.'[40] Accordingly the Committee suggested the appointment of a Vice-Principal to act as 'the Principal's *alter ego*', who should be a member of the academic staff, appointed initially for three years, but eligible for re-appointment. They also recommended the appointment of a Dean, who should be an academic, responsible for the welfare and discipline of the students; of a Domestic Bursar, who should be non-academic, responsible for all domestic matters including those hitherto the province of the Lady Housekeeper; and of a Registrar, who should no longer act simultaneously as Principal's Secretary, an office which should cease to exist but be replaced by that of Principal's Private Secretary, while the Registrar should head a newly created Registry to deal with all the clerical work and official correspondence of the College. These recommendations resulted in the appointment of Miss Beale as Registrar and the advancement of the incumbent Lady Housekeeper, Miss Strachan, to the post of Domestic Bursar. (Her occupancy of the two posts extended from 1937 to 1965). The other offices were filled during the next principalship.

The Committee went on to recommend that the wartime expedient of allotting only one room to each student should be adopted as a permanent measure, and on that basis the number of students should be increased to the full capacity of the building, after the departure of the ATS. The entry of Science students should be encouraged in every possible way, so as to correct the disparity in size between the Faculty of Arts and the Faculty of Science, since for many years there had been

[ 179 ]

nearly twice as many students in Arts subjects. The scope of the College should be increased by the creation of new Departments: Geography, Horticulture, Spanish and Theology were proposed. More encouragement should be given to research, and the Governors should provide clerical help for members of staff whose research was hindered by administrative responsibilities.

Reform of the governing body itself was recommended. The Committee bravely suggested that the appointment of Governors by the Court of Aldermen of the City of London, the Corporation of Windsor and the Corporation of Reading should be abolished on the expiry of the present terms of tenure by their representatives; that a representative Governor should be appointed by the RHCA (whose work for the College should be recognised by the payment of an honorarium to its secretary); that the number of staff Governors should be increased by one, to be appointed from among the permanent members of the academic staff by all those members of staff who were not ex officio members of the Academic Board; and that women should be eligible for appointment as Representative Governors (not, as hitherto, only as co-optative Governors).[41]

In conclusion the Committee pointed out that many of its recommendations could not be put into effect without an amendment of the Trust Deed, and that 'even if none of them commends itself to the Governors, the Committee consider that the present opportunity should be taken to give the College a new and more modern Constitution . . . [and] . . . if (as appears to be the case) a private Bill in Parliament will be needed to amend the Trust Deed it may be the simplest move to provide in the Bill for the making of Statutes for the future government of the College . . .'[42]

The Report of the Post-War Policy Committee was too complex a document to be accepted or rejected by the Governors without many discussions. The coeducation issue was discussed at a special meeting held at Brown's Hotel on 28 February 1945, and a vote was taken. Six Governors supported coeducation, as six opposed it; the Acting Chairman, Sir Henry Marten (Governor 1930-47) gave the casting vote in opposition.[43] However, on 17 May Sir William Marris, who had voted in favour of coeducation, proposed:

That the Governors take steps to initiate a revision of the constitution of the Royal Holloway College generally on the lines recommended by the Post-War Policy Committee, including a provision giving the Governors powers to admit men students if and when they are satisfied by a two-thirds majority of those present at a special meeting of the Governors convened for that purpose that such a step is necessary in the interests of the College.[44]

The motion was unanimously carried, and in this discreet way it was accepted that sooner or later the College would become coeducational; but the existing governing body and staff were not faced with the trauma of an immediate metamorphosis.

Counsel's opinion had already been obtained that a Private Bill would be required to amend the Trust Deed. A Sub-Committee of the Governors, consisting of Sir William Marris, Sir John Cameron and Professor Horton, was appointed to discuss the revisions of the constitution which should be embodied in the Bill.[45]

Fortunately the history of Royal Holloway College during the Second World War was not only a history of hardships, dissensions and inconclusive discussions. The hardships of life in wartime served to show the inner strength of the community and to illustrate its remarkable ability to pursue its normal aims in abnormal circumstances.

Since the College was cut off from the cultural activities and recreations of London, it became more than ever reliant on its own resources, and produced its own flourishing cultural life despite all difficulties. In 1941 Miss Sibyl Barker, Director of Music since 1915, retired, and her place was taken by Miss Joan Scourse, who remained at the College until the foundation of the Faculty of Music in 1969. Miss Scourse immediately perceived her task to be the maintenance of the traditions of College Music in spite of restrictive conditions. At the end of her first year in office she reported:

It is hard to realise that less than a year ago 'Choir', 'Sunday Music', 'Band' and 'Choral' were only names to me. Now I know how much

[ 181 ]

they are a part of College life, and how much enthusiasm and genuine love of music is absorbed and in its turn given out by them.[46]

Concerts and recitals by home-produced musicians were a source of solace and pleasure to the College during the war years. The stimulus of visits by distinguished musicians was continued with music examinations held by Dr Thornton Lofthouse (1940-42) and Sir Thomas Armstrong (1943-5). The latter had a particular admiration for the ability of Miss Scourse, who had been his pupil.

CHARD, too, played its part in maintaining College morale, with ambitious productions in the cramped quarters of the Lecture Theatre, including *Tobias and the Angel*, *Richard of Bordeaux*, and *Thunder Rock*. Of the last production the critic in the *College Letter* commented:

*Thunder Rock* was a tract for the times, the pre-war years 1938 and 1939, when many of us believed that a world war would mean inevitably the rapid destruction of civilisation . . . but now, after five years of world war we find that civilisation goes on much as usual and that . . . it is not stoic heroism that is needed to deal with the problems that arise, but common sense.[47]

This is a striking contemporary comment on the experience of the College in wartime, for in the perspective of history the College appears to have been rather deficient in common sense, for example in the conflicts concerning Miss Bacon, and notably endowed with stoic heroism, illustrated by innumerable details of its daily life throughout the war.

The Botany Department made a heroic gesture on a grand scale by celebrating its Golden Jubilee (1893-1943). It was a defiant assertion of normality to organise an exhibition of fifty years of publications by the Botany School, Memorials of Professor Benson, and a display of her collection of fossils. The Department was 'at home' to all its old students, and tea was provided for them on the lawn in front of the Botany and Physics building (though because of rationing they had to bring their own food). There were nearly a hundred guests, including Miss Higgins, Dame Helen Gwynne-Vaughan and Dr Martha Whiteley. The Department was in a flourishing condition under Miss Blackwell and her

[ 182 ]

Assistant Lecturer Dr M. A. P. Madge (student 1921-6; Assistant Lecturer in Botany 1930; Senior Lecturer 1930-69; Acting Head of Department 1963).

One of Miss Blackwell's greatest achievements before the war had been the re-introduction of Zoology, which had not been taught at Royal Holloway since the retirement of the part-time Lecturer, Miss Florence Buchanan, in 1921. Miss Blackwell consulted with Professor H. L. Jackson, Professor of Zoology at Birkbeck College, and as a result Dr Vera Fretter, then a Demonstrator at Birkbeck, was appointed a part-time Lecturer in Zoology at Royal Holloway, to teach the Intermediate Course, in 1936.

'After two sessions there was a demand for a Subsidiary/General B.Sc. course,' she reported, ' . . . this two-year course continued under my supervision [from 1938] until 1945, and the number in the class averaged fifteen.'[48] In 1940 Birkbeck College was bombed, and 'most of the museum materials, microscopes and microscopical preparations were evacuated to Holloway College and became available for use: only under these conditions was it possible for the more advanced teaching to be carried on.'[49] At the weekends Dr Fretter taught Birkbeck students in London, and in spite of this heavy teaching commitment continued her own research on molluscs and published a number of important papers during and immediately after the war.

In the last year of the war the College was under the capable guidance of the Acting Principal, Miss Fanny Street, whose connection with it had been almost continuous since her student days at the beginning of the century. After achieving First Class Honours in History in 1907, she lectured at Royal Holloway from 1911 to 1917, after which she worked for a short time at the Ministry of Food. In 1920 with Miss Phoebe Walters (RHC Director of Music 1904-15) she founded Hillcroft College for Working Women, Surbiton, of which she was the first Principal (1929-33). From 1933 to 1947 Miss Street was the RHCA Governor of Royal Holloway. She was an admirable choice as Acting Principal, but not eligible to be considered for permanent appointment as she was already sixty-six.

Her view of life was summed up in a pamphlet entitled *Our Christian Responsibility*, in which she insisted that it was the duty of a Christian to be actively concerned in politics. 'There is no such thing as a limited

[ 183 ]

area of specifically religious experience . . . Only in love to God in our neighbour can life be lived to the full.' She had been a suffragist and became a member of the Labour Party as soon as she was eligible to vote. Professor Helen Cam, in a memorial address for her, recalled a characteristic example of her blend of religion and politics.

> Her friends were not unduly disconcerted when at a conference at Somerville, where she was giving us a series of meditations on the Beatitudes in Chapel, she stood up in Hall after dinner and obliged with a rendering of 'The Red Flag.'[50]

The Royal Holloway students, unaware of the details of her career, only knew that she was the sister of A. G. Street, the author of *Farmer's Glory* (1932), a classic autobiography of English rural life. This knowledge of her country background led them to suppose that she could not be a genuine intellectual: 'The conversation [with her] was nothing like so erudite as it was with other members of the Faculty. She infuriated us by reiterating that she was *in loco parentis* and imposing all sorts of pettifogging new rules which she had found necessary with the women at Hillcroft.'[51] Perhaps her coffee party conversation had been pitched to suit the needs of these less intellectual students. The Principal's Private Secretary, Miss A. A. Divine (1941-65), who was well placed to appreciate her qualities, summed her up simply as 'a grand old girl'.[52]

With the arrival of Miss Street the dissensions which Miss Bacon had in one view caused and in the other failed to prevent, ceased, though it was a slow process for the factions which had formed during her principalship to fuse again into a homogeneous community. Miss Street's year of office provided a period in which the process could advance sufficiently to enable the College to present a dignified appearance of unity to its new Principal. The College was the microcosm of the outside world, for there too the end of hostilities was approaching.

'The end of the war had been coming for some days now,' Miss Philippa Moeller (student 1942-5) wrote in her diary entry for 7/9 May 1945, 'and any time anything's happened I've rushed round College telling people – I'm one of the first to hear because I have a wireless . . . We'd been preparing for victory for some time, notably at Choir Practice – last Wednesday we practised the service, and Scourse wailed "We can't *possibly* have peace before Friday – I haven't written out all the parts to 'Now Thank We All Our God'!" '[53]

The ending of the war in Europe was announced on the nine o'clock news on 7 May 1945, and the service of thanksgiving was held as soon as everyone could be gathered together: ' . . . a full throated "Te Deum" pealed out just before 10 p.m. and Chapel was packed in a most unusual fashion.' [54]

'It was a queer night,' wrote Philippa Moeller, 'lightning streaking the sky, but no rain.' Some students went to dance round a victory bonfire on Englefield Green, others dashed up to London to join in the general celebrations. 'Lists went up to be signed, but no one cared what we did or kept any check.' Next day more students and ATS Junior Officers from Royal Holloway, as separate in their rejoicing as they had been in wartime life, made their way to London to join the jubilant crowds which surged round Buckingham Palace to cheer the Royal Family and hear Mr Churchill's victory speech from the balcony. Miss Moeller concluded her account of the celebrations with a reminder that in war and peace university life retained its normal patterns: 'Now Finals calls.'

# LAST YEARS AS A WOMEN'S COLLEGE

## The Principalship of
## Dr Edith Batho
## 1945–62

To think that one should reminisce so soon
Upon that everlasting afternoon . . .
So let it be, for they were royal days
And gracious; let this epitaph be praise
To other eras, and not theirs alone:
They had their glory, flourished, and are gone.[1]

THE new Principal of Royal Holloway College, Dr Edith Batho, who took office on 1 October 1945, was a surprising choice, for she had no previous experience of life in a residential college for women.

Edith Clara Batho was born in 1895 and educated at Highbury Hill High School and University College, London, from which she graduated in 1915. While reading English she developed a liking for Old Norse Literature, and gained some knowledge of Icelandic which she immediately put to use working as a censor during the First World War. After the war she taught at Roedean before returning to University College in 1921 as Quain Student and Assistant in English. In 1927 she published *The Ettrick Shepherd*, a pioneering study of the Scottish poet James Hogg, whose work had long been neglected. Her interest in the Romantic and Victorian periods in English Literature led to her major work *The Later Wordsworth* (1934) and then to *The Victorians and After* (with Bonamy Dobrée, 1938). In 1935 she was appointed Reader in English Literature and awarded the D.Lit. In 1937 she was the first woman to be invited by the British Association to deliver the Warton Lecture on English poetry, her subject being 'The Poet and the Past'. At the same time she did not abandon her interest in Scottish Literature; she edited for the

Scottish Text Society *The Chronicles of Scotland* by Hector Boece, in Bellenden's translation (Vol I with R. W. Chambers, 1936; Vol II with H. W. Husbands, 1941).[2]

Dr Batho's own account of her appointment as Principal of Royal Holloway College was modest:

> There was nobody on the spot who had any real authority, and hence I came in from outside . . . someone from 'that Godless Institution in Gower Street' [University College] . . . I think that after the war people were glad to have a Principal – any Principal.[3]

Though she came from the 'Godless Institution' Dr Batho was far from godless herself. She was a devout churchwoman who relished the Principal's active role in the religious life of Royal Holloway College: 'She took charge of Chapel like the Headmistress taking prayers.'[4] Nor was she altogether an outsider, for she had a long acquaintance with the College which she had first visited in 1912, at the invitation of a schoolfriend who had become a student there. She had met Miss Penrose, after the latter's retirement, had known Miss Higgins quite well, and had been introduced to Miss Bacon on the occasion of her return to College for the presentation of her official portrait. Dr Batho could and did boast that she had known the College since the early years of the century, and met all the Principals except the first; but feeling a certain familiarity with the place was very different from taking command of it, and Dr Batho was aware of the need to feel her way cautiously.

'I probably made some bad mistakes,' she told the author, 'but I didn't make the worst mistake I might have made: I didn't choose the wrong Vice-Principal . . . There I was with an unknown collection of women before me and told that I must choose a Vice-Principal. In the end I realised that they were all admirable women. I realised that two were looked on with special respect by the others, and one of those two with a little more love than respect. And I chose her. And it was the right one.'[5]

Her choice was 'dear Constance West' as she called her, but this expression of affection was retrospective. She determined not to excite jealousy by cultivating any particular friendship, and in her relations with her colleagues she was always reticent and impartial. This cautious

[ 187 ]

attitude carried with it the danger of loneliness, which Dr Batho evidently experienced, for she wrote to the last Principal of Royal Holloway College, Dr Roy Miller (1982-5), on his appointment: 'One great advantage you have – a wife who will support you. I often wished I had a wife.'[6] Dr Batho was nonetheless an intensely private person who found the pressures of residential life irksome. She escaped them by taking a day off once a week to visit her sister, which necessitated a long bus journey to Barnet.

She found the obligation of social contact with the students something of an ordeal. 'I did try to get to know the students,' she said, 'which was difficult because they were shy and I'm rather shy,'[7] – an admission which one cannot imagine that any of her predecessors would have made. Her attempts at friendliness were not always successful, as according to one student: 'Dr Batho was never without a smile and always attempted affability, which I am afraid often came over as being fatuous and meaningless'.[8] But she persevered, resolutely inviting groups of students to coffee, attending performances by Band and Choral, and going to open meetings of most of the student societies, except the political clubs which she thought it correct to avoid. Attendance at the CHARD play is obligatory,' she wrote in a notebook compiled for her successor, 'but sometimes painful – the First and Second Years [in their annual dramatic productions] usually do much better in their less pretentious ways.'[9]

She followed her predecessors in accepting that the Principal's role first and foremost was to be head of the household. Scholarship remained her first love; administration was a chore in which she was sustained by a sense of duty. In appearance Dr Batho was a small stout woman, with iron-grey hair drawn tightly into a bun. Her quiet, precise voice made her occasional flashes of acerbic wit seem the more startling. She was never a commanding figure, but she was respected for being what the College required her to be: competent, conscientious and uncontroversial.

At the end of the Second World War Royal Holloway College, like most other institutional buildings throughout Britain, had a neglected look. For years there had not been money, time or labour for any but the most basic maintenance. With the removal of black-out curtains light flooded the College, but the windows were still covered with dismal lattices of

[ 188 ]

adhesive tape, applied to prevent their being shattered by bomb-blast; hours of labour, in which everyone participated, were spent in stripping off the tape. The grounds were untidy and overgrown, for throughout the war vegetable production and the upkeep of sports fields had taken precedence over the care of lawns and flowerbeds. The grass on the east side of College had disappeared under a sea of asphalt, laid down to provide hard standing for ATS vehicles. Miss Bacon had written a sad little poem, 'To an Eastern Grass Plot', promising

> Though in the years between
> Sad we deplore you
> Some day in springing green
> We will restore you.[10]

Frantic efforts to restore some semblance of pre-war neatness to both College and grounds were made in preparation for a visitation by the University Grants Committee in January 1946. The quinquennial system of UGC visitations, estimates and grants to the Colleges of London University had been established in 1930, and with the passage of years a larger and larger proportion of the income of each College had come to depend on its grant from the UGC. In the years following the Second World War the visitations and resulting estimates became increasingly important, as the UGC was by this time providing three-quarters of the University's funds, from which the Colleges competed for a share.[11] In 1946 Royal Holloway was delighted to secure a grant of £20,000, and the assurance that it was making a constructive contribution to the University's post-war development. As normal conditions of life returned, day-to-day links with the University were restored. Intercollegiate lectures were re-established, and Royal Holloway joined in a reciprocal agreement with other Colleges that fees for these lectures should be waived. Sporting fixtures arranged through the ULAU were resumed, as were the activities of the ULU and the religious societies SCM and LIFCU.

With the departure of the ATS from College in July 1945 the whole of the east side of the building stood empty. It had been left in a deplorable condition, and compensation was requested from the War Office, but renovation could not begin until a sum had been agreed.

However, with only a few weeks left before the beginning of the new session, and with 'no priority for labour or materials', forty rooms at the south end of East I, II and III were made clean and habitable, and most of the Science staff moved across to East.[12] Science students also tended to be housed there, with the unfortunate result of a social dichotomy between the Faculties. Students who had been accustomed to a close-knit community on West also lamented the general dichotomy: 'With this reoccupation the community has lost that sense of corporate well-being which was so marked a feature of the war years. This is inevitable when one section of the community sees so little of the other . . .'[13]

Otherwise internal reorganisation seemed generally advantageous. The Principal's Study on West I was restored to her, but the Principal's Drawing Room continued to be used as the Staff Common Room. Dr Batho, valuing her privacy, chose to live in the South Tower, as Miss Bacon had done; but she moved into its first floor flat, while the previous occupant, Mrs Akehurst, went to live in the bungalow, which then had a private garden and wisteria-covered verandah. Mrs Akehurst's successor as Secretary, Miss Dorothy Hustler (1947-64), used to pin a notice on the main College notice-board when the wisteria was in flower, inviting everyone to come and admire it. The bungalow was never again required as an isolation hospital, for the ATS had installed a Sick Bay at the north end of East I, which the College decided to isolate more thoroughly and retain (and which is now the Health Centre). The recovery of the eastern half of the southern block offered scope for the expansion of the Library; this was now a pressing need, since it had grown to 30,140 volumes by the end of the war, and was constantly increased by purchases and gifts. The Museum was ultimately sacrificed to it without much regret, as its collections had never been systematic, having been formed mostly from travellers' curios and gifts which had no obvious destination. The advancing Library gradually filled the whole of the south range, and two decades later invaded the South Tower itself and displaced its residents. In the meantime the rooms above Dr Batho's flat provided lodgings and a common room for postgraduates, who courteously assured the Principal that they would not disturb her. (At the time of writing the upper rooms of the Tower house the Archives of both Royal Holloway and Bedford Colleges. A trap-door in the ceiling of a fourth floor storeroom gives access to almost the last remaining empty space in College – the shaft of the Tower, which so far has attracted no occupants except unwelcome pigeons.)

Immediately after the war most of the readily available space was required for residence as demand for university places rose. Three-year courses were once more available for eighteen-year-old school leavers; students who had interrupted their courses returned to complete them; mature students who had served in the forces made applications to the universities. After the first post-war phase of applications, the demand continued to grow as university education became more generally available, for increasingly students' fees and maintenance grants came to be paid by local authorities. By the end of the 1950s 70 per cent of London University students were financed by grants.[14]

In the academic year 1946/7 student numbers at Royal Holloway leapt from the previous year's total of 194 to 270, which included a record intake of 135 First Years. The annual report in the *College Letter* included a comment on the resultant overcrowding, which had ensured that the civilised rituals of pre-war life could not be revived:

It is impossible for the whole of the Academic Staff and students to get into the Dining Hall together, and all meals have had to be duplicated . . . The lack of domestic staff has forced the methods of the cafeteria upon us, and the most we can do in the way of formality is to see that the Principal's chair is occupied and Grace said before First and Second Supper during the week and Lunch on Sunday.[15]

At the beginning of the next session, 1947/8, the student community had grown to 330, including twenty-three non-resident postgraduates, eight of whom were men. The arrival of the men, arranged on an individual basis with specific departments, preceded the Parliamentary Bill on which the Governors had resolved, so that when its passing legalised their admission this appeared simply to be an adjustment to accommodate a *fait accompli*. The first step towards the metamorphosis of the College had been taken so quietly as to have been scarcely noticeable.

After its long period of gestation the Royal Holloway College Act received the Royal Assent on 30 July 1949. It embodied many of the recommendations of the Post-War Policy Committee outlined in the previous chapter. Once the Governors had decided that the College should become coeducational at some unspecified future date, it was intended that this should be embodied in the new Act; but at a meeting with Lord Drogheda, the Lord Chairman of Committees, at the House of Lords on 6 April 1949, the Principal and a group of representatives of the College were advised that the admission of men undergraduates should be made the subject of a separate Bill, when the date of their admission should have been decided, and that in the meantime only the admission of men postgraduates should be provided for in the Bill about to be presented. This advice was accepted, so that for the present only a limited measure of coeducation was introduced.[16]

In accordance with the terms of the Royal Holloway College Act (1949) the Board of Governors was dissolved, and replaced by a Council which was to consist of twenty-one members:

(a) the Chairman;
(b) the Principal;
(c) fourteen Representative members, to be appointed as follows:
   One by the Lord President of the Privy Council;
   Two by the Senate of the University of London;
   One by the Court of Alderman of the City of London;
   Two by the Minister of Education;
   One by the Hebdomadal Council of the University of Oxford;
   One by the Council of the Senate of the University of Cambridge;
   One by the Mayor, aldermen and burgesses of the borough of New Windsor;
   Four by the Academic Board;
   One former student of the College, to be selected by the RHCA, and approved for this purpose by the Council;
(d) Six co-opted members.[17]

The first Chairman of the Council was Princess Alice, Countess of Athlone, who had been Chairman of the Governors since 1936. Her husband, the Earl of Athlone* (Chancellor of the University of London, 1932-55) was Governor-General of Canada from 1940 to 1946, and Princess Alice spent this period abroad with him. During her absence

---

* He was born Prince Alexander of Teck, and was brother to Queen Mary.

[ 192 ]

she remained Chairman of the Governors, an Acting Chairman being elected at each meeting. Her return was very welcome, for besides being a woman of charm and energy, she constantly used her influence in the interests of the College. She continued as Chairman of the Council until 1958, when the onset of deafness decided her to resign, though she remained a member of the Council for a further decade. Her informality and humour made her the most approachable of royalties. Dr Batho recalled her saying, 'I have to open a geriatric hospital – horrible word, geriatric! If I have to go into one I won't be a geriatric case – I'll be an Old Woman!' She remained a marvellously lively example of one, almost until her death in 1981, at the age of 97.[18]

On the Council of Royal Holloway College from 1949 onwards women were appointed on the same conditions as men. All representative or co-opted members were to hold office for five years, at the end of which they were to be eligible for re-appointment, except for the representatives of the Academic Board, who were to be appointed annually, but also to be eligible for re-appointment. Of these four, two were to be Professors or Heads of Department, the third neither the one nor the other, and the fourth might belong to either category. Subject to various legal safeguards, and to the approval of the University, the Council was empowered to make new statutes for the College.[19] Among its specified powers were the right to admit men as non-resident postgraduate students, and to change or add to the curriculum. In fact, the Governors had already decided against the additional departments proposed by the Post-War Policy Committee, with the exception of Geography, the foundation of which remained in prospect.

The powers of the Principal were defined as 'the whole internal management and discipline of the College as an institution, subject to the approval of the Council' and also included the appointment of a Vice-Principal and Dean, on the same conditions. Dr Constance West, the first Vice-Principal appointed by Dr Batho, had served for three years and was succeeded by Dr J. M. S. Tompkins; Dr M. A. P. Madge, the first Dean, had already been succeeded by Dr Mary Bradburn, who remained in office. Apart from the admission of a handful of men postgraduates, the effects of the Royal Holloway College Act (1949) were not metamorphic.

However, an invisible revolution was undertaken by Miss Dorothy

Hustler who had succeeded Mrs Akehurst as Secretary to the Governors, and under the Royal Holloway College Act was designated Secretary to the College. Before her appointment she had worked on the administrative staff at Queen Elizabeth College (then King's College of Household and Social Science) and had received the MBE for her work at the Ministry of Production during the Second World War. A short spell as Accountant at Girton preceded her appointment at Royal Holloway. According to her successor, Mr Richard Hardy:

> One of her first tasks was to reorganise the outmoded College accounts ... this was no technical exercise for accountancy's sake, but a successful attempt to establish a sound and practical basis for conducting the College's finances in the future. The principles of her reorganisation of the accounts still apply today.[20]

During the 1950s, as numbers increased and the College outgrew the Founder's Building, Miss Hustler was responsible for negotiating the purchase of surrounding properties, to house expanding departments and provide additional residences. Continued expansion during the next decade led to the establishment of a separate Accounts Department, under Mr K. F. Livesey, in 1969.

Immediately after the Second World War there was a general renewal of the academic community at Royal Holloway College, and especially of the Heads of Departments, following the retirement of many 'Greybeards'. The tradition of long service remained as much a part of College life as it had been in pre-war days so that many of the academics appointed in the late 1940s and early 50s remained in office to provide continuity over the period of metamorphosis to a coeducational college in the 1960s.

In the Faculty of Arts changes began before the end of the war with the retirement of Miss M. E. D. Honey, who was succeeded as Head of the Department of French by Professor H. J. Hunt (1944-66). As a Fellow and Tutor of St Edmund Hall, Oxford, he had published *Le Socialisme et le Romantisme en France* (1935) and *The Epic in Nineteenth Century France* (1941). At Royal Holloway his Balzacian studies enhanced the reputation of his department: in 1957 he published *Honoré de Balzac a Biography*, and *Balzac's Comédie Humaine* in 1959. Professor Hunt was eager to create contacts with France which had been impossible during the war, and with the assistance of Miss G. Brereton (Lecturer in French 1943-65) he arranged a system of exchanges for Royal Holloway students with students from the University of Poitiers.

Immediately after the war, as successor to Professor Sleeman, Professor Hugh Tredennick was appointed to the Chair of Classics, which he held for twenty years (1946-66). For much of this period he was co-editor of the *Classical Review*. His translation of four of Plato's dialogues as *The Last Days of Socrates* first appeared in Penguin Classics in 1954, and was several times revised and reprinted. Able students respected his scholarship and less able ones were grateful for his kindness, and both appreciated his courtesy 'extending even to apologies for any unpleasant smell from the parcel of fish intended for his cats'.[21] Miss Norma Miller joined the Department in 1948 as an Assistant Lecturer, and was appointed Reader in Latin in 1964 and Emeritus Reader on her retirement in 1985. She held at various times the offices of Arts Tutor, Dean of the College and Vice-Principal, and also served on the Academic Board and the Council.[22]

In 1947 the Department of History gained the civilising presence of the seventeenth-century historian Mr Robert Latham, whose 'contribution to College life extended far beyond the History Department. He was seen frequently at Sunday Music, sometimes playing [he was a fine pianist] sometimes just listening for this was an aspect of the creative activity of the College which he particularly valued.'[23] He remained at Royal Holloway until 1968 when he was appointed Professor of History at the University of Toronto, and on his return to Britain became Librarian of the Pepys Library, Magdalene College, Cambridge. At Royal Holloway he had begun his work on the definitive edition of *The Diary of Samuel Pepys*, which has brought him wide acclaim. In 1950 Professor Margaret Deanesly was succeeded as Head of the History Department by Professor Joan Hussey (1950-74), who had been Reader in History at Bedford College since 1947. Already with a high reputation as a Byzantine scholar, Professor Hussey published *The Byzantine World* in 1957, edited and contributed to the Byzantine volumes of the *Cambridge Mediaeval History*, and translated Ostrogorsky's *History of the Byzantine State*. The author of the notice of her retirement in the *College Letter* commented: 'It is easy to see why historians outside College sometimes professed to believe that the entire History Department was little more than a province of the Byzantine Empire.'[24] Byzantine studies continued under her former student Miss Julian Chrysostomides (appointed Lecturer in History, 1965).

The Department of German began to expand after the Second World War with the appointment of Miss S. P. Jenkins as Assistant Lecturer in 1947. Miss Jenkins had just left University College, and was younger than some of her students, who had served in the forces before entering College. She was Vice-Principal from 1960 to 1962, when she married The Revd John Fowles. Dr Richey's retirement in 1948 was followed by the appointment of Dr Ralph Tymms as Reader in German and Head of Department. He was appointed Professor in 1956, served on the Council from 1957 to 1960 and was Vice-Principal from 1969 to 1975. He retired in 1981.

Professor Gladys Willcock continued as Head of the Department of English until 1955, when Professor George Kane was appointed to the Chair of English which he held for ten years, and was also Public Orator to the University. Miss H. A. C. Green and Dr J. M. S. Tompkins both remained throughout his period of office, to make the English Department a particularly strong bastion of College traditionalism.

In the Faculty of Science Dr Joan Thomas (1945-69) was appointed Lecturer in Zoology, in succession to Dr Vera Fretter. With the return to Birkbeck College of the material salvaged after the bombing and used at Royal Holloway during the war, to Dr Thomas fell the responsibility of building up a new collection of museum specimens which were then still regarded as essential to the teaching of the subject.[25] Zoology continued for some years to be taught as a subsidiary course in the B.Sc. General Degree, but it gained its own departmental premises in a series of rooms on East V. These were attics which had never before been used except for storage, and though far from convenient at least they provided Zoology with space in which to expand.[26] The B.Sc. Honours Course in Zoology was established in 1956, following the appointment of Dr P. M. Butler to a new Readership in Zoology. He was Head of Department 1956-72, and Professor from 1962. His particular research interest was in the palaeodontology of mammals, on which he continues to work during his retirement.

In 1946, on the retirement of Professor T. S. Moore, Professor Gwyn Williams was appointed to the Chair of Chemistry (1946-55). At Royal Holloway he pursued his research on reaction mechanism and strong acids, begun at King's College, London, where he had worked since 1939.[27] He was elected to the Council in 1949, and also served on the Finance Committee until 1954. He was a member of Senate as a representative of the Faculty of Science of the University. His ability and influence as an administrator were of great benefit to his department, for he was responsible for planning the new Chemistry Laboratories which were built in 1951. He was also enthusiastic for the establishment of the Honours Course in Zoology, for which he drew up the recommendations which were accepted by the University. An apparently slight illness preceded his sudden death in 1955. His successor in the Chair of Chemistry was Professor E. J. Bourne (1956-74).

In 1947, following the retirement of Professor Horton, Professor Samuel Tolansky was appointed to the Chair of Physics, which he held until his death in 1973. In 1952 he was elected a Fellow of the Royal Society. Professor Tolansky's boundless energy is illustrated by the wide range of his research interests and the volume of his publications. Between 1930 and 1973 he published fifteen books and some 250 papers on four main groups of topics: spectroscopy (mainly hyperfine structure measurements); multiple beam interferometry (especially in relation to the detailed topography of surfaces); diamond physics; lunar dust and the Moon's surface.[28] He established an international reputation through his contributions to spectroscopy, on which he published *Hyperfine Structure in Line Spectra and Nuclear Spin* (1935, revised 1948) and *High Resolution Spectroscopy* (1947). His *History and Use of Diamond* (1962) is a beautifully lucid book for the general reader. But inevitably it was his work on lunar dust and his prediction regarding the nature of the Moon's surface which captured the public imagination:

[At a meeting of the Royal Society in February 1969] He described the results of interferometric examination of tektites, small roughly spherical glassy objects probably associated with the impact of meteors. He suggested that similar objects might be found on the Moon.

[ 197 ]

Samples of moon dust were found to contain an abundance of these particles . . .[29]

The prediction and its successful outcome were widely reported and the general public was enormously impressed, but in writing Tolansky's obituary his erstwhile colleague Professor O. S. Heavens (Reader in Physics, RHC, 1956-64) pointed out that 'his early work on hyperfine structure of spectral lines and especially on multiple beam interferometry were of vastly greater significance'.[30]

Tolansky was of Lithuanian Jewish origin, orthodox in his faith, and an expert on Jewish liturgical music. He made a study of all the musical instruments mentioned in the Old Testament. His apparently limitless range of interests included religions, folklore and optical illusions. He was a fascinating informant on all these topics, and was as widely loved as he was admired. His wife, Ottilie Tolansky, was a successful portrait painter. On his appointment at Royal Holloway he brought with him a group of research students who had previously worked with him at the University of Manchester, and these were the largest contingent of the original male postgraduates.[31]

In 1949 Miss E. M. Blackwell retired from her long headship of the Department of Botany, to be succeeded by Professor Frank Jane (1949-63). As Lecturer and then Reader in Botany at University College he had researched the microscopic algae of freshwater ponds, and research in algal ecology was continued at Royal Holloway by his postgraduate students, one of whom, J. H. Evans (one of the original men postgraduates) was appointed to the staff in 1958. At Royal Holloway Professor Jane's research concerned wood and trees, and he published *The Structure of Wood* (1955). His ambition was to establish a Botanic Garden for London University, and the purchase of Elm Lodge by Royal Holloway College in 1949 provided a starting point. Elm Lodge, almost opposite the entrance gates of the College, was purchased as a staff and postgraduate residence. In its garden Professor Jane was able to establish the nucleus of the University Botancial Supply Unit in 1950.[32] He became Chairman of its Managing Committee, on which both the College and the Senate were represented. With the purchase of more adjacent properties the Botancial Supply Unit was extended from its original three acres to twenty acres, and it is now the University of

[ 198 ]

London Botanic Garden. For the year 1962/3 Professor Jane was appointed Visiting Professor and Temporary Head of the Department of Botany at the University of Ibadan, where he died suddenly in May 1963. Dr M. A. P. Madge became Acting Head of Department at Royal Holloway, until the appointment to the Chair of Botany of Professor Karl Wilson (1963-76).

In 1944 Professor Bevan Baker retired to be succeeded by Professor (now Sir) William McCrea, who held the Chair of Mathematics until 1966. Previously Reader in Mathematics and Assistant Professor at Imperial College, London (1932-6) and Professor of Mathematics at Queen's University, Belfast (1936-44), he arrived at Royal Holloway with a great reputation, and on his resignation to take up another appointment he was described as 'one of the leading cosmologists and relativists in the country'.[33] He was elected a Fellow of the Royal Society in 1952, and was President of the Royal Astronomical Society (1961-3). His publications include *Relativity Physics* (1935), *Analytical Geometry of Three Dimensions* (1942) and *Physics of the Sun and Stars* (1950).

From 1945 Music was listed in the *College Calendar* as an academic department, and students were prepared in Harmony, Counterpoint and History of Music for the BA General Degree. In 1946 Miss Beatrice Pompilia Legge (always affectionately known as 'Pompey') was appointed Assistant Director of Music, and a happy partnership between Miss Scourse and Miss Legge ensued, until they retired simultaneously in 1969. Miss Scourse continued to develop the College tradition of choral singing, and in addition to the Chapel Choir and the Choral Society, founded a Special Choir to perform more difficult works. Miss Legge took over responsibility for Band and 'devoted herself to raising the standards of instrumental music' and to overcoming the perennial complication of 'the variety of musical instruments which could be offered at any one time'. She was successful in developing Band into 'an orchestra some forty strong, with a flourishing wind section'. As College numbers grew and departments began to move out of the Founder's Building, musical activities 'remained one of the chief means of social integration in the community'.[34]

During the principalship of Dr Batho all the newly appointed Professors or Heads of Department were men, with the exception of Professor Hussey (Dr Joan Thomas of Zoology had arrived simultaneously with Dr Batho, and after her retirement no woman was a Head of Department in the Faculty of Science). In 1945/6 there were eleven academic departments with women at the head of six of them; in 1961/2, the year of Dr Batho's retirement, there were still eleven departments, but woman headed only two of them.* There was a corresponding though less dramatic increase in the number of men in other academic appointments. In 1945/6 out of an academic community of thirty-four there were eight men: in 1961/2 out of an academic community of seventy-six there were thirty-five men. The College had become 'co-tuitional' before it became coeducational, with men in almost all positions of authority except the principalship itself, which under the terms of the Royal Holloway College Act (1949) was still to be held by a woman. No regulation had been infringed, but an unwritten custom of a preponderant matriarchy had been abandoned, and this was more metamorphic than any legal change which had yet taken place.

The patterns of social life at Royal Holloway College emerged from the Second World War surprisingly unchanged, despite the stresses and dislocations of the war years.

Mrs Doreen Coker, née Stableton (student 1944-7) shortly after she went down wrote a nostalgic poem describing the teatime gathering of a College Family, which could have described the experience of any group of students from 1887 to 1947 (except for the lines which make it clear that this Family took tea in a study/bedroom). It encapsulates a way of life which was about to disappear:

> The sun beats on the window-sill,
> And scribbled pages glare until
> The clock has ticked to half-past three,
> And then – the ritual of tea.
>
> The volumes, open for a while,
> Are gathered to a tidy pile

* 1945/6: Professor Willcock, English; Professor Deanesly, History; Dr Richey, German; Dr Thomas, Zoology; Miss Blackwell, Botany; Miss Scourse, Music. 1961/2: Professor Hussey, History; Miss Scourse, Music.

And curling pages pressured flat.
The rumpled cushions where I sat
Are plumped upon the wicker stool;
The flowers are lifted from the cool
Of shadowed hearth with careful hand.
(White cow-parsley from Pastureland,
Lords and ladies, clovers, grasses,
Gathered as leisurely one passes
On Sunday afternoon to see
The piglets by the apple tree) . . .

Then turning back to tea once more
I take the kettle to the door
And find the corridor asleep,
Long, carpeted, and buried deep
In dusty sunshine, flooding where
A door stands open. White and bare
The light upon the pantry floor
Dazzles, and quick the football raps
Before the gush of rushing taps.

Then leaps the gas in roaring rings
And heats the kettle till it sings.
And meanwhile, clattering on the stairs
Has come the Family, in pairs,
With butter dish on wooden tray
And milk, the ration for one day
Brought in an individual jug.
They stand the table on the rug
And spread the newly laundered cloth,
And Grace and Honor, laughing both,
Subside upon the bed and chat
And tease and joke of this and that . . .

The bread, from Dallen's, very new
Is hacked to pieces large and few . . .
While complicated debts are paid

[ 201 ]

And candid calculations made
Of how much butter Grace has lent
And what the Family Fund has spent.
Scandal and fantasy are bandied
While second cups of tea are handed.
Muriel gives us her impression
Of Gerald* in a Gothic Session,
And Grace will fill us all with glee
With anecdotes of Little G† . . .

But all too soon the hour is past,
The washers-up begin at last
To pile the plates and sweep the crumbs
And down the corridor there comes
The pantry noise of talk and laughter
Songs and the hush that follows after . . .
The footsteps fade and quiet falls
The sunshine creeps across the walls . . .

To think that one should reminisce so soon
Upon that everlasting afternoon,
And recreate, out of that humdrum hour
The transient beauty of a summer flower!
So let it be, for they were royal days
And gracious; let this epitaph be praise
To other eras, and not theirs alone:
They had their glory, flourished, and are gone.

Many features of College life mentioned in this poem were about to
disappear. The 'piglets by the apply tree' belonged to the last generation
of the College pigs, which had been consuming the kitchen rubbish
since 1887, and providing bacon. During the Second World War they
suffered from poor nutrition and became susceptible to all kinds of
ailments, eventually swine fever. The decision to sell off the remaining

---

* Professor Gladys Willcock was nicknamed 'Gerald' or 'Geraldine'.
† Miss H. A. C. Green was nicknamed 'Little G'.

pigs was taken in the autumn of 1946. The rations of milk and butter (and the College Rolls, not mentioned in this poem) were supposed by many students to have been introduced as a result of wartime rationing, but in fact they had been provided since the earliest days of the College, and were not abolished until the 1960s. The long vistas of carpeted corridors were broken up in the 1950s by the installation of fire doors, which paradoxically became obligatory just as the College was eliminating its coal fires, which by the middle years of the decade had been replaced in all study/bedrooms by gasfires. The Family system itself disappeared in the early 1950s, as a larger and more informal community made such ritualised friendship seem archaic and limiting. The exclusively feminine society which the poem evokes was about to be invaded and transformed.

Miss J. L. Hurn (student 1946-9, Administrative Staff from 1964; Registrar 1970-85) described the impact of the arrival of the men postgraduates:

I was in my room one day getting ready for lunch, and my next door neighbour . . . came tearing into my room and said 'Look, look, men!' And there were two or three young men wearing blazers and standing around [in the quad] . . . And we thought obviously they must be . . . some of Professor Tolansky's postgraduates from Manchester . . . Before I could say much more she had . . . gone out again. So I thought I'd . . . have another look at these beings, and what should I see but my neighbour, Jill, walking along and chatting them up already . . . And about two or three terms later, one vacation I got a letter from herself saying 'Guess what – you'll never guess. I'm engaged.' And it was in fact to one of the men we had spotted from the window. And they were married and are still married. So it really altered the lives of one or two people in the College.[35]

To less enterprising young women the men postgraduates remained, as one student put it, 'rather marginal and peripheral'. Socially they were a far less noticeable male element than the University administrative staff had been during the Second World War. But men were soon to become far less rare beings in Royal Holloway College. Dr Batho had already created conditions favourable to their more frequent appearance. Immediately on her arrival, as she told the author,

My first morning I'd had breakfast in my study and I opened the door and there was a whole crowd of students outside and I said, 'Good heavens, what are you all here for?' and they said, 'Please, we want to be out after ten o'clock' and I said, 'You may all be out after ten o'clock – you needn't bother about it. I will have a book put in the lodge – you can sign when you come in. I trust you not to be later than ten-thirty.' I think that was the first sensible thing I did . . . And I said, 'Yes, of course you may have visitors in your rooms.'[36]

For evenings which were likely to extend beyond 10.30 special permission was still required. At a quarter past midnight the last Green Line Bus from London stopped near the College gates, so that this was regarded as the accepted hour of return after visits to the theatre. The permission to receive visitors applied to visiting men, who were allowed to remain in College until 10 p.m. and to be entertained in students' rooms. College dances ended at 11.30 p.m. and these provided extended time for male visitors to be in College. But at the end of the dance a screen was placed across West I and a member of staff stationed beside it, to ensure that all men left the College by the main entrance.[37]

Apart from the Royal Holloway postgraduates, and students from London Colleges who might be encountered at inter-collegiate lectures and ULU functions, the most available men were those invited in groups to the College dances. In addition to cadets from Sandhurst, the traditional dancing partners of pre-war years, there were also students from Shoreditch Teacher Training College, Englefield Green, (now the Shoreditch Campus of Brunel University) which specialised in the training of craft teachers. Mrs Mary Kennedy, née Charlesworth (student 1950-53; extra-mural lecturer in Women's Studies, University of London, from 1980) gives a feminist perspective on the relations of Royal Holloway with Sandhurst and Shoreditch:

There was rather a conflict, here, of interest, because Shoreditch, being a Teacher Training College, was rather looked down upon, because, after all, we were doing degrees. And at the same time most of us were rather uneasy with army cadets, who weren't nearly as intelligent as we were . . . We were probably only 1 per cent of our generation, so we were brighter, but so disciplined were we, or so well conditioned, that we were

very polite and would remember to ask questions and listen to the men
... And I think that before the Second Feminist Movement started [ie
in the late 1960s] this is very indicative of the way women, and even
women who were going to have degrees, saw themselves.[38]

The women students of the 1950s, who had been small children during
the Second World War, were the daughters of women who had shared
the duties, hardships and dangers of men during the war years, and in
many instances had emerged from them convinced that the domestic
role for women was preferable to the stresses and responsibilities of
equality. Their daughters were conditioned by this reaction. Mary
Kennedy recalls one of her College friends who typified it: 'Her whole
being was set on marriage. She would spend her time looking at women's
magazines ... we were in that sort of ethos ... [39] The resulting reaction
against the traditional values of the College was expressed in a humorous
poem printed in *Erinna*:

> Little Miss Emancipate
> Dost enjoy the newfound state,
> Full of rights, enfranchised, free
> Being a lady of Degree?
> Ever since the world began
> Thou wast better-half to man.
> Now it seems, alack the day
> Thou must work for half his pay!
>
> Lucky Lady, going to College,
> Wearing specs and gaining knowledge,
> Studying odes that lovers yearning
> Wrote to ladies of less learning
> Thy poor lover's hand is frozen
> Dares not write to thee his chozen
> Fearing rightly a refusal
> From thy critical purusal.
>
> Oh brave New World and manners new
> Where ladies may vacate the pew

[ 205 ]

And hang from straps with utmost grace
That weary men may take their place!
'Fie' you say 'What's that to me!
I'm a citizen, I'm free!
Trousered, smoking, drinking ale –
What care I for any male!'

Well, you know, I sometimes wonder,
If perhaps you made a blunder . . .
Don't you find it overrated,
Being a Maid Emancipated?[40]

While what may be termed the 'Feminine Reaction' of the 1950s was strongly represented in College, it did not produce a universal state of mind. There were hard-working and ambitious students; there were students without any motivation, matrimonial, professional or academic. In January/February 1953 the editorial committee of *Erinna* conducted a survey of 'Student Activities', which was equally revealing of student attitudes. One hundred and thirty-nine students out of a community of 362 returned questionnaires. 'Questions were put in an extreme form,' the committee explained, 'and readers may make of them what they will.' A selection of answers reads as follows:

*Do you wish that you had never come to College?* 117 were glad that they had come to College . . . Among the 22 who wished that they had not come the favourite excuse was 'non-academic type' (15 times); 13 had chosen the wrong College and 6 the wrong subject. (The arithmetic is not wrong, several gave more than one reason . . .)

*Do you know what you are going to do when you leave College?* Just over a third (51) did not. Of the rest 34 were going to teach, and the next highest number, 6, besides 5 who were going to earn a living as well, were tackling marriage . . .

*How many times a term do you go to (a) the cinema, (b) the theatre, (c) dances?* In all three categories and with all three years most students went from one to three times: 30 never went to the cinema; 31 to the theatre; 43 to dances. 50 favoured the cinema principally for entertainment, 38 the theatre, and 26 dancing . . .

[ 206 ]

*What else do you spend much of your time on?* . . . Most popular occupation was gossiping (59), followed by knitting (56), eating (32), listening to the radio (32). Suspected committee members gave the names of various College societies, and 4 students supplied the Christian names of their boyfriends . . . 7 openly admitted to idling . . . 11 slept; 12 had no spare time.

*Do you think RHC should admit men undergraduates?* 78 thought it ought, 44 opposed, 17 of them First Years . . .

*Which do you prefer (a) Shoreditch; (b) Sandhurst; (c) University students; (d) Non-Students; or are you (e) not interested?* Shoreditch had 13 supporters, Sandhurst 26. 77 liked university men, and 36 non-students. 20 were not interested. Several students liked *all* men . . .

*How many hours work do you do per day including pracs* [practicals] *and lectures?* 22 did less than 5 hours work a day; 72, 6-7 hours; 33, 8-9 hours, 16 more than 10 hours . . . 27 out of 57 working more than 8 hours a day were Third Years.

*When working are you generally: (a) happy; (b) indifferent; (c) resigned; (d) wretched?* 33 were openly happy, 46 were sometimes. The work of the other 60 was untouched by happiness; 9 of these were altogether indifferent to their work, 22 resigned, 12 wretched, and the rest all had mixed feelings. Remarks from third-year artists included 'Happy in the morning, resigned in the afternoon, asleep in the evening' . . . A scientist wrote 'usually just plain bored.'[41]

The survey reveals reactions ranging from zeal to apathy, a range which would not have been found during the first fifty years of the College, when every girl who went to university was aware that it was a privilege to go. Even though university education was still entered only by a small proportion of women, it no longer had to be fought for against prejudice or paid for by family sacrifice; it could be won by good school results and financed by local authority grants, even without the exceptional attainment of scholarships. In consequence, women who no longer regarded themselves as members of a privileged élite began to take a much less reverential attitude to their education and their College. The students of 1953 composed a new 'Holloway Song' (sung to the tune of 'Men of Harlech'), which contained the lines,

[ 207 ]

We came here 'cos we were made to –
Some of us were even paid to . . .[42]

an eloquent contrast to the 'College Song' of 1907:

There's a College down in Surrey
Southwest of London Town
The best place in all England
Where they wear the cap and gown . . .

Affection for the College remained, but irreverence bred a more critical attitude. The 'Holloway Song' of 1953 contained some satirical lines on College food, and in that year the students staged the first revolt in College history by boycotting lunch, occupying the Octagon under the Central Tower between the Dining Hall and Kitchen, and demanding an improvement in College catering. They invited the local Press to report the event. Unfortunately for the effect of the protest 'they did it on a day when quite a good meal was served, steak and kidney pie, cabbage and potatoes and quite a decent pudding, and the Press came and there was really nothing to report so it fell rather flat.'[43] Miss Strachan, the Domestic Bursar, who had never received any complaints before, reacted with injured feelings, but promised improvement. The improvement was slight, for the catering facilities were stretched to their limits, and in need of reorganisation.

Since the early years of the Second World War lunch had been the main meal of the day, but some of the older members of the staff, attached to the memory of pre-war traditions, still changed into long dresses in the evening. 'They did it,' said Miss S. P. Jenkins, 'partly because they had them and partly because it was so cold that if you had a nice warm long velvet skirt, then why not wear it. And the thing that sticks in my mind with regard to that is Dr Tompkins, who came in a very elegant deep blue velvet dress from time to time, and one student remarked to me that she felt rather sad when Dr Tompkins came in looking so splendid and was then faced with a portion of baked beans on toast!'[44]

This little vignette illustrates the perpetual tension between the forces of tradition and innovation: ever since the social traditions of the College had been invented they had been subject to pressures of change. A point

[ 208 ]

had been reached when some of them were outmoded, and could not for many years longer be retained.

While the Victorian and Edwardian social traditions of the College had suffered irreparably from the effects of the Second World War, its cultural life had gained from the pressures of that period. The necessity of creating an independent cultural life during the war years had encouraged a creative vigour and nourished a spirit of self-sufficiency which were maintained in the years that followed.

The increasing professionalism of College Music under Miss Scourse and Miss Legge has already been mentioned. Besides Band, Choral, Choir and Special Choir, there were musical societies for non-performing enthusiasts too. The Music Club met to listen to weekly papers on musical subjects; the Music Association arranged concerts and recitals by distinguished musicians. 'Orpheus' was a club which collected records and provided twice-weekly gramophone recitals.

CHARD continued to attract the outstanding dramatic talents in the College. Dr Batho's comment that watching the annual CHARD play could be 'painful' may have been occasioned by the 1949 production of T. S. Eliot's *The Family Reunion*, which even a basically kind review in *Erinna* makes clear was beyond the range of an all-female cast.[45] However, in 1951, Garcia Lorca's *The House of Bernarda Alba* with an all-female dramatis personae was acknowledged as the best CHARD production for many years, 'to be additionally praised for its success in putting Royal Holloway College "on the map" with the triumph it scored when performed at the NUS Arts Festival at Bristol during the Christmas vacation.'[46] Play-reading societies, 'Georgians', 'Shakespeare' and 'First and Second Year Poetry and Play-Reading Groups' also flourished. In 1947 Dr Batho and Dr Tompkins joined the Shakespearian Society to read Mistress Page and Mistress Ford in *The Merry Wives of Windsor*.

In the same year the '47 Society was founded as a general cultural society to bring together the staff and students of the Arts and Science Faculties 'in the realisation of a liberal background to special studies'.[47] In 1950, inspired by the '47 Society, the mysterious 'Mr Gillie': 'small and energetic, with sharp ears, beady eyes, deceptively hidden in rather long hair, and he always wears a white fur coat' – began to write and compile a Wall Newspaper, pinned to the main College notice-board. 'His aims were to report on matches, which RHC often won, unknown to any but the teams themselves, [and] to point out events of interest in College . . . When news was scanty he decided to fill in with odds and ends like . . . items of news about past and present students, and occasionally criticisms of plays and films.'[48] The ensuing decade was the heyday of general interest societies. CABAL (1957) which did not define its aims, catered for general interest in the arts. One of its earliest guest speakers was Iris Murdoch on 'The Novel'. GENSCI (1958) was a club chiefly intended for general scientists, which invited speakers on scientific topics but also attempted to recruit members from the Arts Faculty to hear them. MARCH (an anagram of Royal Holloway College Mathematical Association) a long-established society, extended its scope and arranged programmes of lectures, papers and industrial visits far beyond matters of purely departmental interest. All the departmental societies founded in the early years of the College continued to exist, but the less enterprising ones probably relied as they had always done on the obligation of students to belong to them. New societies were formed dedicated to special interests, including Jazz, Chess and Brass Rubbing. An Astronomical Society, under the presidency of Professor McCrea, was founded in 1961.

The Debating Society in the Lent term of that year debated the motion that 'RHC is abnormally Christian' (which was defeated); but it was a tenable view, for in spite of a decline in Chapel attendance in the post-war period, the College continued to have a vigorous and varied religious life. Religious societies, besides SCM and LIFCU, were the Anglican, Catholic and Methodist Societies. Social awareness was represented by the long-standing Women's University Settlement Society and Amritsar Scholarship Fund, to which a branch of the Universities Fellowship for Animal Welfare was added in 1956, and of the Campaign for Nuclear Disarmament in 1961.

Royal Holloway continued to have its old reputation as a non-political college, yet there was sufficient political interest in the post-war years to support the Politico-Economic Club, Conservative and Liberal Clubs and a Socialist Society. Apathy may have been more widespread than enthusiasm, but an exception was provided by Miss Janet Fookes (student 1954-7; Conservative MP for Plymouth Drake since 1979) who came up to College determined since the age of eleven to become a Conservative Member of Parliament. Far from biased, however, she went to hear a

young and handsome Mr Anthony Wedgwood-Benn address the Socialist Society.[49] Miss Fookes took her Finals in the Picture Gallery, which
had been used for this purpose since the end of the Second World War,
when the university cancelled its approval of the use of the lecture
theatre, because of its tiered seats and adjoining desks. Seated beside
Landseer's grim picture *Man Proposes, God Disposes*, she thought its title
unpropitious. Before the end of the decade it was customarily draped
with a Union Jack during Finals, to counteract an increasing superstitious
awe among the finalists.

Royal Holloway College ended the 1950s with 347 resident students
and forty-two non-resident, of whom twenty-one were men postgraduates. After the sharp post-war increase the growth of the College had
been inhibited by the discovery of extensive dry-rot, which necessitated
keeping many rooms empty while the condition was treated. Scaffolding
had veiled one part of the building after another for the better part of
the decade before it emerged as fully habitable again. Within the College
new space was made available for residence with the purchase of two
large houses in Egham Hill, The Beeches and The Chestnuts, which
were to house the Departments of German and French respectively.
The Zoology Department looked forward to its escape from the attics
of East V, following the purchase of Alderhurst in Bakeham Lane, which
was to be converted for its use.

At the end of the 1950s Royal Holloway College still retained much
of its original character as a self-sufficient community with an intellectual
and social life to a large extent self-generating and self-contained.
Change had begun, yet despite the increasing number of men on the
academic staff, despite the growing body of men postgraduates, despite
the liberalisation of the rules which permitted men to visit it by day and
during the evening, it remained a predominantly feminine community,
and retained the ethos of a women's college.


The decision to take in men undergraduates was made in 1960, when
universities throughout the country were planning expansion, as the
children conceived in the 'baby boom' of the Second World War
approached student age. Royal Holloway College anticipated expanding
to become a community of 1,000 students, to be composed of approxi-

mately equal numbers of men and women. The pattern adopted for the intake of men postgraduates – a small number increasing year by year – was to be abandoned in favour of an immediate, massive intake of men undergraduates, changing the character of the College in a single session. The decision to go coeducational, according to Mr Richard Hardy, who succeeded Miss Hustler as Secretary to the College in 1964, was 'as bold and radical in its day as Thomas Holloway's resolve to found the College for the higher education of women'.[50]

Sir Leslie Martin (Professor of Architecture, University of Cambridge, 1956-72) was commissioned to draw a plan for the expansion, including two halls of residence to accommodate 500 men. In the meantime a visitation by the UGC took place on 1 June 1960, attended by the Chairman Sir Keith Murray (later Lord Murray) and also by Sir Douglas Logan (Principal of the University of London, 1948-75). Dr Batho told them that the College had expanded as far as was possible without new buildings for both teaching and residence, and Sir John Cameron (Chairman of the Council 1958-67) stressed the suitability of the site to provide the campus for a much larger residential college. The importance of the Science Departments in the planned expansion was explained to the visitors as they toured the Departments. 'In the Physics Department Professor Tolansky strongly emphasised the reason he supported the admission of men was that a research school could not be built up by the very small number of women students who stayed up to do postgraduate work.'[51] Professor Bourne in the Department of Chemistry made the same point. At the conclusion of the visitation Sir Keith Murray expressed the general approval of the UGC for the College's plans for expansion.

In October Sir Leslie Martin, in conjunction with Colin St John Wilson, presented 'A Draft Plan for the Building Development of Royal Holloway College'. They made the initial point that although the College now possessed land on the opposite side of the road from its entrance gates (ie across the A30) it would be dangerous to build residences separated from the main site by a busy road.

Our proposals therefore concentrate all new developments on the land surrounding the main College building. In our view the main building should remain as both the principal residential accommodation for women students and the symbolic centre of the College – it must

[ 212 ]

always be the dominating building. Around this we consider that the new sectors of residential and teaching accommodation can be arranged in a way which will relate them conveniently to the central building and which will give a formal coherence to the whole layout. The dramatic variety of contours on the site itself and the richly wooded areas . . . provide an opportunity for convenient grouping but at the same time a sense of local seclusion within each particular building group.

While the Founder's Building was to provide residence for women students 'two new halls of residence for men should be grouped together to the east of the main College building but separated from it by the belt of trees that runs . . . diagonally across the site.' New Science Faculty buildings were to occupy the site of the existing ones, and extend further to the east and west of them, where the ground was comparatively level. A new Arts Faculty building was to be sited between the Founder's Building and the Science area. The architects concluded by pointing out that although the projected expansion would not destroy the character of the College's surroundings, it would be advisable to acquire additional land around its boundaries, for it would continue to expand, and 'it is useful to bear in mind that universities accommodating 1300-1500 students have an acreage of 100-147 acres even on central urban sites and that playing fields alone may require 30 to 40 acres.'[52]

The expansion followed the general outlines of Sir Leslie Martin's plan, but not with the immediacy which the College had hoped. Since the end of the Second World War the UGC had provided grants for capital as well as recurrent purposes; and accordingly the College requested the UGC to fund the expansion. In January 1961 a more detailed draft plan was produced, with estimated costs of £2,993,000.[53]

An arrangement had been made for a meeting between representatives of the College (Dr Batho, Sir John Cameron and Miss Hustler) and representatives of the UGC, at which Sir Leslie Martin would explain the expansion plan, with the aid of a model of the site and proposed buildings. But the request for funds led to a cancellation of the meeting by Sir Keith Murray. Sir Douglas Logan, who gave the College all the support he could, asked Murray to reconsider his decision; but the latter replied that 'it would be a waste of the College's time and of [the

[ 213 ]

Committee's] own to enter into detailed discussion at this stage about the College's expansion plans.' Sir Douglas Logan informed Dr Batho of the outcome, and said that he himself, with Mr J. R. Stewart (Clerk of the University Court 1950-82; Principal 1978-83) would meet the representatives of the College and the architects as arranged: 'Our particular interest would be to see whether the "crash" programme which the College has produced could be spread over a longer period than is at present contemplated.'[54] They visited the College on 20 February 1961, and explained that the Treasury grant to the UGC for 1964 and 1965 of £6,000,000 was insufficient to cover the building programme of the whole University. Logan suggested that a phased building programme for Royal Holloway College should be prepared, and presented to the UGC in the summer. In the meantime he 'kindly undertook to promote a Private Bill in the Parliamentary Session 1961-2 to enable Royal Holloway College to admit men undergraduate students'.[55]

The Royal Holloway College Act (1962) received the Royal Assent on 20 May, but the College was no nearer to making provision for its male undergraduates. A discussion was held on the possibility of funding the expansion by a public appeal, and Dr Batho sought Sir Douglas Logan's advice. He replied: '. . . before an appeal has any chance of success I think it is desirable for the planning to have been carried further forward . . . so that there is something fairly concrete to put into the shop window.'[56] Dr Batho and the Council were completely mystified by this colloquialism: did he mean that they ought to build something? The Council resolved that Dr Batho should write to ask him what he meant. He apologised rather irritably, and explained that in his experience completed buildings differed so much from an architect's original model that it could be unwise to launch an appeal before detailed planning had reached a stage 'where models closely resembling what in fact will be erected, can be made and shown to intending benefactors.'[57]

There the matter rested, for Dr Batho was due to retire at the end of the session, and the responsibility for bringing these plans to fruition would fall to her successor. It had the appearance of being an impossible task.

PART FIVE


YEARS
OF
TRANSFORMATION
1962–86

———————————— :>:> 9 <:<: ————————————

# THE GREAT METAMORPHOSIS

## The Principalship of
## Dr Marjorie Williamson
## 1962–73

A welcome was given to us all in the West Ground
Floor Lecture Theatre by the then Dr Marjorie
Williamson,* who being herself an old Hollowegian
at once established a special bond thereby with us and
made you feel that she was a good choice to preside
over the change that coeducation was bringing to the
place ... I was standing by the side of the dais as
she was speaking, and accidentally knocked over a
window-pole. 'The ghost of Thomas Holloway!' she
said, and everyone laughed. She soon put us at our
ease.[1]

I N succession to Dr Batho the Council appointed as Principal Dr
Marjorie Williamson, who had known the College as a student, a
member of staff and a member of Council. Her intimate acquaintance with Royal Holloway College was complemented by broader experience, both as a scholar and an administrator.

Elsie Marjorie Williamson was born in 1913, and educated at
Wakefield Girls' High School. She entered Royal Holloway in 1932 and
gained First Class Honours in the B.Sc. General Degree in 1935. The
following year she won a First in Physics, together with a Driver
Scholarship and the Martin-Holloway Prize for the most outstanding
student. Her doctorate was conferred in 1952. In the meantime Marjorie
Williamson returned to Royal Holloway as Demonstrator in Physics
1936-9, and throughout the Second World War she was Lecturer in
Physics at the University of Wales, Aberystwyth. During the post-war

* She became Dame Marjorie Williamson on receiving the DBE in 1973.

decade, as Lecturer at Bedford College, she worked on Theoretical Physics, and in collaboration with Professor H. T. Flint researched the unification of the Theory of Relativity, Electromagnetic Theory and the Quantum Theory, on which she published a number of papers. In 1955 she was appointed Principal of St Mary's College, University of Durham, where she remained until 1962. In 1958 Dr Williamson became the RHCA member of the Council of Royal Holloway College, an appointment which would have extended until 1963; but when the principalship of Royal Holloway fell vacant on the retirement of Dr Batho, she resigned from the Council and applied for it.

'I enjoyed teaching as much as research,' she told the author, 'and when invited to go to Durham as Principal of St Mary's College, I realised that I had always found people more interesting than Physics, a subject which changes so fast that it requires one's complete commitment . . . I should never have considered leaving Durham for RHC had I not thought that something needed to be done to bring the College out of its backwater and that I would have the chance to do it.'[2]

Her years on the Council had alerted Dr Williamson to the possibility that Royal Holloway College might stagnate in its backwater, but on coming into residence she was still astonished to discover how far the process was advanced. While Dr Batho had accepted the necessity that the College should join the modern world by going coeducational, and had done her best to promote its ambitious plans for doing so, her inherent lack of interest in administration had resulted in her leaving its internal organisation almost untouched, as Dr Williamson realised when she read the little book entitled 'Notes for my successor' which Dr Batho had written for her. The notes held no surprises for Dr Williamson: they conjured up memories of the College in her own student days.

'I was sad about it in some ways,' she recalled. 'I was staggered at just how old fashioned it had become . . . It was still a shadow of the great Victorian house. It had survived handsomely until 1939. It was surprising how much they were still hanging on to. In the morning I still received the same procession that Miss Higgins and Miss Bacon had received . . . At eight I took Chapel, and then went to the Principal's Drawing Room. Pyne brought my breakfast on a tray, with letters . . . At nine o'clock the Registrar came; at nine thirty Sister Moss [with her little notebook recording who had been taken ill]; at some stage Miss Divine and Miss Hustler . . . From nine thirty onwards the Vice-Principal sat quietly in a chair – the idea being that she might have to take over, and must be *au courant*! It was a great waste of time . . . There were a lot of ridiculous rules, and change was resisted with the words "But we've always done it this way" . . .'[3]

Dr Williamson's own recollections of the past gave her a sympathetic understanding of the College's attachment to its customs: 'It was lovable, eccentric and maddening – partly laudable, partly impossible.'[4] Sensitive to the claims of tradition, she nonetheless determined that a thorough-going programme of innovation should metamorphose an old-fashioned college into a modern institution.

During the first term of Dr Williamson's principalship the College received an informal visit by Queen Elizabeth the Queen Mother (Chancellor of the University of London 1955-81). During her tour of the College she met Sir Leslie Martin and saw his model of the proposed new buildings. But however optimistically they might be described, there was no concealing that for the present 'proposed' was all that they could be.

While lack of money for the building programme was the chief obstacle, there was also some opposition within the College to overcome. Dr Williamson was aware that some women academics feared that coeducation would undermine their status: 'in women's colleges it was natural for women to be Professors and Readers – it might not be so thereafter.'[5] But this fear had arisen too late to influence the debate, for the balance of power in academic appointments had passed to men in the previous decade. The most formidable opponent of coeducation was Dr J. M. S. Tompkins, whose views on the virtues of single-sex education Dr Williamson knew and respected. They were both Governors of Bedford College, where the question of coeducation was also being debated. (Dr Williamson recalled someone at Bedford saying that coeducation was needed, but not cohabitation; it was an understandable cause of anxiety to College authorities that the one would lead inevitably to a certain amount of the other.) While Dr Tompkins opposed coeducation with reasoned arguments, her colleague in the English Department, Miss H. A. C. Green, opposed it with intransigent preju-

[ 219 ]

dice, which disappeared after the men undergraduates arrived, when she found them unexpectedly likeable. Older women members of staff were the natural opponents of coeducation, but they found an unexpected ally in Professor Tredennick of the Classics Department, who believed, as Miss Bacon had done, that the College should remain faithful to the Founder's original provisions.

Determination that coeducation should be introduced as rapidly as possible came from the Science Departments which urgently required to recruit new members. Professor Tolansky and Professor Bourne reiterated their arguments that men undergraduates were required in Physics and Chemistry as the raw material of research schools, since too few women students stayed on to do research. Both Professors wrote to the Council stressing this fact, and urged that the College should take in men undergraduates even if finance were not forthcoming for the building programme. If halls of residence could not be built for them, they must live in lodgings: their introduction was too necessary to be deferred while further plans were discussed. This was indeed a desperate suggestion, possibly made only to highlight the urgency of the situation, for it could scarcely have been expected that good male applicants would be attracted to the College unless halls of residence were provided for them.

Dr Williamson, whose appointment carried a special brief to introduce coeducation, held herself aloof from internal debate, and concentrated on the problem of devising accommodation for the men without waiting upon further negotiations with the UGC. The solution which offered itself was for the College to purchase Kingswood, a very large house on Cooper's Hill, overlooking Runnymede, slightly less than a mile distant from the College. Kingswood was not ideal for it would require a great deal of conversion; but it possessed a coach-house which would provide space for additional study/bedrooms, a large garden, and plenty of space for extension. Negotiations proved complex, since four freeholds were involved in the purchase, but the College decided that the acquisition of Kingswood offered the best chance of providing a men's hall of residence by October 1965, the decided date for the admission of men undergraduates. The purchase of Kingswood, pursued with the utmost determination by Miss Hustler, was completed in May 1964.

In the meantime the proposed expansion had received enormous

[ 220 ]

encouragement following the publication in October 1963 of *Higher Education: Report of the Committee appointed by the Prime Minister under the Chairmanship of Lord Robbins, 1961-63*, which has been described as one of the great state papers of this century. According to Mr Negley Harte in his sesquicentennial history *The University of London, 1836-1986*:

> Laid down as the central axiom [of the report] was recognition of the principle 'that courses of higher education should be available for all those who are qualified by ability and attainment to pursue them and who wish to do so.' Calculation of society's needs for professional and other skills was rejected as impractical, and a powerful case was advanced for a massive expansion of higher education based on the growing demand for it.[6]

The Government immediately accepted the main recommendations of the Robbins Report. At the time of its publication there were some 113,000 students in British universities; it proposed that this number should be expanded to 346,000 by 1980/81. In the whole of the higher education sector, student numbers were to be increased from the 216,000 of 1962/3 to 560,000 by 1980/81. This was to be achieved by the expansion of existing universities, the promotion of Colleges of Advanced Technology to the status of Technological Universities, and the foundation of new universities.[7] At the beginning of the 1960s the University of London was the largest university in Britain, and in the twenty years following the Robbins Report it 'underwent a boom that made the development of the new universities elsewhere in the country look small-scale'.[8] From a total of 21,995 full-time internal students in 1960/61 it had grown to a total of 40,280 full-time internal students by 1984/5.[9] Royal Holloway College participated in this expansion, by growing from 387 students in 1960/61 to 1,635 students in 1984/5.[10]

In the eighteen years between the end of the Second World War and the publication of the Robbins Report, universities and individual colleges throughout the country had responded to the growing demand for higher education with expansion schemes which had been consistently hampered by lack of funds. The contrast between the bold scheme commissioned from Sir Leslie Martin at Royal Holloway and the failure to raise the money to realise it had been a typical example. The acceptance by the Government of the recommendations of the Robbins Report resulted in a sudden application of funds for university expansion, from which Royal Holloway benefited, together with London University as a whole, and as part of the national scheme. The purchase of Kingswood was subsequently refunded by the UGC, which in addition made funds available for the new Science buildings which had been part of Sir Leslie Martin's plan. An additional and highly gratifying surprise was the gift of £250,000 by an anonymous donor for the building of a second hall of residence for men. This was the largest donation since the foundation of the College, and the Founder's Building itself had cost precisely this sum to build. The expansion which had seemed impossible to achieve at the time of Dr Batho's retirement suddenly became capable of realisation after all. The College could hope to achieve its target of 1,000 students by 1967.

An anticipated expansion of such magnitude, with equal numbers of both sexes, required not only accommodation for the initial intake of men undergraduates, and thereafter increased accommodation for both men and women students, but also a great deal of internal reorganisation for the change of lifestyle which the expansion would involve. The first necessity was to modernise the catering, which had continued since the Second World War to be run on a system unchanged since the foundation of the College. A kitchen and Dining Hall planned to provide for a community of some 200 still served the needs of one which had doubled in number. The depressing character of College food had become notorious since the war, but the means to improve it simply did not exist. At the same time efforts to provide the homely comforts of College life had persisted. Dr Williamson commented: 'When I was a student cakes were made, little portions of butter were carefully put out, and sugar, and delivered to everyone. Something equivalent was still done when I returned.'[11] It would not have been realistic to expect Miss Strachan, the Domestic Bursar, to re-examine her methods to meet the exigencies of expansion; her retirement, which fell due in 1965, was timely. In her place the College acquired its first Catering Officer, Mr A. J. Boog. (Twenty years after, with the freedom of speech conferred by years in retirement, Dame Marjorie Williamson said to the author, 'One of the best appointments I ever made was getting Tony Boog as Catering Officer. That was much more important than any of the Professors!')[12]

Between the appointment of Mr Boog and the opening of Kingswood only the Long Vacation remained in which to make preparations. In 1962 the College had agreed to join the Universities' Central Council on Admissions, the national scheme for application to universities, which became operative in 1964. With aspiring male candidates entering Royal Holloway College on their 'UCCA Forms' a process had been set in motion which could not be deferred, as Mr Boog was aware when he took up his appointment. The resulting pressure was unforgettable. 'If I had seen Kingswood,' he recalled, 'I would never have started, because it was a total shambles. We were within two months of opening up, and there wasn't anything there – not a thing . . . The site for the kitchen was there, but there wasn't going to be a kitchen in two months, just no chance of there being one . . .'[13]

Mr Boog was keenly aware of the need for general modernisation, and while making something out of nothing at Kingswood may have seemed the most dramatic challenge, he knew that changing the basic assumptions of College catering was the more demanding. His astonishment at the quaintness of the catering arrangements was even greater than that of Dr Williamson, because he had not known the College in pre-war days, when it was still successfully maintaining its Victorian traditions. He saw only the last attempt to perpetuate some echo of them:

Ask any student [of the mid-1960s] and they could tell you precisely what they had on one particular day [of the week] . . . On Sunday it was Sunday roast and it was still carved by the Butler on the High Table . . . The Sunday joint, always a double amount ordered . . . was cut up in little cubes and made into curry. My interview was on the Monday, and I had their curry! And there is nothing worse than . . . roast meat, you can't make it soft in a curry . . . It was always the same, so much so that when I came, the local greengrocer, who had been supplying the College for years, looked at me and said, 'You don't have to worry, I know precisely what you are going to have. You don't have to put in an order' . . . I had to change his views, and all their views, eventually . . .

There were contracts with the local butcher (he also supplied Windsor Castle, so they thought he was the best man to have!). They had purchased from Harrods – nothing but the best! . . .

I told the greengrocer that I was going to get competitive quotes and that he was quite at liberty to quote if he wished, but he felt that he could not compete. The baker, and the 'sticky buns' (ie College Rolls) were stopped. These people were charging retail prices to the College; there was no discount. The baker went bankrupt after that. He used to have on his vans 'By Appointment to Royal Holloway College' and had been serving them for years with 'sticky buns', cakes, bread, the lot, and all at retail prices . . .

It took me five years to get to the prices that the butcher was charging for meat when I went there in 1965 . . .[14]

New contracts with tradesmen, bulk buying and stock control were essential preparations for expansion. The exacting methods of stock control which Mr Boog had previously developed as a Hospital Catering Officer proved their worth at Royal Holloway in the next decade, when his precise knowledge of the quantities of tinned goods the College consumed in the course of a year enabled him to counteract the effects of high inflation by purchasing a year's supply at a time, at prices which had been dramatically overtaken before these stocks were finished. He proved that higher standards of catering could be combined with economies which his predecessors would have regarded as impossible. Mr Boog also modernised the Victorian system which he found still operating below stairs:

When I asked the Butlers* their hours . . . they told me they did eighty hours per week, and during the term they couldn't have a day off . . . As soon as I took over I put them on a forty-hour-a-week five-day week. It was so easy, yet it was 'impossible' because that was how it had always been done . . . Financially they were much better off. I put them on salaries . . . previously they had just been paid weekly.[15]

* Mr Frank Pyne, College Butler 1925-65; Mr Bert Sealey, Under Butler, then College Butler 1936-76.

Mr Frank Pyne had been College Butler for forty years and was about to retire at the age of eighty. He had seen many changes since he had presided at dinner in Miss Higgins' day, wearing white tie and tails. In the lessened formality of the 1950s Mary Kennedy remembered him looking 'like a barrister' in black jacket and striped trousers, and refusing admittance to the Dining Hall to students he considered improperly dressed. With a surprising readiness to accept innovations at the end of a long working life, Mr Pyne offered to defer his retirement for a term, until Christmas 1965, to help in the period of transformation. He was noted for his *bons mots*, and his comment on the streamlined catering introduced by Mr Boog was 'It's not RHC – it's ABC.'[16]

This comment was inspired by the fact that self-service completely superseded surviving attempts at formal meals in Hall which had been summed up by Dr Williamson as: 'I said *"Benedictus benedicat"*. Then they rushed for the hotplates!'[17] The Dining Hall became the main Refectory for women students and members of staff resident in 'Founder's', as the main building was commonly called once other halls of residence had come into being. The rooms beneath the Dining Hall were converted into the Lower Refectory (now the Crossland Suite) where meals could be bought on a cash basis, and multiple choice menus were introduced. The bungalow was extended and converted into a Students' Union building, and provided with a coffee bar. The original men undergraduates were not to be admitted to dine in Founder's; the Dining Hall at Kingswood, when completed, would be large enough to seat 250. The study/bedrooms at Kingswood were at first only sufficient for eighty, so that lodgings in the neighbourhood had to be found for the remaining twenty-one men students of the original intake of 101. Some found themselves in Windsor Castle, in rooms provided by the Dean of Windsor, others in a houseboat on the Thames.[18] The next year the College obtained the lease of the Glanty Hotel on the outskirts of Egham, which housed nineteen men undergraduates.* Those who lived in the Glanty, a community separated from their fellows, enjoyed an

---

* The site of the Glanty, since demolished, is marked by the 'Glanty Loop', where the A30 from London, signposted to Egham, describes a complete circle before doubling under itself and the M25, to approach a small roundabout where a left turn enters Egham and the A30 bypasses the town then leads up Egham Hill to pass the College.

experience so happily memorable that they instituted an annual reunion, the 'Glanty Dinner'.

In the last weeks before the arrival of the men the attention of the College authorities was centred on the conversion of Kingswood, retarded by a wet summer: 'The approaches were a quagmire. Princess Alice came round it walking on planks . . . The men who were coming up were told to bring gumboots!'[19] Dr Williamson asked Mr Robert Latham of the History Department to be Dean of Men, and Dr Roy Miller of the Physics Department to be Warden of Kingswood; each agreed on condition that the other did so.[20] Mr Latham, as previously mentioned, had been on the staff since 1947, and had been an enthusiastic supporter of coeducation; Dr Miller, the future Principal, had come to the College in 1957 as a postgraduate.

Roy Frank Miller, born in 1935, was educated at Wembley County Grammar School, and in 1957 took the B.Sc. Special Honours Degree in Physics as an external student of London University at Exeter (which was then the University College of the South West). He came to Royal Holloway at Professor Tolansky's invitation, and obtained his Ph.D. in 1962. Between 1957 and 1973 he was successively Demonstrator, Assistant Lecturer and Lecturer in Physics; in 1973 he was appointed Senior Lecturer, and in 1982 became Principal of the College. He published twenty-two research papers on the optical and structural properties of thin metal films, and made the first measurements of the Faraday rotation in single-crystal nickel. This work involved electron microscopy, which he also applied to the study of diamond, in collaboration with Professor Tolansky.[21] Dr Miller married Miss Ruth Kenchington (student RHC 1955-8; postgraduate student in Botany 1958-62), whose support Dr Batho envied him when she wrote, 'I often wished I had a wife.'

It was an advantage to Dr Miller that his personal interests involved him in many aspects of College social life: he played the trombone in the Jazz Band formed by the postgraduates, and 'as a pseudo-French Horn in Band under Miss Legge', and sang in the Mixed Choir founded by Miss Scourse when sufficient male voices were available.[22] He made recordings of the Chapel Choir and Special Choir, now in the possession of the Faculty of Music, of which Dr Lionel Pike recalled 'the recording engineer was a handsome young Assistant Lecturer in Physics, who was a great pin-up with the young ladies of the Chapel Choir.'[23] Dr Miller was President of the Staff Cricket Club, for which he played, was actively associated with the Mountaineering Club (founded 1966), and as Principal became President of the Hockey Club (the tradition that the Principal should hold this office dated back to Miss Higgins). Perhaps his greatest assets in his relations with the students, and in particular in the establishment of traditions of coeducation at Royal Holloway, were his calm presence and his capacity to blend a natural authority with a friendly informality of manner.

Even for Dr Miller calm was scarcely possible on the day the men undergraduates arrived. Mr Mike Bayliss (student 1965-8), driven to the College by his father, was the first man to reach Kingswood:

We arrived in the middle of a sunny October afternoon. There was no one around except for a bearded gentleman looking very harassed who was unpacking cardboard boxes containing what looked like crockery. 'Obviously the Caretaker,' I thought. We enquired if he knew where the Warden was, so I could check in. 'I *am* the Warden,' he said. 'Look, we're not really ready yet: can you come back later?'[24]

Mike Bayliss returned later to find that he had a shared study/bedroom in 'A Block' which was the converted coach-house, while the majority of the students were housed in 'B Block', the original house. 'C Block', the extension which would link the two, was no more than a pile of builders' materials. The students were soon told that the old house had once been a convent, which seemed to emphasise their invasion of a female world. That evening they trooped into the temporary dining hall, where supper, which had been cooked in the temporary kitchen, was served by the Warden, the Registrar, and the College Secretary: Spanish catering staff engaged by Mr Boog had not yet arrived. A speech of welcome addressed to the students by Dr Williamson in the Main Lecture Theatre was their formal induction to the College. 'I was standing by the side of the dais as she was speaking,' recalled Mr P. Vianney Waters (student 1965-8), 'and accidentally knocked over a window-pole. "The ghost of Thomas Holloway!" she said, and everyone laughed. She soon put us at our ease.'[25]

While the original men postgraduates had been unobtrusive harbingers of change, the men undergraduates of 1965 were its fulfilment. Their

[ 227 ]

arrival began the metamorphosis of Royal Holloway College into an entirely new type of institution, and they were as aware of being pioneers as the first women students of 1887 had been: 'We ... felt a certain special pride in being pioneers as the first undergraduate male intake, a distinction succeeding intakes did not have, thus marking another clear stage in the evolution of RHC.'[26] The Principal drew attention in the *College Letter* of 1967 to the fact that the eightieth anniversary of the College's existence marked the final passing of the women's college, since it was the last year in which Finals were taken by women only.[27]

To Mr Richard Hardy, the College Secretary, the arrival of the men posed new practical problems:

They knew the college wanted them and there was a sort of house-form of wildness ... they ran over the buildings like mad things. They got into every nook and cranny. The girls would never have bothered ... The boys were in the roof-space. In the attics. We were frightened that they would fall through the ceiling in the Chapel ... We spent a fortune on locks that year to stop them running about where the management felt that they shouldn't be ... They played up a little bit because they knew they were the darlings of the day.[28]

Men legitimately came into Founder's as students of Mathematics, History, Classics and Music, the only departments which were still housed in the building, and to work in the Library, which now occupied the whole of the south range as a self-contained unit (except for the eastern half of the original Museum, which continued to be used as the Music Room). They were permitted to be in women students' rooms until 10.30 in the evening, when they, like visitors from Sandhurst, Shoreditch and elsewhere, were expected to leave; but inevitably 'there were one or two cases of bravado ... where fellows claimed to have secretly spent a night in RHC forbidden territory ...'[29] However, as the decade progressed rules intended for the enforcement of morals increasingly became unenforceable, as young people claimed and acted upon the right to make their own decisions in sexual matters. The acceptance of this right by the College authorities was tacitly acknowledged when twenty men undergraduates were admitted as residents of Founder's in 1970. In 1985 a third-year woman student told the author that she and her boyfriend spent the night in her room in Founder's or his room in Cameron Hall* according to where they happened to be at the end of the evening. Coeducation and cohabitation had become synonymous, at least for some.

A more immediate result of coeducation was a vast expansion in the range of College social activities. In preparation for the introduction of new sports the College purchased Noble's Field, between the southern boundary of the College estate and the then Southern Railway. (Thomas Holloway had hoped to add this field to the College estate, with the intention of building a private railway station; but its owner, appropriately named Lord Field, had refused to sell it.) Students formed stone-picking parties to clear Noble's Field for football pitches. Soccer and Rugby Clubs were founded, and both had successful early seasons, especially the latter, which on formation applied for admission to the University of London League, and won the League Championship in its second season (1966-7). Some long-established sports clubs – Hockey, Cricket, Tennis, Table Tennis, Rowing and Squash – divided into men's and women's sections. Men formed the Mountaineering Club, and members of both sexes joined the new Judo Club. A 'mini-sport' which enjoyed a vogue in the 1960s was Tiddlywinks, which appeared in College as a subsidiary activity of the Jazz Club: 'Jazz Club and Tiddlywinks' (1965). It became affiliated to the English Tiddlywinks Association, and the following year unsuccessfully played Sandhurst and Southampton University, but defeated the Mathematics staff.

With the acquisition of male actors CHARD overcame its perennial weakness, the inadequacy of actresses to play male parts. The CHARD production of 1965 was *Hedda Gabler*, of which the critic in the *College Letter* commented, 'The choice of Ibsen's heroine-dominated play . . . as the first CHARD production to include male undergraduates in the cast might seem somewhat ironic . . .'[30], but Michael Rowan-Robinson as Ejlert Lövborg and David Whitworth as Judge Brack won approval in their supporting roles. Next year CHARD redressed the balance by choosing a play with a star part for a man, Shaw's political comedy *The Apple Cart*, in which Charles Howie acquitted himself well in the demanding role of King Magnus.

* Men's hall of residence, completed in 1969.

All aspects of College Music benefited from the arrival of the men. Choral and Choir extended their repertoire with the acquisition of male voices, and Band was 'reinforced by a very efficient group of wind players'.[31] Mike Bayliss who came up to read French, despite his good A levels believed that he owed his place to an interview with Miss Legge, at which she was delighted to discover that he both played the flute and sang baritone! He recalled that initially the Chapel Choir possessed no music for men's voices: 'We were obliged to sing from little slips of manuscript hastily written by the late lamented Joan Scourse.'[32] It may be remembered that the end of the Second World War had found Miss Scourse writing out the parts for 'Now Thank we all Our God'; the invention of the photocopying machine came too late to help her.

Mike Bayliss and a fellow 'new-intake man' Bob Wardle were founder members of the Savoy Opera Society, which continues to entertain the College with the works of Gilbert and Sullivan. Its first full-scale production was *Trial by Jury* (1967), in which Miss Felicity Lott (student 1965-8), who has since become one of the most famous Royal Holloway alumnae, sang the role of Angelina. She later starred as Yum-Yum in the SOS production of *The Mikado*. Felicity Lott entered Royal Holloway to read French, with the intention of becoming an interpreter. She took singing lessons at College with the visiting teacher, Miss Joan Gray, but not until she was working in Grenoble as an *Assistante d'Anglais* did the encouragement of another teacher, Elizabeth Maximovitch, persuade her to make singing her career. 'I auditioned for a scholarship at the Royal Academy of Music,' she told the author. '. . . I got in, but didn't have much money at all . . . and Royal Holloway gave me a lot of financial help to make me able to be a bit more independent.'[33] A dazzling career followed, in which Miss Lott has sung with the English National Opera, the Welsh National Opera, Scottish Opera, at Glyndebourne and Covent Garden, and in many productions abroad.

While new societies were formed and existing societies invigorated following the arrival of the men, the Students' Union Society was transformed by them. The provision of the extended bungalow as a Students' Union building gave the Union a new sense of cohesion, and created a social centre which, it reported in 1966, 'has helped a great deal in uniting the students of different departments and . . . in extending their extra-academic activities'.[34] To the coffee bar provided by the

[ 230 ]

College authorities the Union added an alcoholic bar and a shop (installed by the manufacturers of Oxford stationery), both of which were run by the Union on a volunteer rota system.[35] In the Lent term of 1966 the Union elected its first male President and Secretary, and many members of staff (not only women) regretted that thereafter women students seemed content to abdicate responsibility for Union affairs, and year after year gave their votes to male candidates for Union offices.[36] In 1966 the College Committee was formed as a joint staff-student body, which met once or twice a term to discuss matters of mutual interest. Union activities became increasingly time-consuming, and in 1968, after five resignations from the Union Committee owing to pressure of work, negotiations were begun for a 'sabbatical' year for the President. The Union's first full-time President, Mr David Coltart, held office for 1969/70.[37]

The same year, following the publication of a Joint Statement of the Committee of Vice-Chancellors and Principals and the National Union of Students on the role of students in the academic community, its recommendations were implemented by the addition of two students to the College Council.[38] One was automatically to be the President of the Union, the other to be elected by the main body of students. The following year student representation was increased by the election of eight students to a panel from which three were to be picked at random in the event of the meeting of the Council's *ad hoc* Disciplinary Committee. Lord Longford, who was Chairman of the Council for the brief period 1969 to 1971, expressed concern that all eight of these students were men.[39] These developments took place over the period of student unrest which reached its high point in 1968; but at Royal Holloway College, though the increased political activism of students had its effect, relations between the students and the authorities were free from the violence which occurred in some other colleges.

The 1960s witnessed a transformation in the religious life of Royal Holloway. The increasing secularisation of society which followed the Second World War was mirrored in College by a continuing decline in Chapel attendance. Membership of the Chapel Choir was freely admitted to have been sought in some instances for musical rather than religious reasons. Dr Williamson changed the time of Chapel from 8 a.m. to 8.45 a.m., both to encourage attendance and to facilitate Chapel-goers who were not resident in Founder's. Among the religiously inclined there was less sectarian attachment and an increase of interest in Christian Unity, which was a general result of the Second Vatican Council (1962-5), at which the Roman Catholic Church had given unprecedented encouragement to the ecumenical movement. Services of prayer for Christian Unity were held in the College Chapel, and in 1964 a Roman Catholic Mass was celebrated there for the first time in College history – an event made possible by the non-denominational status of the College, but one which the Founder could scarcely have foreseen. In 1966 following the recommendations of a working party which studied religious life in College, appointed by the Council on the initiative of Dr Williamson, a Joint Chaplaincy was set up. Four Honorary Chaplains were appointed, one Roman Catholic, one Church of England, and two Free Church, an arrangement which provided pastoral care for students, which had not been attempted in the early years of the College when Church membership and a religious background at home had been assumed to provide it. Sunday morning services conducted by visiting clergymen were discontinued.

In the course of the decade most of the traditions or customs which had characterised Royal Holloway as a small and isolated women's college fell victim to the effects of expansion and coeducation. To those who had known the College in earlier years (for example, the older members of the RHCA) it might have seemed in danger of losing its individuality together with its ladylike ethos. However, the coeducational Royal Holloway developed a new individuality and new traditions, some invented by the authorities to provide an appropriate social framework for a changed community, some evolved by the students themselves.

In 1966 Mr Boog suggested to Dr Williamson that a Farewell Dinner should be held for the students who were going down. It was a splendid occasion graced by the use of some new College silver, which Mr Boog had been able to purchase as a result of a rather unusual deal:

> I found a room chock-a-block of old jerries [chamber-pots], all brand new, with the wash basin, bowl and the jerry, which was the standard issue, all with the RHC crest on it. And I thought that if I could sell these, I could perhaps replace the silver cutlery ... I sold the whole lot to a baker in Richmond ... who immediately put Easter eggs in

[ 232 ]

the jerries and sent them to America. And the wash basins, he found an hotel who had got the same initials RHC, they got those . . . So I upgraded my silver, and I had sufficient over to bring in the candelabra. Most people think that those candelabra are something . . . from the old days when it was a Victorian College. But not so, because in those days . . . they had these beautiful electric lights, one of the first places in England to have electric lights. And they never had candelabra at all.[40]

The success of the Farewell Dinner led to the inauguration of the Year Dinners, for First Years in the first term of the session, for Second Years in the second term, for Third Years in the third. While formality had been abandoned of necessity in the daily life of a large and crowded community it returned in the form of celebration dinners, and 'played a very important part in the social life of the students in teaching them how to conduct themselves in . . . formal life. It was incredible how nervous they were. You could actually see some of them shake through fear at those meals.'[41] However, they attended enthusiastically, and for the most part accepted the convention of formal dress: 'Most of the men wore suits. One or two of the girls tried to come in bare-footed . . . This was like part of the 1960s fashions . . .'[42] In the 1970s a taste for formality began to return, with the men willingly donning dinner jackets and the women long frocks.

In the course of the 1960s women members of staff moved out of Founder's, so that it ceased to be a mixed community of students and academics and became a hall of residence. Dr Williamson, who had begun her principalship in the flat previously inhabited by Dr Batho in the South Tower, moved into Settrington in Bakeham Lane, which the College purchased from the executors of Miss Taylor as an official Principal's House. In 1968 Dr Williamson commented:

Perhaps the biggest problem with which we are faced is that of sustaining the general life, apart from the academic, of a residential College . . . [A] new system of appointing Resident Tutors does ensure that there is one senior person available in the Founder's Building, in case of need in the evening or at the weekends . . . The question is how long we shall be able to find people able and willing to undertake these duties. We realise now just how much was done, without reward and as a matter of course, by the long succession of resident academics in the past . . .[43]

For the staff the social cohesion provided by communal dining in the past was now provided by formal dinners on special occasions, such as the Christmas Feast, the St Cecilia Musicke Feaste (a medieval banquet with musical entertainment) and the departmental dinners. A staff Dining Club was founded, and the more exclusive Thursday Club with an all-male membership – the existence of which perfectly exemplifies the metamorphosis of the College. Dr Williamson was a member as an 'honorary man', and the author has had the honour of being the club's only female guest.* Towards the end of Dr Williamson's principalship Mr Boog suggested the inauguration of an annual Foundation Dinner; two were held in successive years, but the financial stringency of the 1970s caused this nascent tradition to be abandoned.

In the second half of the 1960s more students became car-owners, and as a result they did not remain in uninterrupted residence throughout the term. Increasingly there was an exodus from the College each weekend, and consequently student societies began to arrange all their meetings on weekday evenings to ensure attendance. A vicious circle ensued: the complaint that nothing happened in College at the weekend encouraged the exodus. This remains an unresolved problem. Sunday Music has been mentioned in a previous chapter as a casualty of weekend absence, but the tradition of concerts by students and music staff continues as Campus Concerts many of which are given during weekday lunch hours.

There are, however, certain enterprises organised by the Students' Union Society which draw the student community together: the production of *Château* (the College newspaper), the Summer Fête, Rag Week and the Summer Ball. The expansion of the College led to the demise of 'Mr Gillie', the Wall Newspaper, since there was no longer a focal point where it would be seen by all the students. At first 'Mr Gillie' descended from the notice-board and was circulated as a small duplicated news-sheet, before being scrapped in favour of *Château*, a more ambitious

---

* The Thursday Club has since entertained Dr Mary Bradburn and Miss J. L. Harn.

weekly newspaper founded in 1968 and intended 'to provide a useful forum for argument and discussion involving all members of the College'.[44] The Summer Fête, in support of a selected charity, originated after the Second World War as a midsummer entertainment to replace the College Garden Party, which after one post-war revival proved too costly to continue. Rag, also with charity as its pretext and pleasure as its purpose, likewise began after the war, when Dr Batho's liberalisation of the rules made it possible for the students to appear in a Rag Procession through the town centre of Windsor. The procession provided an annual outing for the College mascot Colossus, an appropriately named stuffed grizzly bear. The expansion of the College in the 1960s enormously increased the scale of Rag, to a week of fund-raising stunts and functions. In 1970 the SUS reported a Rag Procession 'which disturbed the peace in all surrounding districts', and profits for charity of £1,500.

1970 was also the occasion of a memorable Summer Ball:

The evening was transformed into a really grand occasion. The best possible use was made of all available space, considerably increased since the construction of the New Halls,* and Dinner in Founder's Dining Hall was followed by coffee served in North Quad to the background music of a Steel Band, while music and dancing for all tastes was provided throughout the College. The evening gained momentum and breakfast was provided and enjoyed by many in the misty greyness of the following morning.[45]

The great metamorphosis of the College, from the exclusively female 'orderly Christian household' of the Founder's vision, into the modern coeducational College with its social freedoms, was complete.

'As student numbers increase,' declared a brochure published by the College in 1964, and designed to attract male applicants, '. . . the range of subjects taught in the College will be extended by the addition of new departments . . . With a highly successful academic organisation in

---

\* Cameron (for men) and Athlone (for women), both completed in 1969.

[ 235 ]

being, an ideal setting, and ample room for further expansion, Royal Holloway College has everything in its favour.'[46]

These words expressed the optimism which swept the universities following the publication of the Robbins Report; but that optimism was sadly fleeting, and in Royal Holloway, as elsewhere, it had begun to evaporate long before the expansion was complete. Though the cuts in Government spending from which the universities have suffered are particularly associated with the Conservative Government elected in 1979, the first hint of financial stringency came well before the end of the 1960s.

'This has been a year both of achievement and disappointment,' the Principal reported in 1966. '. . . Disappointment and frustration set in with the Government announcement in July 1965 of the six months moratorium on public spending . . . The moratorium was followed by announcements of less generous capital provision for university building generally and so, in spite of the goodwill and generous support of the Court of the University, our building programme is, once again, in question. There is no doubt that the financial climate is steadily worsening. This turn of events has come at a most unfortunate time for Royal Holloway College, and we can only be thankful that we have at least got started and try to maintain a cautious optimism.'[47]

In the event, this cautious optimism proved justified, and the College was able to carry out its intention of founding new departments. Italian was introduced in 1966, under Mrs A. C. Miller; Biochemistry in 1967, under Dr J. B. Pridham (appointed to the Department of Chemistry, 1964; Professor of Biochemistry from 1970); Statistics and Computer Science in 1968, under Professor H. J. Godwin. In 1969 Miss Joan Scourse retired, and was succeeded as Director of Music by Mr I. W. A. Spink (Professor of Music from 1973). Dr Lionel Pike (appointed to the Department in 1964) became Chapel Organist and Choirmaster. Since 1965 a degree course in Music and Mathematics had been available; a single honours course in Music was offered in 1970, and the Department became the Faculty of Music. Mr Spink commented on this development, 'It will mean that some things will become more professional: sad perhaps to those who prize (rightly) the enthusiasm of the gifted amateur which has kept College music vital for so long, but inevitable and not incompatible with the traditions of the past.'[48] The foundation of the Faculty was indeed the fruition of past aspirations.

The expansion and dispersion of the departments were succinctly described by Dr Williamson in 'RHC 1970', a contribution to the *College Letter* of that year:

> The departments of Classics, History and Mathematics are still accommodated in Founder's Building, but all others have moved out. The Chemistry Department has its original laboratory (subsequently named the Moore) in the grounds, close to the newer Williams Laboratory, and this session a new Chemistry laboratory has been opened a little way to the south-east of the old Physics/Botany laboratory. The latter is now used by the Physics Department only, which also occupies Sutherland House on the other side of Egham Hill just below the Pack Horse.* Walking up Egham Hill from there one passes The Chestnuts (Departments of French and Italian), The Beeches (German Department), and Elm Lodge, a small hall of residence for men students and also the headquarters of the University of London Botanical Supply Unit, in whose care are the grounds of all the neighbouring houses mentioned above. Crossing Harvest Road one reached Woodlands on the corner (now used by the Music Department for academic work for the BA Music and M.Mus. courses, while the North Tower remains the centre for vocal and instrumental tuition and practice), Chevithorne (English Department) and Highfield.† Between Woodlands and Chevithorne is the base of a high and much needed bridge, which carries pedestrians safely, if slowly, to and from College across the A30. The remaining departments are housed some little way down Bakeham Lane: Botany in Huntersdale and Zoology in Alderhurst . . .[49]

In the academic year 1970/71 student numbers reached 1,087 (507 men and 580 women). Fortunately provision for residence had kept pace with expansion largely through the generosity of the anonymous donor, whose initial benefaction for a hall of residence for men was increased to provide another hall for women. The New Halls, both completed in

---

* Now renamed the Royal Ascot.
† Administered by the SUS as accommodation for married students.

1969, were Athlone Hall for women and Cameron Hall for men, named in honour of Princess Alice, Countess of Athlone and Sir John Cameron, who had chaired the Council successively. In November 1970 the New Halls were visited by Queen Elizabeth, the Queen Mother, who was received by Princess Alice in the Hall named after her. The Queen Mother toured the new buildings, was shown a sample of Moon Dust by Professor Tolansky, and attended a cocktail party in Athlone Dining Hall.

The next session, 1971/2, was the penultimate of Dr Williamson's principalship, and the last of the current financial quinquennium. The *Report of the Council* commented: 'That this, the last year of the quinquennium, should once again be a year of uncertainty about the next five years was less a matter of surprise than of resignation. In spite of the bleak financial outlook, the College continued hopefully to plan its future course of consolidation and modest expansion . . .'[50]

November saw the completion of a new building designed to house a CDC 1700 satellite computer. An additional hall of residence, to contain 118 study/bedrooms, financed by a loan, was planned for completion by October 1973. It was named Williamson House after the retiring Principal. Her official portrait, painted by Ottilie Tolansky was hung in the Founder's Dining Hall. Though its light colours and informal style contrast appropriately with the sombre formality of her predecessors' portraits, it scarcely conveys the dynamism of the subject. The DBE bestowed on Dr Williamson in 1973 was a fitting accolade to a great achievement: the metamorphosis of the College had been undertaken in circumstances which at first had seemed challenging, which had become favourable, and which at last had become increasingly problematic. Dame Marjorie Williamson's successors took office in a period which imposed greater trials and demanded unprecedented adaptability to change.

# FORCES OF CHANGE

## The Principalships of
## Dr Lionel Butler
## 1973–81
## and
## Dr Roy Miller
## 1982–5

> In our history we [the College] have filled two success-
> ive roles: to be one of the distinguished colleges for
> women in the University of London; and then to
> play our part in the national expansion of university
> education and research in the last two decades. My
> advice is that we should . . . agree on and achieve a
> new (and radically revised) role soon.[1]

IN the years which followed the publication of the Robbins Report
the University of London underwent the most recent of its periodic
phases of self-examination and self-metamorphosis. Royal Holloway
College, as one of its thirty-four constituent Schools, participated in, or
was affected by, the resultant changes in constitution and organisation.

The Robbins Report was critical of the shortcomings of the system of
government in a large federal university:

> Power tends to become concentrated in the centre, and the link
> between the central authority and the places where teaching and
> research are actually carried on becomes increasingly tenuous. To
> counter this it becomes necessary to set up a system of boards and
> committees that consume time and distract academic staff from their
> primary function. Moreover, the intervention of the University be-
> tween the basic academic unit, the College, and the national system
> makes for delay and inhibits decision . . .[2]

The Robbins Committee thought that the resulting 'problems and inconveniences' called for 'investigation and remedy', and the Report suggested that if the University could not resolve these problems for itself, then 'we recommend that these should be the subject of an independent inquiry.' This, Mr Negley Harte pointed out, in *The University of London, 1836-1986*, 'was a threat the University could not ignore. A process of critical self-examination was unleashed. The possibility of the dissolution of the University was being put forward in various quarters, and so the first issue that had to be addressed was whether the constituent parts of the University were in favour of preserving the basic federal structure. The views of the Schools were sought, and their replies in 1964 indicated that they all favoured the continuation of the federal link.'[3]

However, while these replies clearly expressed the desire of the Schools to retain the federal relationship, many of them contained harsh criticisms of its methods of organisation. Accordingly the need for structural modification was addressed initially by the Robbins Report Steering Committee, and then by the first Committee on Academic Organisation (1965-6), chaired by Professor Sir Owen Saunders (Professor of Mechanical Engineering, Imperial College, and Chairman of the Academic Council; Vice-Chancellor of London University, 1967-9; Chairman of the Council of Royal Holloway College, 1971-85). Under the resultant 'Saunders Reforms' the Schools gained more control over their own teaching arrangements. In the Faculty of Science a new degree structure based on 'course units' was introduced, and new 'School-based' degrees replaced the former rigidly centralised system. Boards of Studies were broadened so that their membership included all permanent members of the academic staff, and not as formerly only the most senior ones. Rules governing the 'recognition' of teachers by the University were liberalised, Schools were given more freedom to choose their own postgraduate students, and the academic committee structure of the University was made more responsive to the views of both the Schools and the teachers.[4]

While academic reforms were generally welcomed, constitutional reforms proved more difficult to achieve. The immense growth of the University since the passing of the University of London Act (1926) and the Statutes of 1929 suggested that the heads of some of its newer institutions should be added to the Senate, a proposal first made in 1951; but Convocation refused to accept increased institutional representation, unless its own representation was also proportionately increased. By 1965 Convocation had moderated its position and was willing to accept an increase in the number of heads of Schools in the Senate, but still would not accept a reduction in the number of its own seats. Constitutional changes would require the amendment of the University of London Act (1926) and of the ensuing Statutes, and the fact that these changes could not be agreed upon within the University led to the setting up in 1970 of the Committee of Enquiry into the Governance of the University, chaired by Lord Murray of Newhaven and appointed jointly by the University and the UGC.[5]

The Murray Report, published in 1972, expressed firm commitment to the federal system, but commented that the thirty-four constituent Schools formed 'an almost bewildering complex of institutions' and suggested that it might be advantageous if the Schools were organised into 'half a dozen or so largish groups of roughly comparable size'. In this context the report proposed 'some kind of amalgamation' of Bedford, Queen Elizabeth, Royal Holloway and Westfield Colleges: 'What we envisage is a physical and academic integration. One possibility would be the fusion of Bedford, Queen Elizabeth and Westfield Colleges . . . It would then be necessary to expand Royal Holloway College to at least double its present size in order to give it sufficient strength and range to maintain itself as a viable academic unit. Another possibility would be to move one of the three Colleges situated in London out to Egham and merge it with Royal Holloway College . . .'[6] Such reorganisation was rejected at the time, only to be revived a few years later for very different reasons.

On the central government of the University the Murray Report proposed that the diarchy of the University Court and the Senate should continue in its present form, but with the membership of the Court increased from seventeen to thirty-seven, and that of the Senate from fifty-nine to between eighty and eighty-five. Members of the Senate should be elected by the Schools and the Boards of Studies, and there should also be student members. It was proposed that the Vice-Chancellorship should become full-time, instead of being as hitherto a part-time and short-term appointment. These proposals caused enormous controversy, as they tended to strengthen the centralised authority of the University, when the Schools would have preferred a devolution in the governmental process as well as in academic organisation. The result was the appointment of the Murray Consultative Committee, which on the basis of its consultations produced five reports between 1973 and 1975.[7]

Though the Murray Report was not accepted its proposals influenced the moderate restructuring of the University which was ultimately embodied in the new University of London Act (1978):

New Statutes had consequently to be produced, and the long processes of negotiation and drafting and redrafting were prolonged until 1981, when the first phase of the new statutes finally came into effect . . . The creation of a full-time salaried Vice-Chancellor attracted especial difficulties, as did the proposed 'over-representation' of Convocation, and the arrangements proposed for the election of teachers to the Senate on the dual basis of constituencies based on Boards of Studies and on Schools. At length . . . Convocation was appeased, and the objections to the full-time Vice-Chancellorship were overcome . . . The University's present system of government was achieved by a process of hard-fought compromise . . .[8]

In 1973, the year following the publication of the Murray Report, Dame Marjorie Williamson was succeeded as Principal of Royal Holloway College by Dr Lionel Butler. The appointment of a man as Principal had been sanctioned by the Royal Holloway College Act (1962); the appointment itself marked a final severance with the matriarchal tradition of the College.

Lionel Butler was born in Dudley, Staffordshire, in 1924. He was educated at Dudley Grammar School and, after war service in the RAF, at Magdalen College, Oxford, where he took a first in History. Following a short period there as Junior Lecturer and Senior Mackinnon Scholar, he was elected a Fellow of All Souls, and it was during his years at All Souls that he formed a lifelong interest in the history of the Knights Hospitallers of St John, and chiefly of their occupation of the Island of

Rhodes between 1306 and 1522. His research in the subject itself gained him a reputation as an expert on it, but did not lead to the major work which might have been expected. Professor J. S. C. Riley-Smith (Head of the Department of History, Royal Holloway College 1984/5; Royal Holloway and Bedford New College from 1985), commented in his memorial address for Dr Butler:

> ... a study of the government by Western Europeans of a Greek island just off the coast of Turkish Asia Minor involves a knowledge of Western, Byzantine and Islamic institutions. No historian has ever yet written a full scale history of the Order in the later Middle Ages and one very knowledgeable scholar has stated that it is in fact too great a task for one man. It is possible that it could be done by someone who is not too much of a perfectionist and is prepared to devote himself single-mindedly to the enterprise. But Lionel Butler's interest in people, delight in teaching and concern for administration meant that he could not give his research the attention that might have led to an early book.[9]

In 1955, at the age of thirty-one, Dr Butler was appointed the first Professor of Medieval History at the University of St Andrews, where he remained, latterly as Vice-Principal, until his move to Royal Holloway in 1973. This period covered years during which his subject was not generally popular, despite the expansion of the universities: as Professor Riley-Smith put it, 'the swinging sixties swung away from medieval history.'[10] But this trend was not reflected at St Andrews, where Dr Butler's subject was enormously popular, and his Department continually expanded. One explanation was that in the Scottish universities students applied to the Faculties and not the Departments, so that they had freedom to gravitate to the subjects which attracted them; naturally they gravitated to a Department run by a man who genuinely enjoyed teaching and lecturing, who found time to interest himself in the problems and aspirations of individual students, and who encouraged his junior colleagues to do likewise. As a lecturer he was extremely popular, for his attractive manner, command of style and mellifluous voice all communicated his enthusiasm for his subject, and 'he had an enthusiasm for just those aspects of history – the sweep of events, the clash of personalities, the irony and contradiction of human situtations – that most excite those with a general interest.'[11] At Royal Holloway College his friend and colleague Professor Katharine Worth (Head of Department of Drama, RHC, 1979-85; RHBNC from 1985) commented on his tolerance of 'what many people would have called boring meetings, because he was so interested in the interplay of personalities'.[12]

Dr Butler found Royal Holloway College a congenial community, for despite its expansion it had retained the ethos of a civilised collegiate life which he had appreciated at Oxford and St Andrews. This, he would have recognised, was because the expansion had taken place under the leadership of a Principal who had appreciated the importance of the past and understood that modernisation required not that tradition should be jettisoned but that it should be adapted and recreated to suit the needs of an enlarged community. This was his own view, for he had an innate love of order, tradition and ceremony which made the College's past immensely appealing to him. He researched its history and gave a series of lectures on the early Principals. His brilliant capacity for lecturing extempore from very brief notes resulted in there being no texts of these lectures, and they were not recorded, which must be regretted as a great loss to College history.[13] However, a lasting result of his interest in it was the commissioning from Miss Jeannie Chapel of a catalogue and historical account of Thomas Holloway's picture collection, *Victorian Taste: The Complete Catalogue of Paintings at the Royal Holloway College* (1982). Dr Butler's *pietas* towards the College's past extended to small things such as the removal of *Erinna* from her desolate position by the tennis courts to the shelter of the Chapel cloister, where she remains, protected from erosion by the weather.

Dr Butler's enthusiasm for the College and identification with its interests won him the respect of the academic community as a whole; his warmth of personality won him the affection of many members of it. More than one of these has described him as a man who possessed a genius for friendship. Liking his fellow human beings he desired to be liked by them, and it was a resultant weakness that he could be over-conciliatory, for a reluctance to make enemies paradoxically can permit enmities to proliferate. An unhappy example of this was a dispute which had arisen over the conduct and tenure of a member of the Library staff, which caused him immense distress and created enmities which he was never able to reconcile. Only after his death was the problem solved and reason restored, when the situation was inherited by Dr Roy Miller. Dr Butler's last years were troubled by ill health, as he struggled against the crippling effects of severe asthma, to which he eventually succumbed. The College's official portrait of him, painted posthumously from a set of photographs, fails to convey a vital impression of his tall and bulky figure or of his benignly humorous face.

His humour was endlessly fuelled by an unmalicious enjoyment of human foibles, on which he frequently jotted down impromptu verses, characterised by intricate rhyme schemes. For example, when a foreign student, seated next to the Principal at a College dinner, inconveniently announced that she was a vegetarian, Dr Butler's Private Secretary, Miss Janet Christie, hurried away to organise something acceptable for her to eat, and later received from him the following limerick:

> A Second Year Chemist from Brunei
> Said 'Out East, at the full of the Moon, I
> Eschew long-pig*, real swine,
> Chow-chow and Chow-mein.
> My boyfriend has custard; a prune, I.'[14]

Many of his verses concerned more significant events in College, but were frequently inspired by circumstances too complicated to make them easily quotable. It was fortunate that Dr Butler possessed and retained a sense of humour, for as his principalship progressed events in the universities provided less and less subject-matter for laughter.

When Dr Butler took office at the beginning of the academic year 1973/4 student numbers had risen to a total of 1,291 (including forty-nine part-time postgraduates), divided among the three Faculties: 494 in Arts, 718 in Science and 79 in Music. While the Science Faculty had now outgrown the Arts, women students continued to form the majority,

---

* He added this note: 'You'll remember from your brothers' boys' adventure stories that "long-pig" is the name in the Indies and the South Seas for the staple diet of cannibals.'

THE HISTORY OF ROYAL HOLLOWAY COLLEGE

with 715 women to 576 men. The academic staff numbered 160: the Principal and the staff of fourteen Departments.[15] Among such a large group of academics long service to the College was a less general characteristic than it had been in the years before the expansion, since many of the younger staff naturally regarded teaching and research at Royal Holloway as a step on the ladder of advancement not as an entire career, for not everyone could expect eventually to become Senior Lecturer or Head of Department, as had been the case when each Department was staffed by two or three.

In the Faculty of Arts the Department of Classics remained the smallest, with five members of staff. It was headed by Professor J. F. Healy, who had succeeded Professor Tredennick in 1966. His special interest is in metallurgy and numismatics in the Ancient World; for example, in 1973/4 he gave a paper to the Royal Numismatic Society on 'Greek Refining Techniques and the physical properties of gold, silver and related alloys'. In the same session Miss Norma Miller, Reader in Latin, a member of the Department since 1948, was elected the first woman member of the *Academia Latinitati inter omnes gentes fovendae*.[16]

The Department of English numbered eleven members of staff, including two readers, in English Language and Literature, and eight Lecturers, one of whom was Dr Katharine Worth, who later became Professor of Drama and Theatre Studies. The Head of Department was Professor Francis Berry, who had fairly recently succeeded Professor Barbara Hardy (1965-70) and had been appointed to Royal Holloway from a personal chair at the University of Sheffield. He held office until 1981 when he was succeeded by Professor Alan G. Hill. According to the notice of Professor Berry's retirement in the *College Letter*:

> ... the chief characteristics of Francis Berry while at the College ... were his intellectual curiosity and the breadth of his interests: one could hear him discoursing on anything from place-names to St Augustine or Norse etymologies ... A similar breadth of interest is seen in his writings, which comprise well over a dozen books, including a substantial body of highly distinctive poetry.[17]

*The Galloping Centaur* (1952) contains his collected poems from 1933 to 1951; it was followed by *Ghosts of Greenland* (1966) and *From the Red*

[ 246 ]

*Fort* (1984). For relaxation he turned to cricket, and a game of his own invention called 'crolf', a cross between golf and croquet.

The Department of French numbered thirteen members of staff, including its three visiting *lectrices*. After the brief headship of Professor J. Gaudon (1966-70), who had resigned to take a chair at Yale, Professor B. V. Juden had been appointed Head of Department. His publications while at Royal Holloway include *La France Littéraire de Charles Malo (1832-1839) et de Pierre-Joseph Challamel (1840-1843). Présentation, répertoire et notes* (1974), and *Traditions orphiques et tendances mystiques dans le romantisme français (1800-1855)* (revised second edition, 1982) and numerous papers. Italian continued to be taught by three members of staff, and was a 'sub-department' of French under the headship of Professor Juden. The Department accepted its first student in Single Honours Italian in 1974/5.[18]

The Department of German, though greatly expanded since the days when Dr Delp had taught the subject single-handed, remained small, with eight members of staff, including three visiting *assistentinnen*. Professor R. V. Tymms, appointed as Reader in German and Head of Department in 1948, and Professor in 1956, held office until his retirement in 1981. He had served on the Council from 1957 to 1960 and was Vice-Principal at the time of Dr Butler's appointment to the principalship; this office he held from 1969 to 1975. On his retirement no appointment was made to the Chair of German. Dr M. E. Gibbs, a specialist in Medieval German Literature, appointed to the Department in 1964, became Acting Head and then Head of Department in 1981/2.

The staff of the Department of History numbered thirteen when Professor J. M. Hussey retired at the end of the academic year 1973/4. Professor G. N. Sanderson (appointed to the Department in 1965; Professor of Modern History from 1970) was Acting Head until Professor P. R. L. Brown took up his appointment as Professor of History and Head of Department in May 1975. He published *The Making of Late Antiquity* (1978) and a number of papers on this period before leaving at the end of the Lent Term 1978 to become Professor of Classics at the University of California. He was succeeded as Head of Department by Professor Sanderson, who held office until his retirement in 1984. During the Second World War Professor Sanderson had been commissioned in the RAOC and had served in Egypt; thereafter he taught at the Gordon Memorial College, later the University of Khartoum, and founded the Sudan Research Unit, which became the Institute of African and Asian Studies. At Royal Holloway he taught modern British, European, African and Islamic history. His publications include *England, Europe and the Upper Nile 1882-1899* (1965), and *Education, Religion and Politics in Southern Sudan (1899-1964)*, in collaboration with his wife Lilian Passmore Sanderson (1981). He was a contributor to the recently completed *Cambridge History of Africa*. He was succeeded as Head of Department by Professor J. S. C. Riley-Smith, who joined the Department in 1978 and whose publications include many contributions to studies of the Crusades: for example as a subject editor and contributor to the *Lexikon des Mittelalters* (Artemis Verlag, Munich).

While Professor Hussey's successors held office as Heads of Department for short periods, in general the History Department was remarkable for the long service of its staff. Dr Enid Stoye, appointed in 1960, was the longest serving member when she reached retirement in 1982. The notice of her retirement in the *College Letter* commented that she typified the earlier traditions of the College:

> She was . . . a resident don, keeping up a long and worthy tradition that is now, alas, almost defunct. With her profound Christian faith, her commitment to moral values, and her refusal to be fobbed off by the slick and second-best, she stood for something very valuable in the life of the history department and of the College as a whole.[19]

Mr R. W. Lockyer, a specialist in seventeenth-century history, joined the Department in 1964; his acclaimed biography *Buckingham: The Life and Political Career of George Villiers, First Duke of Buckingham, 1592-1628*, was published in 1981. Miss Julian Chrysostomides and Miss P. K. Crimmin were appointed to the Department in 1965; Dr J. P. Croft and Dr J. R. Dinwiddy in 1969. Dr G. Alderman, a specialist in Jewish history, joined the Department in 1972, and Dr F. C. R. Robinson, a specialist in Islamic history in 1973. All these members of the Department held their appointments throughout the remaining years of Royal Holloway's existence as a separate College.

In the Faculty of Science, by the time of Dr Butler's appointment to the principalship, the two youngest Departments had both grown rapidly from their small beginnings. Biochemistry, established as a separate Department from Chemistry in 1967, continued under the headship of Professor J. B. Pridham, and had grown to a Department with eight members of staff, with additional teaching given by external lecturers. Research activities included an investigation by Professor Pridham and his colleague Mr D. Davies of the role of sex hormones in the metabolism of fructose and the possible relationship between dietary sucrose and atherosclerosis. They publicised their research by taking part in a BBC *Controversy* programme on sugar and heart disease.[20] The Department of Statistics and Computer Science, founded with five members in 1968, continued under the headship of Professor H. J. Godwin, and by 1973/4 had a staff of eight. In 1979/80 a Single Honours degree in Computer Science was introduced, and in 1981/2 the Computer Centre was extensively modified and doubled in size and a new DEC VAX 11/780 computer was installed. At the end of this academic year Professor Godwin took early retirement, and received the title of Emeritus Professor. He was succeeded as Head of Department by Mr A. R. Davies (appointed 1968). The Chair of Statistics and Computer Science remained unfilled until the appointment in 1984 of Professor Thomas Beth, from the University of Erlangen, West Germany.

The Department of Botany had nine members of staff in 1973/4, and was headed by Professor Karl Wilson, who had succeeded Professor Jane in 1963. In addition to overseeing the expansion of the Department which followed the admission of men undergraduates and the move to Huntersdale in 1967, Professor Wilson pursued his own research on algae and plant cell walls, and completely revised Professor Jane's book *The Structure of Wood*. He was elected the College's first Dean of Science, and was a member of Council from 1965 to 1968. He retired in 1976 and received the title of Emeritus Professor of Botany.[21] Mr P. A. Dixon (appointed 1965) was Acting Head of Department until the appointment of Professor John Dodge in September 1977. Professor Dodge established a dinoflagellate research group, and also took over the posts of secretary and treasurer of the long-established journal *Annals of Botany*, which previously had been held by Professor Wilson. Its editorial office was established in the Department in 1984. Continuing expansion of the Department led to the addition of the Garden Wing to Huntersdale, which was opened on 21 May 1981 by Professor J. P. M. Brennan, Director of Kew Gardens, at a ceremony attended by the Mayor of Runnymede and by Sir Henry Abel-Smith, and his wife Lady May, the daughter of Princess Alice.[22]

The Department of Chemistry in 1973/4 was the second largest of Royal Holloway's Departments, with seventeen members of staff. There had been only three when Professor E. J. Bourne was appointed Professor of Chemistry and Head of Department in 1956. Following his sudden death in 1974, Dr Lionel Butler, who had known him only for a year, was asked to give the Memorial Address at a Service of Thanksgiving for his life and work. 'I have been trying to imagine his own thoughts on the holding of a service of thanksgiving for him,' Dr Butler said. 'Because he was fond of us he would surely have allowed us to proceed, adding though, with that slow, diffident warm smile of his, "Well, if you are going to speak about virtue and utter praise, exaggerate neither" '[23]

That modesty characterised the man as much as achievement was illustrated both by Dr Butler's memorial address and the elegant biographical essay by Dr Helmut Weigel, Professor Bourne's colleague in the Chemistry Department, which was published in the journal *Advances in Carbohydrate Chemistry and Biochemistry*.[24] Of one thing Professor Bourne was proud: the deep roots of his family in the county of Staffordshire, where he was born at Cannock in 1922. He was educated at Rugeley Grammar School and Birmingham University, where he researched the chemistry and biochemistry of carbohydrates under the Nobel laureate Sir Norman Haworth. At Birmingham he became a Lecturer at the age of twenty-two, Doctor of Science and Reader of Organic Chemistry at thirty-three. He was only a year older when he was appointed to the Chair of Chemistry at Royal Holloway. Professor Bourne wrote of his own work: 'I and my colleagues, with pupils of many nations, have found challenge and satisfaction in techniques, syntheses and reaction mechanisms, whilst at the same time helping to unravel the intricate processes of Nature and so strengthen the scientific basis of medicine and agriculture.'[25] With these ends in view the range of his research was formidable. It covered polysaccharides and their chemical and enzymic transformation; the interaction of carbohydrates with a variety of elements, especially those implicated in medical disorders and soil deficiencies; cyclic condensation products of carbohydrates in different stereochemical situations; radiation-induced transformations; the development of new reagents; infra-red spectroscopy; and methods of separating and identifying different carbohydrates.

Besides pursuing his research, Professor Bourne was a member of the Council, the Academic Board, the Finance Committee, and for a time held the office of Vice-Principal. When the expansion of the College permitted the construction of a new Chemistry building, 'He worked very closely with the architects, discussing in detail everything from the siting of the whole building to the positioning of taps on the benches; and the design of the building was greatly influenced by ideas which Bourne pressed on the architects, including the need to allow for unforeseen change and growth. The completed building . . . erected at a cost of £800,000 . . . has been acclaimed in journals of architecture and chemical education in many parts of the world. In recognition of his work he was elected a Fellow of the Royal Society of Arts.'[26] After his death the building was named the Bourne Laboratory in his honour, and the Bourne Medal for postgraduate distinction in Chemistry was established.

He was succeeded as Professor of Chemistry and Head of Department by Professor Trevor G. Bonner, who had been appointed to the Department in 1948, and had the title of Professor of Organic Chemistry conferred on him in 1968. Bonner's chief research interest was the study of reaction mechanisms in organic chemistry, on which he published many papers. He was an enthusiastic supporter of universities in developing countries, and he travelled widely to establish co-operation between chemistry departments in British universities and those overseas. His travels took him to the Sudan, Tanzania, Egypt, Ghana and Nigeria. He retired in 1981, and died suddenly the following spring.[27] He was succeeded as Head of Department by Professor K. Singer, Professor of Physical Chemistry, who had joined the Department in 1947 and retired in 1982. The Chair of Chemistry remained vacant, but the Headship of Department passed to Dr Helmut Weigel who had come to Royal Holloway from Birmingham with Professor Bourne in 1956. He shared with Professor Bourne much of the detailed planning of the Bourne Laboratory, and also his research on carbohydrates: 'but his interests have ranged widely, with particular emphasis on applications to processes which would be beneficial to mankind. Characteristic is the current

[ 251 ]

project on the development of dyes used to enhance X-ray images in the early detection of breast cancer.'[28] When Dr Weigel became its head, the Chemistry Department was already working in close conjunction with the corresponding Department at Bedford College, with which it was soon to merge, in circumstances which will be described later in this chapter. In the period leading up to the merger he acted as chairman of the joint Department. Dr Weigel has always been a great supporter of College traditions; at one time he played the flute in Band.

The Department of Mathematics was the largest Department in 1973/4, with twenty members of staff. Professor of Mathematics and Head of Department was Professor H. G. Eggleston, who had succeeded Professor McCrea in 1966. Educated at High Storrs Grammar School in his home town of Sheffield, and at Trinity College, Cambridge, he came to Royal Holloway from Bedford College, where he had been Professor of Mathematics since 1958. He had already published *Problems in Euclidean Space* (1957), *Convexity* (1958) and *Elementary Real Analysis* (1962). The Department continued to expand under his headship, and a University Professorship of Applied Mathematics was established at Royal Holloway, to which Professor M. R. C. McDowell was appointed in 1969. McDowell was Dean of the Faculty of Science in 1973/4, and he became Head of Department in January 1982, following Professor Eggleston's retirement. For a number of years he was co-editor of *Case Studies in Atomic Physics* and of *Comments in Atomic and Molecular Physics*. He also researched on Simulation Models of Conflicts in Traffic. In 1980 he was appointed to the chair of the Atomic and Molecular Physics Committee of the Institute of Physics and to the Board of the Atomic Physics Division of the European Physics Society.[29] He continued as Head of Department over the difficult period of the merger with Bedford College, and simultaneously found the time to serve as a JP. His distinguished career was brought to an end by disabling illness.

The tradition of long service to the College was represented in the Mathematics Department by Dr Mary Bradburn (appointed 1945) and Dr Barbara Yates (appointed 1948). Dr Bradburn, as previously mentioned, had been a student at the College before the Second World War. She retired in 1980, and the author of the notice in the *College Letter* commented: 'Through the years of expansion she played a vital part in preserving something of the character of RHC as she first knew it, while at the same time her breadth of vision and clear thinking made full use of the opportunities for development within the wider framework.'[30] Dr Yates retired in 1982. A graduate of Trinity College, Dublin, who had gone on to work at Queen's University, Belfast, and the University of Aberdeen, 'she had not been brought up in the tradition of residential colleges, but throughout her career she had a deep appreciation of the value of a liberal education outside the narrow confines of a single academic discipline and she adapted easily to living at the College. She took advantage of the many cultural opportunities, sang in Choral and supported concerts . . .'[31] Both she and Dr Bradburn were influential in ensuring the survival of some of the traditions of earlier years in the post-expansion decade.

Professor Tolansky died in March 1973, and at the time of Dr Butler's appointment, Dr V. I. Little (appointed Senior Lecturer 1965, Reader in Experimental Physics 1969) was Acting Head of Department. The new Physics building, which extended and vastly enlarged the original Physics and Botany building,* was nearing completion; in October 1974 it was formally opened by Dame Marjorie Williamson, and named the Tolansky Laboratory in the late Professor's honour. An elegant and unusual memorial plaque, incised with symbols illustrating his research interests, was put up; it was designed by Dr A. M. Moore (appointed Lecturer in Physics 1969), who continues Tolansky's research in diamond physics. In January 1974 Professor D. W. O. Heddle was appointed to the Chair of Physics and Headship of Department. The title of Professor of Theoretical Physics had been conferred in 1970 on Dr Ernest Hütten, 'in recognition of his many distinguished contributions to theoretical physics and in particular to the Philosophy of Science. Professor Hutten previously worked in Berlin, Cambridge and several university and industrial institutions in the USA. He knew and worked under Einstein, Shrodinger and Rutherford.'[32] He joined the Department in 1947, and retired in 1977, with the title of Emeritus Professor.

The Department of Zoology in 1973/4 had eleven members of staff, including its first Head, Professor P. M. Butler, who had retired two years earlier, but stayed on as an Honorary Research Fellow. His successor was Professor P. A. Jewell (1972-7), who has been described

* Used by Physics only since Botany had moved to Huntersdale.

as 'a man of great charm, as well as a highly individual sense of dress'.[33] His special interest was in the social organisation and behaviour of large herbivorous mammals, and he was a member of a team of scientists which studied the primitive breed of Soay sheep on the island of St Kilda. He and his collaborators Dr C. Milner and Dr J. Morton Boyd published *Island Survivors: the Ecology of the Soay Sheep of St Kilda* (1974). Professor Jewell kept his own small flock of Soay sheep in the paddocks at Alderhurst, where they remained after he left to take a research chair of animal physiology at Cambridge. Another of his research interests was the population dynamics of mammals. The Departmental Report for 1973/4 explained: 'In order to study the population dynamics of mammals it is valuable to be able to control completely the numbers in a population . . . To this end, two large enclosures have been built in the grounds at Alderhurst which are designed to be vole-proof, and into these two enclosures foundation populations of the Bank Vole have been put.'[34] (The enclosures were known as 'Voleditz', for this was the period of the popular television serial *Colditz*, set in the German prison of that name.) The study of the voles was undertaken by Dr J. H. W. Gipps, Jubilee Research Fellow.

When Professor Jewell left the College, Dr G. I. Twigg (Assistant Lecturer and Demonstrator 1959; Lecturer 1962, Senior Lecturer 1973) became Acting Head of Department. His book *The Black Death: A biological reappraisal* (1984) captured wide public interest, and he appeared on the television programme *Timewatch* to discuss his new interpretation of the biological and historical evidence that the Black Death was not caused by plague, as previously believed.[35] In September 1978 Professor C. T. Lewis became Professor of Zoology and Head of Department; he was appointed Vice-Principal of Royal Holloway College, the last to hold that office, in 1982.

The Faculty of Music, promoted to that status in 1970, was in 1973/4 still numerically equivalent to a small Department, with eight permanent members of staff. But it had in addition fifteen visiting teachers, and reckoned that 'more than 200 instrumental and vocal lessons were given weekly [during the session] by visiting teachers – approximately a third of them to College students not enrolled for Music degrees.'[36] Professor I. W. A. Spink continued as Professor of Music and Head of Department. Dr Lionel Pike, Lecturer in Music and

[ 254 ]

College Organist, was appointed Senior Lecturer in 1980. His book *Beethoven, Sibelius and The 'Profound Logic'* (1978) was named as one of the three best academic books of the year by *Choice*, the publication of the American Library Association. Each year the musical events organised by the Faculty, with staff and student performers and with visiting artists, were frequent and varied, each term with its traditional highlights. For example, in 1973/4, 'The St Cecilia Musick Feast was marked by a concert performance of John Weldon's "opera" *The Judgment of Paris* (Libretto by Congreve); the first, so far as is known, since the early eighteenth century, and specially edited from manuscript for the occasion by Mr G. O'Reilly, a postgraduate student.'[37] Felicity Lott returned to College to sing the role of Pallas. Enthusiasm for new music was fostered by Mr B. J. C. Dennis (Lecturer in Music 1972), who directed THEME (The Experimental Music Ensemble). During 1973/4 a number of his own compositions were broadcast on BBC radio and television, and his *Cantata In Memoriam Jackson Pollock* was performed in Beverley Minster.[38] Despite the increasing professionalism of the College's Music students, the Faculty's report for 1983/4 commented: 'Naturally every music student is, or should be, caught up in music making. But not only music students; the participation of non-music students in the musical life of the College has always been strong . . . This is only to be welcomed for we like to think that it is one of the things that make life here better than at other places.'[39]

The Students' Union Society saw its chief purpose in making life, if not 'better than at other places', at least as good as possible for its members. According to its 1973/4 report:

The Union plays a prominent role not only in the life of the College as a whole but also in the life of each individual student, providing a wide range of activities to suit the needs of most minority interests in College. These were extended during this year to include a Women's Rights Society and a Gay Soc. But perhaps the best example of the way the Union sought to look after its membership was the creation of a post of Welfare Officer. This is now an elected position on the Union Council . . . [and] . . . provides a new source of information for those unwilling to visit the College-based areas of help.[40]

The Women's Rights Society and Gay Soc were not of course exclusively College phenomena; both mirrored changing attitudes in society as a whole: the rise of the Second Feminist Movement and the social acceptance of homosexuality. In the latter context it is worth remarking that social changes do not only affect those who participate in them, they also act retrospectively: College alumnae who told the author of their ignorance of homosexuality before the Second World War, or of its unmentionability, were able to discuss it in a free and unprejudiced manner in their old age. The election of a student Welfare Officer indicated the development of a student community no longer willing to rely exclusively on the guidance of its mentors, but confident of its ability to solve its own problems.

In 1973/4 the SUS reported the appearance of a new problem, and its own successful intervention on behalf of its members.

Racing inflation brought the College finances into dire straits and the students were faced with a residence fee increase from £78 to £120, but after full consultation with the students a figure of £105 was agreed. Here, once again, the good relations that exist between the College authorities and the students, and the willingness to conduct full negotiations, which even included the Principal speaking at a General Meeting, saw the College safely through what could have been a very difficult time.[41]

In January 1975, when Dr Butler gave his Memorial Address for Professor Bourne, he recalled their last conversation, after the ceremonial opening of the Tolansky Laboratory:

He and I walked after tea the short distance from Physics to Chemistry. The rain was pouring down on Egham Hill; and I think now of how he swung round, in front of the great glass doors of his domain and said 'You know, we're all very sorry for you.' What he meant was that the opportunities and finances for significant new ventures by the College had dried up almost immediately on my arrival. He spoke, I knew, for the College. I replied, 'If you are sorry for me, I need never be sorry for myself.' I hoped then that I would be capable of becoming as good a member of the College as he.[42]

[ 256 ]

The Picture Gallery: Mr C.W. Carey lecturing to students, 1937.

Professor Hilda Johnstone, with a group of research students, 1937.

(*Opposite above*): Royal Holloway College Jubilee, 1937. Left to right, Princess Alice, Countess of Athlone, Chairman of the Governors, Queen Mary, Miss J.R. Bacon, Principal of Royal Holloway College 1935–1944.

(*Opposite below*): Princess Alice, Countess of Athlone, at the presentation of the Powell Gates, 1958. Princess Alice stands under the umbrella which had sheltered Queen Victoria at the opening of the College in 1886. Seated behind her are left, Dr Edith Batho, Principal of Royal Holloway College, 1945–1962, right, Sir John Cameron; on the extreme left is the latter's sister, Miss Cameron.

Miss Fanny Street, Acting Principal, 1944–1945.

Dinner in honour of Miss Dorothy Hustler MBE, on her retirement, left to right:
Princess Alice, Countess of Athlone, Dr Marjorie Williamson, Principal of Royal
Holloway College, 1962–1973, Sir John Cameron.

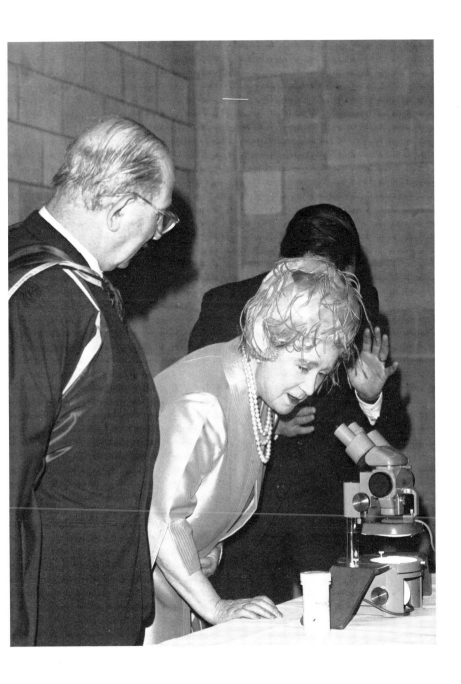

Professor Tolansky shows moondust to Queen Elizabeth the Queen Mother, November 1970.

Students taking their finals in the Picture Gallery: the Union Jack covers Landseer's Man Proposes, God Disposes, believed by students to bring bad luck if uncovered.

The Department of Zoology at Alderhurst, with Professor Jewell's Soay Sheep in the foreground.

Dr Lionel Butler, Principal of Royal Holloway College, 1973–1981.

The partnership agreement between Royal Holloway College and Bedford College, 26th July 1982: standing in the background, Dr Roy Miller, Principal of Royal Holloway College 1982–1985, Professor Dorothy Wedderburn, Principal of Bedford College, 1981–1985; the signatories, left, Sir Owen Saunders for Royal Holloway, right, Sir Cyril Clarke, for Bedford.

Dr Butler was a man of expansive ideas, who had come to Royal Holloway with the belief that he would be able to continue the expansion which the College had achieved under Dame Marjorie Williamson. Despite his staunch response to Professor Bourne he was deeply disappointed by the reversal of the conditions which he had expected. This reversal was described in sombre words in the *Annual Report* for 1973/4:

> We realised that 1973/74 . . . would be a year of stringency, with money in short supply, and the [University] Court reminding all schools of the University that the size of their recurrent grants depended, year by year, on their success in achieving the agreed rates of expansion in student numbers; but we hardly anticipated the scale of the national economic emergency which began in November 1973, and its severe results for higher education. The government cuts in public spending in December 1973 included the suspension of the system of monetary compensation to the Universities for inflation, while rising costs and prices sharply reduced the value of our fixed grants.[43]

The *Annual Report* also contained the comment that 'discussion of the Murray Report has continued within the University, but the Report's suggestion that one of the other smaller schools of the University might be amalgamated with the Royal Holloway College at Egham appeared to have become a dead letter by the end of the session.'[44] However, the proposal, made initially for the purpose of economy in administration, though it might be submerged for a time, was certain to resurface when short-term economies proved insufficient to counteract the effects of the economic emergency. Miss J. L. Hurn (RHC Registrar 1970-85) explained, 'The Arab-Israeli oil war was followed by enormous inflation. What money we did have did not any longer meet our needs. It was not a matter of what are now called "Government Cuts" whether they are or not: after that date the quinquennial system failed because the Government could no longer estimate so far ahead.'[45] 1972-7 was the last effective Quinquennium: in November 1974 the UGC made its five-yearly visitation, and expressed interest in the plans which the College outlined for 1977-82, but it could not promise capital provision for the building projects which the College had regarded as essential

[ 257 ]

to maintain its hoped-for expansion. These included more student residences, increased accommodation for the Library, the Faculty of Music and the Biological Sciences, a new Students' Union Building to replace the cramped quarters provided by the converted Bungalow, and a Great Hall. Little encouragement was forthcoming and according to the *Annual Report*: 'What is to be expected of or provided for the Universities nationally in the later seventies, to look no further ahead, seemed in 1974 and 1975 to be as obscure to the UGC and the University of London as it was to the College.'[46]

The College responded to these difficult circumstances by formulating its own programme of stringent economies: ' . . . the struggle to keep the accounts in balance and the cashflow healthy without lowering academic standards, or charging the resident students (75 per cent of the whole student body) more than they could or should pay for board and lodging was waged strenuously, but inevitably *ad hoc* . . . Reductions in staff were made only where factors like retirement or resignation created "casual" vacancies . . . but even a major chair, falling vacant, did not escape being "frozen" . . .'[47]*

The Principal reported the next session 1975/6 as 'the third successive year to present acute financial difficulties . . . the savings, as before, were made chiefly by the selective "freezing" of posts falling vacant among academic and non-academic staff; cutting down resources for libraries and laboratories; reducing maintenance, decoration, telephone services and consumption of energy . . . In 1973/4 economies could be in themselves often salutary and worthwhile; in 1974/5 they created discomfort and harder working conditions; but in 1975/6 they began to threaten standards (the quality of teaching and research, the good management of buildings, grounds and equipment); and our ability to see reasonably far ahead was lost . . .'[48] The Principal acknowledged the College's debt to Mr Boog, who in recent years had developed the College as a conference centre during the vacations, an enterprise which assisted the College to balance its accounts: '1975/6 was a year of record turnover, bringing exceptional benefit to the College from the profits of conferences, summer schools and banquets.'[49]

By 1977 it seemed impossible to make any further plans: 'With

* The Chair of German, on the retirement of Professor R. V. Tymms.

the close of the Quinquennium 1972-7 and the petering out of the quinquennial system of University planning, the College had strictly no targets . . . However, the last agreed target – 1,474 for October 1976 – was exceeded in October 1977 with the likelihood that the 1,500 mark would be reached a year later.'[50] It was, in fact, exceeded, with a total of 1,514 students (including sixty part-time postgraduates) in October 1978: 629 in the Faculty of Arts, 787 in the Faculty of Science, and 98 in the Faculty of Music. The balance of the sexes was drawing closer to equality with 799 women and 715 men.

In these difficult circumstances, 'almost against the tide' as Dr Butler described it, the Department of Drama and Theatre Studies was founded, under the headship of Dr Katharine Worth, 'with enough teaching, technical and secretarial staffing and teaching collaboration from members of other Departments to enable us to admit 21 students to commence the BA course in English and Drama and Theatre Studies in the autumn of 1978'.[51] The new Department was at first squeezed into Chevithorne, then occupied by a section of the Faculty of Music; later it moved into Sutherland House, further down Egham Hill, which had previously housed an offshoot of the Physics Department. In 1979 London University's only Chair of Drama and Theatre Studies was established at Royal Holloway, to which the Head of Department was appointed.

One of the first generation of Drama students, Miss Alison Chard (student 1978-81) described to the author the Department's first production:

The first play of the department was indicative of the daring nature of our activities at the time – Euripides's *Hippolytus*, performed in the incongruous splendour of the Picture Gallery. We encountered many difficulties in production – rehearsal time and space, limited budget, not to mention interpretation of the play and the notoriously thorny problem of the classical chorus . . . To give you some idea of our involvement, I juggled the offices of deputy stage manager, props mistress . . . spotlight operator and the role of the avenging goddess Artemis (that last peculiar combination was brought about by desperate necessity at the technical rehearsal, but was acclaimed, in the way of these things, as a brilliantly symbolic representation of the goddess

[ 259 ]

directing the fate of the mortals! Of course we simply accepted the praise without demur!)[52]

This improvisation and successful outcome could be regarded as symbolic of the College's progress throughout the uneasy decade.

The chronic financial problems of the universities worsened with the election of the Conservative Government in 1979. Dr Roy Miller described its particular effect upon Royal Holloway College:

The gradual decline in the financial resources of the College started with Lionel's principalship. It really came to a head with the run-up to the 1978/9 cuts. It was quite clear that the Government had the intention of reducing public expenditure, and universities are always a soft target. The cuts were to be in the order of fourteen to fifteen per cent. For universities nationally this was serious enough, because the budget of a university is seventy-five per cent salaries. The increase in the cutting rate was Government policy . . . also there was the demographic prediction of a fall in numbers of students. They [the cuts] were on such a scale that institutions which had used up their resources were going to have to cut staff. It was serious for RHC as we were one of the smaller Colleges, and we had relatively small Departments; if we were going to have to cut one in seven staff this could have made it difficult to cover teaching, let alone research.[53]

Royal Holloway's situation was not unique; the other smaller Schools of the University could have described their own situations in similar terms. In 1980 Lord Annan, the Vice-Chancellor of the University (Provost of University College 1966-78; Vice-Chancellor of London University 1978-81), 'attempted to force the University to confront the need for structural change'.[54] On his initiative a new Committee on Academic Organisation was set up, under the chairmanship of Sir Peter Swinnerton-Dyer (Professor of Mathematics, University of Cambridge, from 1971; Master of St Catharine's College, Cambridge, 1973-83; Chairman of the UGC from 1983). The Committee expressed the view that there was 'nothing absurd about a university 10 per cent smaller

[ 260 ]

and 15 per cent cheaper than London now is'.[55] In December 1980 it issued a first Discussion Document outlining the financial background and requirements, which was sent to the Colleges of the University for their comments. On 1 March 1981 Sir Peter Swinnerton-Dyer sent round an additional letter asking the effect of a thirteen per cent drop in income for the two ensuing academic years.

After full discussion, initiated by the Principal, Royal Holloway College accepted the inevitability of a reduction of staff by one in seven. The Academic Board decided at this stage that even if the Departments were reduced in size, still it should be possible to retain all academic subjects. However, a group of senior academics decided to mount an operational research exercise. This 'role-playing exercise under the supervision of operational research experts', organised by Professor McDowell in the summer of 1981, and carried out by Professor K. C. Bowen (Visiting Professor, Department of Mathematics), produced the conclusion that 'this College ought to combine with another of the smaller Colleges. It was decided we could not survive on our own; it would be impossible to cover the academic range with a reduced staff.'[56] Accordingly a Liaison Planning Group was formed, to explore the possibility of establishing a consortium of small Colleges on the Egham site. Since the Principal was not a member of the Group, the senior academics of Royal Holloway had the freedom of action to meet their counterparts in other Colleges and discuss the possibilities without official commitment.

In the meantime representatives of the College were invited to meet the Swinnerton-Dyer Committee, to discuss its proposals. Dr Butler, Dr Miller, the Vice-Principal, Miss J. L. Hurn, the Registrar and Mr Richard Hardy, the Secretary of the College were the representatives who attended the meeting in Senate House. Dr Butler made an extempore speech on behalf of the College, in which he described it as being unique among London Colleges in being integrated and residential, and he stressed the advantages of its location. He added that it would be disastrous to lose the Science Departments (which were regarded as vulnerable since they were comparatively small already). Dr Butler was dissatisfied with his speech to the Swinnerton-Dyer Committee; but Dr Miller considered it a perfectly adequate performance.[57] In fact, the case for the College, based on similar arguments, had been clearly and fully set out the previous year, in the College's official reply to the Committee's

[ 261 ]

first enquiries. The perennial criticism that the College was inconveniently far from central London had been answered, and the advantages of its location defended:

We are 22 miles from central London. Is it costly to be so distant? Travel costs are minor items in our budget, which neither prevent our staff from playing a full part on the central committees, Boards of Studies and examining bodies of the University, nor keep our students away from inter-collegiate lectures and seminars . . . If the cost of being at Egham is insignificant the location has advantages. We offer residential life on a semi-rural campus in an academic community with a strong sense of cohesion and identity. That is what many applicants for student places want. Time and again they say they wish to be in the University of London, but in a college outside the metropolis yet with reasonable access to the centre, its libraries, theatres and concert halls. Our 1150 residence places are in the greatest possible demand; residences and catering pay their way, aided by the College's success in vacations as a centre for the conferences of outside organisations.[58]

The College's success, measured by the wide range of its students' careers, was impressive in itself, and of particular interest in comparison with the small range of careers open to the early women students of the College:

We try to measure our academic success by looking at the employment our graduates secure after leaving us. The pattern in recent years is that nearly half took up employment in industry and commerce: the largest group went into engineering, the others into agriculture, forestry, the oil and chemical industries, building, transport, accountancy, banking, insurance, publishing, librarianship, the museum service and entertainment. Ten per cent of our graduates went on to take higher degrees. Twenty per cent embarked on teacher training or other further training (our Mathematics Department produces a very large number of mathematics teachers for the schools). Eight per cent, an impressive proportion, were appointed to the Civil or Diplomatic Service, and a similar number went into local government or hospital service. Some joined the armed forces. Five per cent were appointed to posts in universities, technical colleges or schools. Meanwhile, so far as we can discover, the proportion still unemployed six months after graduation did not amount to three per cent.[59]

However, neither advantages nor achievements made the College proof against either the economic pressure to form a merger in order to survive, or the Committee's conclusion that mergers were absolutely necessary for the good of the whole University. In July 1981 the Liaison Planning Group recommended the establishment of a consortium, principally for Science, on the Egham site, with Westfield, Queen Elizabeth and Chelsea Colleges, and with the possible addition of Bedford College. The LPG suggested that the Principal should put this recommendation to the University Court, and in the first instance to the Vice-Chancellor. The Principal agreed, and a letter outlining the proposal was sent to Lord Annan. He was about to retire, but encouraged Dr Butler to pursue the matter with his successor.[60]

The autumn of 1981 was a time of great change in the University. The first phase of the new Statutes which had followed the University of London Act (1978) were about to come into force. Following Lord Annan's retirement, Professor (later Sir) Randolph Quirk was appointed as the first full-time Vice-Chancellor (Professor of English, University College, London 1960-81; Vice-Chancellor of London University, 1981–5). At the same time the new and enlarged Senate came into being. It was even larger than the Murray Report had proposed. It had 120 members, and included all heads of Schools in receipt of grants from the University Court; three heads of Schools not receiving such grants, and of Senate Institutes; twenty-five teachers elected according to their membership of Boards of Studies; fifteen teachers elected according to the institutions at which they held their posts; ten other teachers; twenty members of Convocation; twelve student members (including the President of the ULU and the immediate Past President); and five co-opted members.[61] One member of the new Senate was to sit for Royal Holloway and Westfield, and obviously Royal Holloway was eager to secure the membership. Dr Roy Miller, with the full support of Royal Holloway, the larger College, was elected, and Dr Geoffrey Alderman of the RHC History Department became a co-opted member. Dr Butler,

[ 263 ]

however, failed to secure election to the University Court, which he had hoped for; in autumn 1981 the only representative of the smaller Colleges on this important body was the newly appointed Principal of Bedford College, Professor Dorothy Wedderburn (Professor of Industrial Sociology, Imperial College 1977-81).

The Liaison Planning Group, with the Principal's approval, approached the other Colleges with whom it was hoped that a consortium could be formed. Westfield, of which Royal Holloway had had the highest hopes, was not receptive. Its Principal, Dr Bryan Thwaites, had recently hoped to form a merger between Westfield and Bedford under his own principalship; though Bedford had preferred independence under Professor Wedderburn he remained opposed to other alliances for his College.[62] Neither Queen Elizabeth nor Chelsea was enthusiastic, and Bedford entered negotiations with King's College. Royal Holloway, though it had been early in recognising the necessity for either a merger or a consortium, appeared at this point to have been left in isolation.

In 1979 Bedford College had responded to its financial problems by launching a Public Appeal for funds, and Dr Butler contemplated following its example with an appeal to the alumni, on the subject of which he wrote a humorous verse:

> From Windermere to Pegwell Bay
> The call goes forth '*RHCA*
> Take up your pens, re-write your Wills
> (The Prin has drafted codicils)
> No money,.please, for useless knowledge
> But cash for plays, tunes, games in College.'
> Among the trees on Egham Hill
> RHESUS* was born, and scratches still
> Its pate, and tries to write *its* Will –
> Intentions generous; assets nil.
> What hope in this for RHC?
> It's wondered. Howe's† raised VAT.[63]

* RHESUS – Royal Holloway Ex-Students' Union Society – was an alternative alumni association, formed by post-expansion students who found the predominantly elderly membership of RHCA uncongenial. The two associations subsequently merged.
† Sir Geoffrey Howe, Chancellor of the Exchequer.

But though he remained capable of jesting about a desperate situation, in the stressful circumstances of the summer and autumn of 1981 his health seriously declined. Following an episode of suspected arson in the College, he went to investigate the aftermath of the fire, and suffered from breathing the fumes caused by burning plastic bags. As a result of his worsening asthma it was noticed that he was 'almost consciously having to force air in and out of his body'. His colleagues began to wonder how much longer he would be able to carry out his responsibilities.

In October 1981 another possibility of merger appeared, with an approach from Brunel University. At the beginning of the Session Professor R. E. D. Bishop (Kennedy Professor of Mechanical Engineering, University of London, 1957-81) had been appointed Vice-Chancellor and Principal of Brunel, the Technological University, founded in 1966, which has its main campus at Uxbridge, Middlesex, and had recently taken over the site of the former Shoreditch College of Education, Engleford Green. Professor Bishop's aim was to develop Brunel into a new 'University of West London', an aim which would have been assisted by a merger with Royal Holloway. Particularly by the acquisition of the latter's Arts Departments. The moment was propitious to initiate discussions, since Royal Holloway's Liaison Planning Group had so far made little progress in its approaches to the other London Colleges. Professor Bishop and Mr David Neave, Secretary General of Brunel University, lunched with Dr Butler and Dr Miller, and discussed the possibilities of co-operation in general terms. Shortly afterwards Professor Bishop made a firm proposal for the institutional merging of Royal Holloway and Brunel. This was a far more radical proposal than that of any merger between London Colleges, for it would involve an entirely new relationship between Royal Holloway and the University of London, or possibly its secession from it. On the Academic Board of Royal Holloway the representatives of the Arts Faculty expressed alarm at the idea of being absorbed into an institution which would be predominantly scientific, but discussions continued, still on an informal basis.

On 19 October Professor Bishop and Mr Neave entertained Dr Butler and Dr Miller to dinner in Windsor, and Professor Bishop invited them to attend a meeting of the Senate of Brunel University the following morning, which they agreed to do. Professor Bishop warned his Senate that in the near future half-a-dozen small universities might face closure, and that Brunel could not discount the possibility of being one of them; Brunel needed to be larger in order to survive, and a merger with Royal Holloway might provide a means advantageous to both. He introduced Dr Butler and Dr Miller, and invited the former to address the Senate. Dr Butler outlined the present situation of Royal Holloway, mentioned the Murray Report's suggestion of an amalgamation of small Colleges on the Egham site, and stressed that the site was vested in the College and not the UGC or the University of London. He suggested that 'an amalgamated Royal Holloway and Brunel could perhaps become like Imperial College which retained links with the parent University but received its grant from the UGC quite separately.'[64] The Senate invited the Vice-Chancellor to continue discussions with Royal Holloway, and authorised him to extend them to include other such persons or bodies as he and Dr Butler might consider appropriate.[65] So the discussions between Royal Holloway and Brunel became official, and the possibility of a merger between them was reported in the *Guardian* under the heading 'New University of Windsor mooted'![66] Dr Butler remained wary of any plan which would involve the secession of Royal Holloway from the Federal University, and continued to favour a relationship with it like that of Imperial College, which he had mentioned to the Senate; Professor Bishop, however, issued a 'Discussion Paper for Brunel-RHC talks' in which he stated, 'By far the most adventurous plan would be to strike out on our own . . . Undeniably there is enormous potential, given the goodwill.'[67] Talks continued, and an arrangement was made for a meeting of the Principals of Royal Holloway and Brunel with Dr Edward Parkes, Chairman of the UGC, on 30 November. But this meeting was destined never to take place.

Thursday, 26 November was University Foundation Day, the first occasion on which Princess Anne was to appear as Chancellor of the University, to present the Honorary Degrees. She had just succeeded her grandmother, Queen Elizabeth the Queen Mother, as Chancellor, after a disputed election in which her candidature had been preferred to those of Jack Jones and Nelson Mandela.[68] Dr Roy Miller and his wife drove up to Senate House to attend the ceremony. They had expected to see Dr Butler, and noted his absence with anxiety. Late in the evening, Dr Miller recalled, 'we drove home, and as we drove up to the balcony steps at Kingswood, my son Stephen was hovering on the steps. I knew, as soon as I saw him, something must have happened. He said, "Mr Hardy's been phoning. The Principal's dead." '[69]

Dr Butler had died in London that afternoon.

The following morning Dr Miller in his capacity as Vice-Principal assumed authority, which he described as 'like being dumped at the controls of an aircraft'.[70] He had been Vice-Principal since 1976, and had been closely associated with Dr Butler in all the recent negotiations; it was appropriate, indeed obvious, that he should be made Acting Principal. The following year he was appointed Principal of Royal Holloway College, an appointment which satisfied the innovative principle of male leadership and the traditionalist principle of the headship of a former student. (He was the third Principal to have been a student of Royal Holloway; the fourth, if the Acting Principal Miss Fanny Street be included.) Dr Miller chose as his Vice-Principal Professor C. T. Lewis, Head of the Department of Zoology, as a man well regarded by members of all three Faculties.

On 3 December Dr Butler's funeral took place at St Jude's Church, Englefield Green, and the College began to come to terms with the shock of his death. On 9 December Dr Miller had a meeting with the Vice-Chancellor. 'I was anxious he should know what we were doing,' said Dr Miller, 'and that our voice should be heard in the Senate House, particularly our policy of merging. Our options were beginning to crystallise.'[71] One of these options Professor Quirk strongly discouraged: any relationship with Brunel which would involve the secession of Royal Holloway from London University. He reminded Dr Miller that any University institution had to have the permission of the Court and Senate to change its status, and he would oppose such permission for Royal Holloway.[72] Discussions continued, but by the beginning of 1982 no other option appeared promising. On 22 January, Dr Miller requested another meeting with Professor Quirk, and telephoned a preliminary statement that Royal Holloway needed to grow bigger in order to survive, that the attempt to form a consortium at Egham had gained little support and that since Brunel was willing to negotiate a merger this was the course which Royal Holloway would have to follow. Dr Miller later

[ 267 ]

explained to the Vice-Chancellor at greater length that even though the severance of the College from the University would cause enormous controversy, yet it appeared to offer the only solution. The Vice-Chancellor asked if Dr Miller had discussed a Royal Holloway and Bedford merger with Professor Wedderburn; Dr Miller replied that they had met on 11 January, and concluded that the Colleges were too far apart for a merger to be practicable. However, negotiations between Bedford and Kings had by now broken down: the Vice-Chancellor recommended that talks between Bedford and Royal Holloway should begin. He telephoned the Principal of Bedford to arrange an immediate visit. 'That, indeed,' said Dr Miller, 'was the beginning of the merger.'[73] On 10 February the two Principals and the Vice-Chancellor met again, in Senate House, and discussed the possibility of Bedford College leaving its site in Regent's Park and joining Royal Holloway at Egham.

The merger was a difficult exercise in diplomacy, which the Vice-Chancellor facilitated by visiting both Bedford and Royal Holloway and persuasively addressing the assembled Colleges. The Bedford academics, many of whom lived in North London, were naturally reluctant to leave their central site, and would have preferred to remain there and form a convenient merger with Westfield or Kings. Professor Quirk astonished them by pointing out that the M4 motorway link had eliminated the proverbial remoteness of Egham: he had driven there in twenty-two minutes! But there were other arguments, which Bedford was helpless to resist. Following the Swinnerton-Dyer Committee's conclusion that the University could and must shrink, Subject Area Review Committees (SARC) had been set up, which made recommendations as to how staff in the University should be deployed, and how Departments might be moved from one College to another. The Senate accepted the general recommendation that teaching and research in Science should be concentrated on five sites: Imperial College, Kensington; Kings College and University College, Bloomsbury; Queen Mary College in East London; and Royal Holloway College at Egham. Since neither Westfield nor Bedford figured in this five-point plan, and Bedford no longer had the option of a merger with Kings, the move to Egham began to seem inevitable. The obvious alternative of remaining *in situ* and attempting to survive alone was clearly impossible: most of Bedford's property was held on a Crown Lease which had only thirty more years to run, and on renewal the rent of £1,500 a year was likely to increase enormously.[74] Professor Quirk commented, 'The signs were that the Crown Commissioners were going to be as fierce as any commercial property company. But worse than that, I established that, even if we negotiated successfully with the Crown Commissioners, the chances of planning permission from either Westminster or the Department of the Environment were negligible. The site was landlocked on somebody else's land.'[75] Since growth was impossible in Regent's Park he stressed the encouraging possibility of growth elsewhere: 'The University had gone through a period of low morale, with Annan accused of encouraging Swinnerton-Dyer to talk about closures. I saw my role as being concerned with heightening morale as rapidly as possible. I turned the argument round to growth – growth in the context of contraction – by picking upon the points usable as growth areas.'[76] Participation in this enterprise was at least a happier prospect for Bedford than an ultimately doomed struggle to survive alone.

With the reluctant withdrawal of the most powerful Bedford opposition, Professor Wedderburn was able to persuade the Council of Bedford to join the Council of Royal Holloway in issuing a 'Declaration of Intent to seek a union of the two Colleges, as rapidly as proves practicable'. The Declaration was signed on 30 March 1982. Nonetheless, the remaining opposition refused to give up, and a hard-fought 'Save Bedford' campaign was pursued during the spring and early summer. But on 22 July a meeting of the Bedford Governors resolved that it 'approved in principle the proposed merger with Royal Holloway College' and 'the taking by the Council of such steps as it may consider appropriate to achieve such a merger'.* On 26 July 1982 the Chairmen of the two College Councils, Sir Owen Saunders for Royal Holloway and Sir Cyril Clarke for Bedford, signed a Partnership Agreement, by which they bound themselves to 'co-operate as closely as possible in the teaching of students registered in each College and to share the use of existing Royal Holloway buildings and facilities at Egham Hill – the intention of the Councils of the Colleges being to seek a union of the

---

* Unlike Royal Holloway Bedford had both Council and Governors, the Council being the executive body, the Governors a very much larger group, whose main function was to act as guardians of the constitution.

Colleges resulting in the formation of a new single institution incorporated by Act of Parliament.'[77]

The actual process of the merger was painful for both Colleges. In Dr Miller's words 'people who leave their site feel like refugees, the people on the receiving end feel invaded'.[78] Yet the process was undeniably more painful for Bedford, for two reasons: firstly, a beautiful site, invested with all the College's history and traditions, was taken over by an alien institution (Regent's College, the London company formed by Rockford College, Illinois, USA, which also took over the Crown Lease); and secondly, Bedford College was not transferred to Egham in its entirety, but suffered a process of disintegration, with Dutch and Aegean Archaeology transferred to University College, Philosophy to Kings College, and Mathematics staff and research students dispersed among several Schools of the University. However, there was accretion to counteract disintegration: the Geology Departments from Kings and Chelsea Colleges were eventually brought to Egham, together with chemists, physicists and mathematicians from both Chelsea and Westfield, so that some elements of the previously proposed consortium were brought together in the end.[79]

At Royal Holloway the problem was that of accepting invasion, which some Departments found more difficult than others. The process began with the transfer of the Bedford Chemistry Department to Egham in August 1982, which Dr Miller described as 'something of an act of faith'. The Departments of English, History, Botany, Biochemistry and Zoology followed in August 1983. In November 1982 Powell, Moya and Partners were appointed as Consulting Architects on the building programme necessary to house the enlarged departments and the increased student numbers. Their Development Plan included projected buildings for Electron Microscopy, Earth and Life Sciences, and also new accommodation for Arts and Mathematics Departments, Library, Students' Union and Residence for two hundred students. The initiation of this ambitious building programme ensured that the later stages of the merger would take place in conditions of mud, noise and chaos. Mr Philip Howard wrote a vivid description of it in *The Times*: 'If moving house is hell, moving a huge organisation is ... the lowest Circle of Hell ... the private confusion is increased by geometric progression. The show must go on, but it is difficult working from a Portakabin in a greenfield site muddier than Passchendaele, files scattered to the four winds, and ever the dreadful music of the pneumatic drills . . .'[80]

Looking back over the whole period of the merger, from 1982 to 1985, and taking into consideration the stress which it had imposed on individuals, Dr Miller commented:

> Many people here just wanted things to go on as before. Like water rising through a floor, only when they get their toes wet do they realise that they're going to be flooded. It hit people in turn. What I am sorry about is the people who have been hurt. In so far as I am political at all, this is what I find it hard to forgive the Government for . . .[81]

Neither College had desired the merger, yet both looked forward to its completion. A period of anxiety and turmoil was ended with the passing of the Act of Parliament which created Royal Holloway and Bedford New College on 1 August 1985. For Royal Holloway sadness that the College had existed for ninety-nine years and not a full century was accompanied by acknowledgement that Dr Miller, in the words of Mr Richard Hardy, had 'most honorably brought RHC to its conclusion'.[82]

Neither Royal Holloway nor Bedford College wished to think of its history as concluded. Royal Holloway and Bedford New College was conscientiously if cumbrously named to indicate that the new institution would remember the history and continue the traditions of both its predecessors. Sir Randolph Quirk (whose encouragement of the merger had led to the jocular suggestion that the new college should be named St Quirk's) commented: 'In many ways it was the ideal merger . . . in enabling two smallish colleges to become one medium-sized viable college, on its own land, in an area which was promising both demographically and economically'.[83]

The first Principal of the new college, Professor Dorothy Wedderburn, designated 1986 a Celebration Year, to honour the centenary of Royal Holloway's foundation and the inauguration of RHBNC. Nostalgia blended with optimism in a series of events which included a centenary play, *College Voices* by Chrys Salt, in which Miss J. L. Hurn played the part of Queen Victoria, and a visit by Her Majesty the Queen, who in a speech in the Chapel recalled the opening of Royal Holloway College by her great-great-grandmother, and expressed her hopes for the new college's future which, Professor Wedderburn pledged, would include 'a special concern for women's education'.[84]

The mood of the Celebration Year was captured in a verse by Professor K. C. Bowen, entitled *Name Dropping*:

> Two famous names have now been syndicated
> With a strange third. Who thinks of us as New?
> Our title could not be more complicated,
> The whole too long, any one part untrue!
>
> Rich in our ancestry, and rich in knowledge,
> Time for a challenge, space in which to grow,
> With pride in what we were, we are *The* College:
> For future history, let us make it so.[85]

# NOTES AND REFERENCES

*Preliminary Note*

Since 1 August 1985 Royal Holloway and Bedford Colleges have been merged as Royal Holloway and Bedford New College. However, the Archives of the two Colleges remain separate, and therefore references to the Royal Holloway College Archives have been abbreviated as RHC Archives, with classification numbers referring to the Catalogue compiled by Derryan Paul (1973).

Papers from the Holloway Sanatorium, following its closure in 1981, were deposited with the Surrey Record Office. These include the Thomas Holloway Personal Papers, some of which have been classified, while others remain unlisted. References to these papers have been abbreviated as SRO THPP, with classification numbers or the word (unlisted) in brackets.


CHAPTER ONE

1. *The Story of Thomas Holloway*, anonymous author, published by the Governors of Holloway Sanatorium (1933), p.26.
2. *Malta Times*, 23 July 1877.
3. John Morley, *Life of Gladstone* (1903), Vol. II, p.459.
4. Gwennol Gwaynten, 'Thomas Holloway of Penzance', *Old Cornwall*, Vol. IV, No. I (Summer 1943), p.28: 'He became an apprentice of Mr Joseph Harvey a chemist who had a business, established in 1762, on the Terrace where the International Stores now stands.'

   Gwennol Gwaynten was the Cornish pseudonym of Miss Olive Martin, a writer on Cornish history. Dr A. Harrison-Barbet, researching a biography of Thomas Holloway, wrote to her, and as she was very old and 'simply cannot remember' where she obtained this information, she passed Harrison-Barbet's letter on to Mr P. G. Laws, a lecturer in Cornish subjects at the University of Exeter. On 20 May 1981 he wrote to Harrison-Barbet as follows: 'There certainly was a family of chemists/

druggists in Penzance called Harvey established in 1772 (according to Courtney) and still there a century later (Joseph Harvey). In 1872 the shop was 11 Market Jew Street (next to Warren's) and the International Tea Company in 1942 when Miss Martin wrote. I can find no reference to Joseph Harvey in the town of the Regency when Holloway was said to have been apprenticed, say 1816. But there was a chemist called William Harvey in 1817.'

5. RHC Archives GB/130/1, *Letter Book of Thomas Holloway 1874-1877*. Holloway to Mr L. Lambert, 15 April 1875.

6. *The Story of Thomas Holloway*, p.2: 'In later years when living in the Ascot neighbourhood, he used to receive as his guest at regular intervals an old Frenchman with whom he had associated in the days of his sojourn in the north of France.'

7. 'Mr Thomas Holloway', *The Chemist and Druggist*, January 1884, p.11.

8. George C. Boase, 'Thomas Holloway, Pill Maker and Philanthropist', *The Western Antiquary*, Vol. IV, June 1884 to May 1885, p.184.

9. *Pall Mall Gazette*, 19 January 1884, letter from anonymous correspondent, signed J. H.

10. He lived long, and probably in poverty as he died in St Giles's Workhouse. This was reported as having occurred 'a few years ago' in the article on Thomas Holloway in *The Chemist and Druggist* referred to in note 7.

11. The formula was:

| | |
|---|---|
| Yellow Beeswax (cera flaval) | 5.5% weight |
| White Beeswax (cera alba) | 5.5% weight |
| Resin | 15% weight |
| Lanolin (adeps sus.) | 30 % weight |
| Olive oil | 44 % weight |

An original pot of Holloway's Ointment was analysed by Mr R. G. Davis CRSC, F. Inst. Pet.

12. SRO THPP 2620/9/(3), *Private Letter Book 1869-1872*. Holloway to J. Bowen May (his solicitor), 21 Mary 1870: 'I had read the leader in *The Times* to which you are so good as to call my attention . . .' SRO THPP (unlisted) Diary 1877, *passim*.

13. A reference to a debt of £600 by Thomas Holloway to his mother is made

[ 274 ]

in her Will, in which the debt is also forgiven him.

Holloway's family may have followed him to London, as his father died in Bermondsey in 1836. Holloway's mishaps with advertising and consignment to a debtors' prison so closely resembled episodes in the career of Felix Albinolo that George C. Boase made the ingenious suggestion that Albinolo was merely a pseudonym of Holloway! (Boase, op.cit., p.184.) Boase evidently did not know of Albinolo's notice in *Town*, or of his death in St Giles's Workhouse, which establish his separate existence.

14. The formula was:

| Aloes | 37% weight |
|---|---|
| Rhubarb root | 18.75% weight |
| Cinnamon | 4.5% weight |
| Cardamom | 4.5% weight |
| Ginger | 18.75% weight |
| Saffron | 2.5% weight |
| Glauber's Salt (sodium sulphate) | 4.5% weight |
| Potassium sulphate | 9.5% weight |

'plus confection of roses in sufficient quantity'

This analysis appeared in *The Chemist and Druggist*, 15 July 1880.

15. SRO THPP (unlisted), 'verbatim Copy of Mr Holloway's letter to Mr Driver dated 14 October 1877'. The letter is followed by a list of Holloway's employees and a record of their wages, calculated on a daily basis. It concludes with the words 'Examined and approved Oct 21 1877' and bears Thomas Holloway's signature.
16. *A Sketch of the Commencement and Progress of Holloway's Pills and Ointment*, by the Proprietor, 1863 (one page only).
17. Gwennol Gwaynten, loc cit.
18. George C. Boase, op.cit., p.184.
19. *A Sketch of the Commencement . . .*
20. SRO THPP (unlisted).

21. Hilda Johnstone, 'The Founder', *The Royal Holloway College 1887-1937* p.10.
22. 'Mr Thomas Holloway', *The Chemist and Druggist*, 15 January 1884, p.11.
23. Genealogical table compiled by Vere Langford Oliver, son-in-law of Sir George Martin-Holloway.
24. Information given to the author by Dr A. Harrison-Barbet. References to Dr Lee in SRO THPP (unlisted), Diary 1877, *passim*.
25. George C. Boase, op.cit., p.185.
26. Ibid.,' p.184.
27. *A Sketch of the Commencement . . .*
28. SRO THPP 2629/9/(1), Travel Diary 1848.
29. Ibid. At the end of the narrative Holloway listed the places he had visited, with the dates, so that it is easy to follow his intricate wanderings on a map.
30. SRO THPP (unlisted), Travel Diary 1853.
31. Hilda Johnstone, op.cit., p.11.
32. SRO THPP (unlisted), Travel Diary 1853.
33. *A Sketch of the Commencement . . .*
34. Broadsheet advertising Holloway's Ointment and Pills, undated but probably shortly after 1867, as Holloway's address is given as '533 Oxford St (Late of 244 Strand), London.'
35. R. C. Bell, 'The Tokens of Thomas Holloway', *British Numismatic Journal*, Vol. XXXVI, 1967, p.186.
36. SRO THPP 2620/9/(3), Private Letter Book 1869-1872. Holloway to Editor of *Kentish Observer*, 9 October 1871.
37. Hilda Johnstone, op.cit., p.12.
38. George C. Boase, op.cit., p.185.
39. SRO THPP (unlisted), Diary 1877, *passim*.
40. Denys Sutton 'Robert Langton Douglas', Part III, *Apollo*, June 1979.
41. Jeannie Chapel, *Victorian Taste: The Complete Catalogue of Paintings at Royal Holloway College* (1982), p.13.
42. W. H. Crossland, 'The Royal Holloway College', *Transactions of the Royal Institute of British Architects*. New Series Vol. III, part III (1887), p.148.
43. Edwin Hodder, *The Life and Work of the Seventh Earl of Shaftesbury, K.G. (3 Vols, 1886), Vol. III, p.119.*
44. Ibid., p. 121.
45. *The Story of Thomas Holloway*, p.17.
46. Ibid., pp.19-20, f.n. Further evidence of Lord Shaftesbury's connection with the Sanatorium is provided by the fact that he is represented in one of the stained glass windows of the Sanatorium Chapel.

47. The bequests were:

| | |
|---|---|
| Henry Holloway (brother) | £300 |
| Matilda Holloway (sister) | £300 |
| Caroline Young (sister) | £150 |
| Mary Jane Hutchings (sister) | £150 |
| James Bennett | £30 |
| Captain George Chellew | £30 |
| Mary Ann Driver | £30 |
| Clara Ewbank | £30 |

Captain George Chellew was obviously a maternal relative, but the exact relationship has not been established. James Bennett may have been Thomas Holloway's godson. Dr A. Harrison-Barbet has traced the birth certificate of a James Thomas Holloway Bennett of appropriate age; though there is no proof that this was the same person, the name is suggestive. James Bennett was a rather tiresome wastrel in whose welfare Holloway interested himself, using Captain George Chellew as an intermediary (see SRO THPP 2620/9/(3), Private Letter Book 1869-1872, *passim*). Clara Ewbank may have been either a relative or a family servant. The author is indebted to Dr A. Harrison-Barbet for the details of the Will.

48. J. Mordaunt Crook, 'Architecture and History', *Design and Practice in British Architecture: Studies in architectural history presented to Howard Colvin* (1984), p.556; J. Mordaunt Crook to Caroline Bingham, undated letter, November 1985.

49. W. H. Crossland, op.cit., pp.141-2. Crossland's account of Royal Holloway College is prefaced by a short account of the building of the Sanatorium.

50. SRO THPP 2620/9/(3), Private Letter Book 1869-1872. Holloway to Donaldson, 25 October 1871.

51. W. H. Crossland, op.cit., pp.142-3.

52. SRO THPP 2629/9/(1), Travel Diary 1848. 'My Trip to Chambord' is copied into the remaining blank pages of the Travel Diary, and is annotated 'This is the handwriting of the late Sir George Martin Holloway'/V.L.O.

Jan 1900/. The initials stand for Vere Langford Oliver, Martin-Holloway's son-in-law.

53. Marion Pick, *Social Life at RHC 1887-1939* (revised version of unpublished memoirs), typescript, p.7. The author is indebted to Dr Ida Bushbridge for the loan of this typescript. (RHC Archives RF/131/7 comprises the unrevised version, in four files.)

54. *The Royal Holloway College for Women*. Prospectus, 1895, p.5.

55. *The Story of Thomas Holloway*, p.29. The volume of Holloway's Diary from which these words are quoted has now disappeared.

56. *Waterford Mirror*, 12 October 1876.

57. RHC Archives RF/126/1, Press Cuttings Book 1876-1900, *passim*.

58. *Oudh Akhbar*, Lucknow, 28 July 1877. Trans. Dr M. S. Ahmed and Dr Francis Robinson; Dr Robinson to Caroline Bingham 5 March 1985: 'As far as I know, the first women's college [in India] for Moslems at least, was not founded until 1914.'

59. *Guardian*, St Helena, 9 May 1877.

60. *Standard*, Buenos Aires, 9 June 1877.


CHAPTER TWO

1. John H. Ellison, 'Early days', *The Royal Holloway College 1887-1937*, p.22. Randall Davidson, Dean of Windsor and later Archbishop of Canterbury, and a Governor of the College, addressed these words to The Revd John H. Ellison, Prebendary of Windsor, who became a Governor in 1915. He dated Davidson's remarks 'I should suppose about the year 1884'; but as Davidson referred to Holloway in the present tense, and Holloway died in 1883, his words must belong to that year at the latest.

2. Alfred, Lord Tennyson, *The Princess* (1847, reprint 1851) p.7. Gilbert and Sullivan amusingly burlesqued *The Princess* in *Princess Ida* (1884), which is now far more familiar. Tennyson's noble and humourless poem with its slightly absurd story was easily distorted to ridicule the idea of higher education for women.

3. Josephine Kamm, *Indicative Past: A Hundred Years of the Girls' Public Day School Trust* (Allen and Unwin, 1971), p.43.

4. Ibid., p.15.

5. *Some Small Memories as to the Origin of Holloway College for Women! being Mr Holloway's Address on meeting some Friends to explain his views, and some*

*correspondence with Mr James Beal as to its Initiation* (Privates Printed by G. Stahl, London, no date), p.14.

6. J. Mordaunt Crook, *Mr Holloway's Château*, RHC Centenary Lecture, No.1, 15 January 1986.

7. RHC Archives GB/130/1, *Letter Book of Thomas Holloway 1874-1877*. Holloway to Professor Henry Fawcett, 10 April 1875.

8. W. H. Crossland, op.cit., p.144.

9. Edward R. Linner, *Vassar: The Remarkable Growth of a Man and His College*, ed. Elizabeth A. Daniels (Vassar, 1984), p.18.

10. *Historical Sketch of Vassar College* (S. W. Green, New York, 1876) p.3.

11. RHC Archives GB/130/1, *Letter Book of Thomas Holloway 1874-1877*. Holloway to Chadwick, 6 September 1875.

12. SRO THPP (unlisted) *Diary 1877*, and ensuing quotations, *passim*.

13. W. H. Crossland, op.cit., p.148.

14. C. W. Carey, 'The Buildings', *The Royal Holloway College 1887-1937*, p.16.

15. C. W. Carey, 'Chronicles of College', *Erinna*, 1940, p.29.

16. Ibid., p.32.

17. Jeannie Chapel, *Victorian Taste: the Complete Catalogue of Paintings at the Royal Holloway College* (RHC, 1982), pp.101-2.

18. Ibid., pp. 108-9.

19. Ibid., pp. 83-90.

20. C. W. Carey, 'Chronicles of College', *Erinna*, 1940, p.32.

21. Jeannie Chapel, op.cit., p.92.

22. *Historical Sketch of Vassar College* pp.4-5. Full text of Matthew Vassar's speech.

23. RHC Archives GB/130/1 *Letter Book of Thomas Holloway 1874-1877*. Holloway to Chadwick, 8 February 1875.

24. Holloway's Pills and Holloway's Ointment were bought up by Beecham Pills Ltd in December 1930, at which date the company operated from Chipstone St, London W1. In July 1939 it was transferred to McLean's Ltd, which Beecham had acquired the previous year, in premises on the Great West Road. Production of Holloway's Ointment was discontinued shortly after the outbreak of the Second World War, and the company itself, Holloway's Pills was liquidated in 1952. Information given by Mr Greg Ernest, Beecham Group PLC, (Group Communications) to Caroline Bingham, 10 July 1985.

25. W. H. Crossland, op.cit., p.148.

26. W. E. Delp, *Royal Holloway College 1908-1914* (printed pamphlet, text of

lecture given at RHC to the 'Professors' Wives Club', 21 January 1969), p.1.

27. Walter Armstrong, 'A Women's University' (pamphlet reprinted from the *Art Journal*, January 1885), p.10.

28. C. W. Carey, 'Chronicles of College', *Erinna*, 1940, p.29: ' . . . the earth excavated . . . from the tunnel was brought to make up the hockey and tennis lawns, the trucks being pulled up the ascent by horses.'

29. Walter Armstrong, op.cit., p.8.

30. Ibid., p.10.

31. W. H. Crossland, op.cit., p.148.

32. Walter Armstrong, op.cit., p.11.

33. Ibid., p.12.

34. W. H. Crossland, op.cit., p.147.

35. Ibid.

36. Vera Tsaritsyn, 'A Woman's Walks No. XCVI. The Training of Rosebuds', *The World*, 8 July 1891.

37. *Queen Victoria and the Royal Holloway College 1885-1886: Letters and Papers from the Queen's Archives at Windsor Castle*, transcribed and edited by Lionel Butler and Janet Christie (RHC, privately printed 1977). No. I, Martin-Holloway to Ponsonby, 20 July 1885.

38. Ibid. No. IV, Count Gleichen (signature 'Victor Hohenlohe') to Sir Dighton Probyn, 18 February 1886.

39. Ibid. No. XXIII, Martin-Holloway to Ponsonby, 28 Mary 1886.

40. Ibid. No. XXIX, Martin-Holloway to Ponsonby. Undated, but mid-June in sequence of letters.

41. Ibid. No. V, Thring to Ponsonby, 1 March 1886.

42. Ibid. No. VIII, Davidson to Ponsonby, 7 April 1886.

43. John H. Ellison, 'Early Days', *The Royal Holloway College 1887-1937*, p.22.

44. *Queen Victoria and the Royal Holloway College* . . . No. XIII, Benson to Ponsonby, 15 May 1886.

45. Ibid. No. XIV, Ponsonby to Queen Victoria, 16 May 1886.

46. Ibid. No. XV, Ponsonby to Benson, 18 May 1886.

47. Ibid. No. XVI, Martin-Holloway to Ponsonby, 18 May 1886.

48. Ibid. Letter No. XXI, Thring to Ponsonby, 21 May 1886; RHC Archives GB/140/3, 'the Royal Holloway College' (Brochure), p.26.

49. *Queen Victoria and the Royal Holloway College* . . . No. XXXVI, the Queen's Diary, 30 June 1886.

50. [Miss Blackwell] 'RHC Reminiscences – Mr Carey', *Erinna*, 1944, p.7.

51. *Queen Victoria and the Royal Holloway College* . . . Letter No. XXIX, Martin-Holloway to Ponsonby, 7 July 1886.

52. Count Gleichen to Sir George Martin-Holloway, 22 June 1887. (Letter in the possession of Gerald Oliver Esq.)

## CHAPTER THREE

1. RHC Archives GB/110/1, *Minutes of Governors' Meetings No. 1*, Principal's Report on the First Year of the College Work, 14 July 1888.
2. *Moonshine*, 3 July 1886.
3. cit. Martha Vicinus, *Independent Women: Work and Community for Single Women 1850-1920* (Virago History, 1985), p.128.
4. John H. Ellison, 'Early Days', *The Royal Holloway College 1887-1937*, p.23
5. RHC Archives GB/110/1, *Minutes of Governors' Meetings No. 1*, 17 March 1887. The other three interviewed were Miss Borchardt, late Headmistress of Devonport High School; Miss Kennedy, Principal of Leeds High School; and Miss Kensington, Secretary of Girton.
6. Alice Luxton, *Matilda Ellen Bishop, A Memoir* (Arden Press, 1914), p.10.
7. Ibid., p.12.
8. Martha Vicinus, op.cit., p.135.
9. In 1881 Miss Maynard almost despaired of the difficulties which beset the foundation of Westfield, and sought an interview with Thomas Holloway, with a view to applying for the principalship of his College. She was excited at seeing the great building in progress, and confided to her diary, 'I wanted it for the Lord', but she was shocked to learn that it was to be non-denominational; and after a crisis of conscience, she resolved to continue her struggle to found an Evangelical women's college. The outcome was successful, and Westfield opened five years before Royal Holloway. Miss Maynard was a pillar of Evangelical respectability, but her unpublished autobiographical writings contain details of homoerotic if not homosexual relations with close friends. *vide* Martha Vicinus, op.cit., pp. 157-162.
10. 'A Sectarian Dodge', *The Nonconformist and Independent*, 5 January 1888.
11. *Pall Mall Gazette*, 25 February 1888; *Daily News*, 25 February 1888. (Anonymous letters of protest signed 'A Radical'.)
12. 'Perversion of the Royal Holloway College', *The Freeman*, 10 February 1888.
13. RHC Archives GB/110/1, *Minutes of Governors' Meetings No. 1*, 20 May 1887.

14. 'The Staff', *The Royal Holloway College 1887-1937*, p.28.
15. RHC Archives GB/110/1, *Minutes of Governors' Meetings No. 1*, 20 May, 1887, 22 July 1887, 20 August 1887.
16. 'The Staff', *The Royal Holloway College 1887-1937*, p.28.
17. Emily Daymond, 'Early Days', ibid., p.22
18. E. C. Higgins, 'Miss Knowles' (obituary), RHCA *College Letter*, 1939, pp. 82-3.
19. RHC Register of Students Vol. I, *passim*.
20. 'Careers', *The Royal Holloway College 1887-1937*, pp. 61-2.
21. Eric Hobsbawm, 'Inventing Traditions', *The Invention of Tradition*, ed. Eric Hobsbawm and Terence Ranger (Cambridge University Press, 1983), p.2.
22. 'Chronicles of College' (interview with Dr Martha Whiteley), *Erinna*, 1938, p.18.
23. RHC Archives GB/110/1, *Minutes of Governors' Meetings No. 1*, 29 October 1887. At this meeting the Governors agreed to provide *The Times, Spectator, Nineteenth Century, Edinburgh Review, Quarterly Review, Classical Review* and *Nature*. By 1891 thirteen more papers and periodicals had been added, including *Revue des deux Mondes, Blackwood, Art Journal* and *Punch*. Students paid a fixed subscription of one shilling per term to the College newspaper fund, out of which additional papers were purchased. (RHCA *College Letter*, March 1891, pp. 5-6.)
24. 'Games', *The Royal Holloway College 1887-1937*, p.53.
25. Marion Pick, *Social Life at Royal Holloway College 1889-1939*, typescript p.110 (revised edition loaned to Caroline Bingham by Dr Ida Busbridge).
26. Ivy Compton Burnett to her cousin Katie, 1 May 1903, cit. Hilary Spurling, *Ivy When Young: The Early Life of I. Compton Burnett, 1884-1919*. (Victor Gollancz, 1974), p.14.
27. Marion Pick, op.cit., pp. 115-16.
28. Lilian Faithfull, *In the House of My Pilgrimage* (Chatto and Windus, 1924), pp.92-3.
29. Marion Pick, op.cit., p.3.
30. Lilian Faithfull, op.cit., p.89.
31. Marion Pick, op.cit., p.68.
32. RHC Archives GB 110/1, *Minutes of Governors' Meetings No. 1*, 24 February 1890; GB/110/2, *Minutes of Governors' Meetings No. 2*, 23 February 1895.
33. 'Chapel Services and Religious Societies', *The Royal Holloway College 1887-1937*, p.38.
34. Ibid.

35. RHC Archives GB/110/2, *Minutes of Governors' Meetings No. 2*, 27 May 1897.
36. RHCA *College Letter*, December 1897, pp. 3-7.


CHAPTER FOUR

1. RHCA *College Letter*, December 1907, pp. 6-9. Speech by Miss Hayes-Robinson at the unveiling of Miss Penrose's portrait on 2 November. The portrait, by Philip A. Laszlo, is in the College Dining Hall.
2. *University Degrees for Women: Report of a Conference convened by the Governors of the Royal Holloway College and held at the House of the Society of Arts on Saturday 4 December 1897* (printed for the College by Spottiswoode and Co., London, 1898), p.10.
3. Ibid., p.11.
4. Ibid., p.16.
5. Ibid., pp.17-19.
6. Ibid., pp.30-1
7. Ibid., pp.32-3.
8. Ibid., p.42. Sir Joshua Fitch said that Thomas Holloway had seen Vassar, Bryn Mawr and Wellesley, and had been impressed by their scale and facilities. But he seems to have been mistaken, for though Thomas Holloway had been in America in 1853, this was twenty years before he expressed any interest in women's education, and before the foundation of these Colleges. However, George Martin who had visited Vassar on his behalf, may have visited them also.
9. Ibid., p.34.
10. Vera Brittain, *The Women at Oxford: A Fragment of History* (George G. Harrap and Co., 1960), p.121.
11. Vera Furnell, *A Somervillian Looks Back* (privately printed by Oxford University Press, 1948), p.35.
12. Vera Brittain, loc.cit.
13. Marion Pick, *Social Life at Royal Holloway College 1887-1939*, p.113.
14. Letter from Professor Dominica Legge to Caroline Bingham, 18 June, 1985.
15. Marion Pick, op.cit., p.99.
16. RHC Archives GB/110/2, *Minutes of Governors' Meetings No. 2*, 27 January 1898.
17. Ibid., 28 May 1898.
18. Ibid., 29 April 1899.

19. RHC Archives GB/110/3, *Minutes of Governors' Meetings*, No. 3, 24 June 1899.
20. RHC *Calendar* 1900/01, p.99: 'The following Members of the Staff have been recognised by the Commissioners as Teachers of the University in the subjects specified: Miss K. S. Block, English; Miss A. G. Corry, German; Mr E. H. Donkin, Classics; Miss C. Frost, Mathematics; Mr S. L. Loney, Mathematics; Miss M. A. Péchinet, French; Miss E. Penrose, History; Mr J. Solomon, Philosophy; Miss M. E. J. Taylor, Classics; Miss M. Benson, Botany; Miss F. Buchanan, Zoology; Mr W. Cassie, Physics; Miss E. E. Field, Chemistry.'
21. Marion Pick, op.cit., p.102.
22. Ibid., p.111.
23. RHC Archives GB/110/3, *Minutes of Governors' Meetings No. 3*, 12 July 1900, Librarian's Report for the Year 1899/1900.
24. RHC *Calendar* 1900/01, pp.125-6. 'Donations to the Library' details fifteen Greek and Latin texts donated by Miss Dabis.
25. W. E. Delp, *Royal Holloway College, 1908-1914*, p.3.
26. Ibid., p.4.
27. Ibid., p.3.
28. Letter and memoir from Miss Marian Crout (student 1912-15) to Caroline Bingham (undated), summer 1985.
29. Letter from Miss Eleanor Barnes (student 1928-31) to Caroline Bingham, 22 July, 1985.
30. RHC Archives (unclassified), typescript of autobiographical memoir by Miss E. M. Blackwell, with alternative suggested titles 'Women or co-educational?' or 'Residential or non-residential?', p.3, footnote on Miss E. M. Rowell and her work.
31. Hilary Spurling, *Ivy when Young: The early life of I. Compton Burnett, 1884-1919* (Victor Gollancz, London, 1974). Appendix Two, 'Helen Cam's key to Dolores', pp.280-3. (The first edition of *Dolores*, with Helen Cam's key pencilled on the back endpapers, is in RHC Archives.)
32. Ibid., p.150.
33. 'Research', *The Royal Holloway College 1887-1937*, p.31.
34. Ibid.
35. Ibid., pp.33,34,35.
36. RHCA *College Letter*, December 1907, p.14.
37. RHC Archives AS/142/3, 'A College Song' (1907), *Selections from RHC 'College Album' 1898-1930*, p.5.
38. W. E. Delp, op.cit., pp.2-3.
39. 'Music', *The Royal Holloway College 1887-1937*, p.47.

[ 284 ]

40. RHCA *College Letter*, July 1905, pp.9-15.
41. 'Social and Political Societies', *The Royal Holloway College 1887-1937*, p.43.
42. RHCA *College Letter*, December 1898, p.11.
43. 'Chapel Services and Religious Societies', *The Royal Holloway College 1887-1937*, pp.39-40.
44. Marion Pick, op.cit., p.139.
45. Ibid., p.123.
46. W. E. Delp, op.cit., p.8.
47. Ibid., p.12.
48. M. F. Richey, 'Evening Episode', *Collegiate Causeries* (Basil Blackwell, Oxford, 1949), pp.7-8.
49. *Bedford College Magazine*.
50. Marion Pick, op.cit., p.119.


CHAPTER FIVE

1. RHC Archives A.56. *Papers of Miss E. M. Blackwell relating to RHC ...* 'The Draft of a speech made in the Jubilee Year 1937, possibly a reply to the toast of 'The College' made at an RHCA luncheon' by Miss E. M. Rowell (Miss Blackwell's typescript of Miss Rowell's notes).
2. Six Oxford Honour Moderations, fourteen London BA or B.Sc., one Oxford Final Honours and London BA (Honours) (E. C. Higgins). RHC Calendar (cumulative edition) 1957/8, pp.91-2.
3. 'Games', *The Royal Holloway College 1887-1937*, p.56.
4. Miss A. A. Divine (student 1921-5; Principal's Private Secretary 1941-62), interview with Caroline Bingham.
5. Professor E. S. Waterhouse, Memorial Address for Miss E. C. Higgins, 5 January 1952, RHCA *College Letter*, December 1952, pp.42-3.
6. Ibid.
7. W. E. Delp, *Royal Holloway College 1908-1914*, p.1.
8. Professor E. S. Waterhouse, loc.cit.
9. M. F. Richey, 'For E. C. H. Whom former students named The Chief', *Collegiate Causeries*, p.33.
10. RHCA *College Letter*, December 1952, pp.43-4.
11. W. H. McCrea, 'Miss E. C. Higgins', *Nature*, Vol. 169, 2 February 1952, p.178 (reprinted in RHCA *College Letter*, December 1952, pp.41-2).
12. Mrs Amy Mummery née Beazeley (personal maid to Miss Higgins), interview with Caroline Bingham.

13. RHC Archives GB/110/4, *Minutes of Governors' Meetings No. 4, University of London Report of the Persons Appointed to Report on the Organisation and Administration of Schools of the University in the Faculties of Arts and Science (S.M. 2226 of May 13 1908) with Reference to the Royal Holloway College* (minuted at meeting on 26 November 1910).

14. RHC Archives GB/110/4, *Minutes of Governors' Meetings No. 4, University of London Inspection of Departments and Schools of the University Under Statute 76*, (minuted at meeting of 26 November 1910), p.6.

15. Ibid.

16. Ibid. p.7.

17. RHCA *College Letter*, May 1978, p.9. Obituary of Dr W. E. Delp by Margaret L. Mare (student 1919-22).

18. RHC Archives GB/110/4, *Minutes of Governors' Meetings No. 4, University of London Inspection of Departments* . . . , p.8.

19. Ibid.

20. Ibid., p.9.

21. RHCA *College Letter*, December 1968, pp.23-4. 'In Memoriam M. P.'

22. RHC Archives GB/110/4, *Minutes of Governors' Meetings No. 4, University of London Inspection of Departments* . . . p.8.

23. Ibid., p.4.

24. Ibid., p.7.

25. Ibid.

26. Ibid., p.5.

27. RHC Archives AS/142/3, *Selection from RHC 'College Album' 1898-1930*, p.8, 'Song of the Senior Student' (1927).

28. RHC Archives GB/110/4, *Minutes of Governors' Meetings, No. 4, University of London Inspection of Departments* . . . p.5.

29. RHC Archives GB/110/4, *Minutes of Governors' Meetings No. 4*, 30 January 1908.

30. Ibid. Letter dated 26 February 1909 (minuted at Governors' Meeting on 13 March 1909).

31. Ibid. *Times Law Report* (minuted at meeting on 27 November 1909). Mr Justice Swinfen-Eady as Lord Swinfen, Master of the Rolls, was a Governor of Royal Holloway College 1918-19.

32. *Final Report of the Committee of Enquiry into the Governance of the University of London* (1972), Chapter Two, 'Outline of Constitutional History', p.8, para 23.

33. Ibid., pp.8-9, para 24.

34. RHC Archives GB/110/5, *Minutes of Governors' Meetings No. 5, Memorandum Presented by the Governors of the Royal Holloway College to the*

*Departmental Committee appointed by the Board of Education in Connection With the Report of the Royal Commission on University Education in London* (minuted at meeting on 29 November 1913), p.2.

The Memorandum includes the following comparative table of the standards attained by women students at four London Colleges in the years 1903-12:

| | Average annual No of registered women students | Total No of Honour Degrees | Total No of First-class Honours. | Total No of open University Scholarships, Studentships, &c. |
|---|---|---|---|---|
| University College (Women only) | 147 | 133 | 29 | 28 |
| King's College and King's College for Women (Women only) | 80 | 54 | 13 | 3 |
| Bedford College (Women) | 203 | 171 | 35 | 11 |
| Royal Holloway College (Women) | 143 or 25.1% of whole | 214 or 37.4% of whole | 42 or 35.3% of whole | 28 or 40% of whole |

35.  Marion Pick, *Social Life at Royal Holloway College 1887-1939*, p.160.
36.  RHCA *College Letter*, December 1914, p.28.
37.  RHCA *College Letter*, July 1908, p.13.
38.  'Social and Political Societies', *The Royal Holloway College 1887-1937*, p.43.
39.  RHCA *College Letter*, July 1911, p.35.
40.  Frances Lloyd George née Stevenson, *The Years that are Past* (Hutchinson, London, 1967) pp.32-3.
41.  Miss A. I. G. Hewitt (Student RHC 1910-13), interview with Elizabeth Bennett, Archivist of Royal Holloway and Bedford New College, July 1986.
42.  Frances Lloyd George, loc.cit.
43.  W. E. Delp, op.cit., p.12.
44.  'The Staff', *The Royal Holloway College 1887-1937*, p.29.
45.  W. E. Delp, op-cit., p.4.
46.  RHCA *College Letter*, December 1914, p.20.
47.  Ibid. December 1916, 'The Potato Patch', p.25.
48.  Ibid. December 1914, p.21.
49.  Ibid. 'The Women's Song' p.44-5.
50.  Ibid. December 1915, pp.22-3, 27.

51. Ibid., p.24.
52. Mrs Rachel Teschemaker née Dawson (student 1915-18), letter to Caroline Bingham, 12 August 1985.
53. RHCA *College Letter*, December 1915, pp.19-20.
54. RHC *Calendar* (cumulative edition) 1957/8, p.12.
55. RHCA *College Letter*, December 1914, p.24. The writer of these words was D. A. Tennant (student 1912-16).
56. RHCA *College Letter*, December 1915. 'Women's Labour in Wartime', pp.63-6.
57. RHCA *College Letter*, 1953, pp.48-9. Speech by Dr Whiteley at the Summer Luncheon, in response to the toast 'The College'.
58. Marion Pick, op.cit., p.209.

CHAPTER SIX

1. 'The Staff', *The Royal Holloway College 1887-1937*, p.29.
2. They were: Miss M. S. Sim (1898-1901), Miss E. M. Boyd (1901-09), Miss A. Martin-Leake (1909-16), Miss D. M. H. de Grave (1916-18).
3. Marjorie Milsom, 'In Memoriam Ulrica Dolling, 1884-1969', *Journal of the Ladies' Alpine Club* (1970), pp.57-8.
4. Ibid.
5. RHCA *College Letter*, December 1969, pp.18-19.
6. 'The Staff' *The Royal Holloway College 1887-1937*, p.29.
7. Miss Muriel Glyn-Jones (student 1919-22) to Caroline Bingham, 22 September 1985. Miss Glyn-Jones became a Superintendent Inspector of the Children's Department at the Home Office, from which she retired in 1955.
8. Mrs Kathleen Lathbury née Culhane (student 1918-22), to Caroline Bingham, 26 June 1985.
9. RHC Calendar 1957/8 (Cumulative edition), pp.147-50.
10. Mrs Kathleen Lathbury, 'Women in Industry: Experience of a Woman Chemist' (lecture 1946). Exhibitions: 1960, pictures in Paris Salon; 1961, Royal Society of Portrait Painters; 1979, one-man show by invitation of Free Painters and Sculptors; 1982, pictures in Salon de Nations, Paris; 1985, one-man exhibition, The Maltings, Farnham.
11. Miss Phillippa Moeller (student 1942-5) to Caroline Bingham, 5 June 1985.
12. RHC Archives AS/142/3, *Selections from RHC 'College Album' 1898-1930*, 'Shopping' (1929), p.10.

13. Mrs Doreen Coker née Stableton (student 1944-7), to Caroline Bingham, 3 August 1986.
14. Marion Pick, *Social Life at Royal Holloway College 1887-1939*, p.219.
15. W. E. Delp, *Royal Holloway College 1908-1914*, p.14. (Dr Benson retired after the First World War and did not sever her connection with the College for some years after her retirement. Despite the title of Dr Delp's pamphlet, the reference to Dr Benson does not refer to the pre-war years.)
16. 'Social and Political Societies', *The Royal Holloway College 1887-1937*, p.43.
17. RHCA *College Letter*, November 1939, p.51; RHCA *College Letter*, November 1941, p.38.
18. Miss Rosemary Manning, interview with Caroline Bingham.
19. Lady Linstead to Caroline Bingham, 6 October 1985.
20. 'The Staff', *The Royal Holloway College 1887-1937*, p.29.
21. Marion Pick, op.cit.
22. Mrs Kitty Hawkes née Griffiths (student 1930-33) to Caroline Bingham, 1 July 1985.
23. RHC Archives GB/110/6, *Minutes of Governors' Meetings No. 6*, 1 December 1921.
24. 'The Staff', *The Royal Holloway College 1887-1937*, p.30. The four were Miss Honey, Miss Taylor, Miss Barker and Miss Willcock. Miss Taylor moved into Settrington, a large detached house in Bakeham Lane, alongside the west boundary of the College grounds. After her death it was purchased to provide an official residence for the Principal of the College, its first occupant being Dame Marjorie Williamson (Principal 1962-73).
25. Marion Pick, op. cit., p.202.
26. Ibid., p.204.
27. RHCA *College Letter*, July 1914, p.3.
28. RHC Calendar 1957-8 (Cumulative edition) p.77.
29. RHCA *College Letter*, November 1939, pp.13-14, 175.
30. RHCA *College Letter*, December 1963, pp.17-18.
31. RHCA *College Letter*, December 1954, p.44.
32. Ibid., p.45.
33. RHCA *College Letter*, May 1972 p.11. Continuation to obituary by Mrs M. C. Vincent née Pitman (student 1927-33).
34. RHCA *College Letter*, December 1955, p.23.
35. Ibid.
36. 'Research', *The Royal Holloway College 1887-1937*, pp.32-3.
37. RHCA *College Letter*, May 1972 p.10. Obituary by Miss H. A. C. Green and Dr J. M. S. Tompkins (signed with initials only).

38. Miss Doreen Coker (student 1944-7) to Caroline Bingham, 3 August 1986. (Poem attributed to Miss Marjorie King, student 1945-8.)
39. RHCA *College Letter*, December 1967, p.24.
40. Dr J. M. S. Tompkins, interview with Caroline Bingham.
41. M. F. Richey, 'Thoughts on the Wisdom that Endures, as Inspired by Two Masters', *Collegiate Causeries*, pp.14-15.
42. 'Professor Helen Maud Cam', obituary in *The Times*, 12 February 1968.
43. 'Research', *The Royal Holloway College 1887-1937*, p.33.
44. 'Royal Holloway College: The Department of Physics', S. Tolansky and E. M. Williamson, *Chemistry and Industry* 13 July 1963.
45. Ibid., 'Department of Chemistry'.
46. Professor John D. Dodge, *History of the Royal Holloway College Botany Department 1893-1985)*, (privately printed by the Department), pp.4-5.
47. W. E. Delp, *Royal Holloway College 1908-1914*, p.5.
48. Dr Grace Waterhouse to Caroline Bingham, 14 August 1985. Of these ten women, four had been connected with the Botany Department at Royal Holloway College: 1928, Dame Helen Gwynne-Vaughan (staff 1905-7); 1938, Miss Kathleen Sampson (student 1911-16); 1942, Miss E. M. Blackwell (Head of Department 1922-49); 1961, Dr Grace Waterhouse (student 1924-8).
49. Dr Ida Busbridge to Caroline Bingham, 10 June 1985 and 24 July 1985.
50. RHCA *College Letter* November 1924, p.12.
51. RHCA *College Letter*, November 1944, p.14.
52. Miss Rosemary Manning, interview with Caroline Bingham.
53. 'The Staff', *The Royal Holloway College, 1887-1937*, p.29.
54. 'Music', op.cit., pp.47-8.
55. Dr Lionel Pike, 'One Hundred Years of Music at Royal Holloway College' (Centenary Lecture, 1986), typescript p.8. Text of lecture kindly given by Dr Pike to Caroline Bingham.
56. RHC Archives GB/110/7, *Minutes of Governors' Meetings No. 7*, 'Report of the Music Examiner' (Dr Harold Darke) appended to minutes of Governors' Meeting 27 May 1933.
57. Music Report, 1949.
58. Dr Lionel Pike, op.cit., p.13.
59. 'Music', *The Royal Holloway College 1887-1937*, p.49.
60. RHC Archives GB/110/6, *Minutes of Governors' Meetings No. 6*, 'Principal's Report on the Easter Term 1921', appended to minutes of Governors' Meeting 27 October 1921.
61. *Final Report of the Committee of Enquiry into the Governance of the University*

*of London*, Chapter Two, 'Outline of Constitutional History', paragraph 33, p.12.

62. Ibid., paragraph 35, pp.12-13.
63. Ibid., paragraph 36, p.13.
64. RHC Archives GB/110/7, *Minutes of Governors' Meetings No. 7*, 'Memorandum presented to the Statutory Commissioners on the University of London by the Governors of the Royal Holloway College', appended to the minutes of the Governors' Meeting of 29 October 1927.
65. Dr Edith Batho, interview with Caroline Bingham.
66. Dr J. M. S. Tompkins (staff 1934-65), interview with Caroline Bingham.
67. Miss Kathleen Vinall to Caroline Bingham, 8 August 1985.
68. Miss Doreen Urwick to Caroline Bingham, 27 August 1985.
69. Miss E. B. Leggett to Caroline Bingham, 10 October 1985.
70. Dr J. M. S. Tompkins, interview with Caroline Bingham.

CHAPTER SEVEN

1. Dr J. M. S. Tompkins, interview with Caroline Bingham. The allusion was to Tacitus' statement concerning the Emperor Galba, that none would have doubted his capacity to govern, had he never governed.
2. Tim Severin, *The Jason Voyage* (1985).
3. Dr M. F. Richey, 'Valedictions: for J. R. B.', *Collegiate Causeries*, p.23.
4. Interview given by Dame Marjorie Williamson and Miss A. D. Thompson to Caroline Bingham.
5. Miss A. A. Divine, Principal's Private Secretary (1941–65), interview with Caroline Bingham.
6. Mr Bert Seeley, interview with Chrys Salt.
7. Mrs Lucy Ben-Levi née Fowles (student 1942–5) to Caroline Bingham, 10 June 1985.
8. Miss A. D. Thompson, interview with Caroline Bingham.
9. 'Genius Loci', signed 'JRB', *Erinna*, 1939, p.2. The key is as follows: GREEN, Miss H. A. C., (Department of English, 1928-67); WEST, Dr Constance, (Department of French, 1928-65); WOODWARD, Miss Avery (Department of Classics, 1928-53); MOSS, Sister M. G., (Sister-in-Charge, 1935-65); PLANT, Dr Millicent, (Department of Chemistry, 1933-47); HONEY Miss M. E. D., (Department of French, 1905-43); PICK, Miss Marion, (Department of Mathematics, 1911-46); WILLCOCK, Professor Gladys (Department of English, 1915-55); LEGGE, Miss M. D., (Department of French 1938-42); FAIRWEATHER, Miss H. M., (Assistant Secretary

to Governors, 1921-46); BAKER, Professor Bevan, (Department of Mathematics, 1924-44); BACON, Miss J. R., (Principal, 1935-44); COLES, Miss M. G., (Botanical Gardener, 1935-41); RICHEY, Dr M. F., (Department of German, 1918-48); MOORE, Professor T. S., (Department of Chemistry, 1914-46).

10. Mrs E. M. Higman née Turner (student 1934-7) to Caroline Bingham, 11 July 1986.

11. RHC Archives RF/113/1, Notes of Professor Mackail's speech, provided by himself.

12. Marion Pick, *Social Life at Royal Holloway College, 1887-1937*, p.182.

13. RHC *Calendar*.

14. RHCA *College Letter*, November 1939, 'University News', p.61.

15. RHC *Calendar* 1957/8 (cumulative edition), p.13.

16. Mr David Kennard to Caroline Bingham, 11 September 1985.

17. RHCA *College Letter*, November 1940, p.29.

18. RHCA *College Letter*, November 1939, 'University News', p.61.

19. RHC Archives GB/110/8, *Minutes of Governors' Meetings No. 8*, Letters from Brigadier the Hon. M. A. Wingfield CMG, DSO, Director of Quartering, to the Principal, 18 April 1941, minuted to Governors' Meeting of 15 May 1941.

20. RHCA *College Letter*, November 1941, 'The College in Wartime', pp. 16-17.

21. Ibid., p.16.

22. Ibid.

23. Extracts from *The Official History of the Auxilliary Territorial Service*, published by the War Office, by the authority of the Army Council, and 'Restricted' (1949). The History was compiled by Colonel J. M. Cowper (late ATS and WRAC), and the extracts communicated to Caroline Bingham by Major (Retired) D. R. M. Parker, curator of the WRAC Museum, Queen Elizabeth Park, Guildford, Surrey.

24. Frances Head, 'ATS Officers in the Making', *Erinna*, 1942, pp.16-17.

25. *Official History of the ATS*, p.143.

26. RHCA *College Letter*, November 1944, p.16.

27. Miss Frieda Winter to Caroline Bingham, undated memoir 1985.

28. Sister M. G. Moss to Caroline Bingham, 4 November, 1986.

29. Miss Philippa Moeller to Caroline Bingham, 5 June 1985.

30. 'Food Flash', signed 'J. R. B.', *Erinna*, 1943, p.13.

31. Miss Gillian Harris (student 1940-43) to Caroline Bingham, undated letter, 1985.

32. Dr Mary Bradburn to Caroline Bingham, 26 June 1986.

33. Ibid.
34. RHC Archives GB/203/2, *Report of the Committee appointed by the Governors to Consider the Post-War Policy of the Royal Holloway College* (Privately printed, December 1944, and marked 'Confidential – for the Information of the Governors of the Royal Holloway College'), Interim Report, paragraphs 1-5, pp.5-6.
35. Ibid., para 2, p.5; para 8, p.7.
36. Ibid., paras 43, 45, 47, 48, 52, 54, pp.13-16.
37. RHC Archives GB/110/9, *Minutes of Governors' Meetings No. 9*, Her resignation was accepted with conventional expressions of regret, at the Governors' Meeting on 1 April 1944.
38. RHC Archives GB/203/20, *Report of the Committee appointed by the Governors to consider the Post-War Policy* . . . paras 151, 153, pp.38-9.
39. Ibid., paras 158, 161, p.40.
40. Ibid., para 92, p.25.
41. Ibid., Appendix B 'Summary of Recommendations', pp.47-50.
42. Ibid., paras 170, 176, pp.42,44.
43. RHC Archives GB/110/9, *Minutes of Governors' Meetings No. 9*, 28 February 1945.
44. Ibid., 17 May 1945.
45. Ibid.
46. RHCA *College Letter*, October 1942, J. C. Scourse, 'Music and Music Societies 1941/42' pp.26-7.
47. RHCA *College Letter*, November 1945, p.25.
48. Dr Vera Fretter to Caroline Bingham, 5 August 1986.
49. Ibid.
50. RHCA *College Letter*, December 1962, 'Fanny Street, 1878-1962', pp.69-71.
51. Miss Philippa Moeller (student 1942-5) to Caroline Bingham, 5 June 1985.
52. Miss A. A. Divine, interview with Caroline Bingham. (Miss Divine was styled 'Assistant Secretary to the Principal' until the Post-War Policy Committee abolished the post of Principal's Secretary and created that of PPS.)
53. Miss Philippa Moeller, extracts from diary, kindly provided with letter to Caroline Bingham, 5 June 1985.
54. RHCA *College Letter*, November 1945, p.14.

## CHAPTER EIGHT

1. Mrs Doreen Coker née Stableton (student 1944-7), poem on College life sent to Caroline Bingham, 20 September 1985.
2. Dr Edith Batho, obituary, *The Times*, 10 February 1986.
3. Dr Edith Batho, interview with Caroline Bingham, 1985.
4. Miss J. L. Hurn (student 1946-50; Administration staff from 1964; Registrar 1970-85), recorded interview with Chrys Salt.
5. Dr Edith Batho, interview with Caroline Bingham, 1985.
6. Dr Edith Batho to Dr Roy Miller, 2 October 1982 (copy of letter given by Dr Miller to Caroline Bingham).
7. Dr Edith Batho, interview with Caroline Bingham, 1985.
8. Mrs Doreen Coker née Stableton (student 1944-7) to Caroline Bingham, 20 September 1985.
9. RHC Archives (unclassified), 'Notes for my successor', a manuscript notebook written by Dr Batho for Dr Marjorie Williamson (Principal 1962-73) and presented by the latter to the Archives.
10. 'To an Eastern Grass Plot', signed 'J. R. B.', *Erinna*, 1942, p.3.
11. Negley Harte, *The University of London 1836-1986*, p.255. By 1953, Sir Douglas Logan (Principal of London University 1948-75) described the quinquenniel estimates as 'almost a matter of life and death'. loc. cit.
12. RHCA *College Letter*, November 1945, p.15.
13. 'History of Holloway', *Erinna*, 1947, pp.19-20. This short piece is subtitled 'Chapter XXII Post-War Changes'. *Erinna* had printed none of the Chapters of this elusive 'History'; previous historical pieces had appeared as 'Chronicles of College', by various authors. This piece is signed 'M. K. M.', identified by the author as Mrs M. K. Ritchie née Mort (student 1944-7; returned 1950-52; MA 1952).
14. Negley Harte, op.cit., p.255.
15. RHCA *College Letter*, October 1947, p.17.
16. RHC Archives GB/110/10, *Minutes of Governors' Meetings, No. 10*, 'An Interview with the Lord Chairman of Committees (Lord Drogheda) . . . at the House of Lords, 6 April 1949' minuted to Governors' Meeting on 12 May 1949. The representatives of the College were: Sir John Cameron, Miss L. F. Nettlefold, Mr E. L. Tanner, Dr Edith Batho and Miss Dorothy Hustler.
17. RHC Archives GB/110/11, *Minutes of the Council No 1*, 'Royal Holloway College Act', 30 July 1949.
18. 'HRH Princess Alice, Countess of Athlone', obituary by Dr Edith Batho, RHCA *College Letter*, May 1981, p.11.

19. RHC Archives GB/110/11, *Minutes of the Council No 1*, 'Royal Holloway College Act, (1949)', para 5, pp.7-8.

20. 'Miss Dorothy Hustler MBE', memorial address by Mr Richard Hardy (Secretary to the College 1964-85), RHCA *College Letter*, May 1977, pp.8-10. (Mr Hardy continues in office as Secretary to Royal Holloway and Bedford New College.)

21. 'Professor Hugh Tredennick' obituary, RHCA *College Letter*, May 1982, pp.10-11.

22. RHC *Annual Report* 1984-5, p.32.

23. RHCA *College Letter*, December 1968, p.26.

24. RHCA *College Letter*, 1975, p.5.

25. Dr Vera Fretter to Caroline Bingham, 5 August 1986.

26. Dr Joan Thomas to Caroline Bingham, 5 September 1986.

27. 'Royal Holloway College: the Department of Chemistry' reprinted from *Chemistry and Industry*, 13 July 1963.

28. R. W. Ditchburn FRS and G. D. Rochester FRS, 'Samuel Tolansky 1907-1973', *Biographical Memoirs of Fellows of the Royal Society*, Vol. 20, December 1974, pp.436-7.

29. Ibid, pp. 442-3.

30. 'Professor S. Tolansky', obituary, *The Times*, 17 May 1973, by Professor O. S. Heavens.

31. B. T. M. Willis, 'Physics Department, Royal Holloway College, 1947-1950: A Memoir' (typescript lent to Caroline Bingham by Dr A. Moreton Moore, Department of Physics). The postgraduates were: D. G. Avery, W. Bardsley, R. C. Faust, C. J. Griffin and J. Holden. B. T. M. Willis joined the group the following year, after graduating from Cambridge.

32. John D. Dodge, 'History of the Royal Holloway College Botany Department 1895-1985' (privately printed by the Botany Department 1985), pp.7-8.

33. RHCA *College Letter*, December 1966, p.24.

34. RHCA *College Letter*, December 1969, pp.14-15.

35. Miss J. L. Hurn, recorded interview with Chrys Salt, 1985.

36. Dr Edith Batho, interview with Caroline Bingham, 1985.

37. Miss S. P. Jenkins (Mrs Fowles), recorded interview with Chrys Salt, 1985.

38. Mrs Mary Kennedy, recorded interview with Chrys Salt, 1985.

39. Ibid.

40. 'Doddles and Ditties', signed 'J. R. H., D. C. M.'; *Erinna*, 1950, p.12.

41. 'Student Activities: from a survey held in College January-February 1953', *Erinna*, 1953, pp.17-18.

42. 'Holloway Song', *Erinna*, 1953, pp.2-3.
43. Miss S. P. Jenkins (Mrs Fowles), recorded interview with Chrys Salt.
44. Ibid.
45. 'The Eumenides at Home', M. M. Morgan, *Erinna*, 1949, pp.26-7.
46. RHCA *College Letter*, December 1951, p.28.
47. RHCA *College Letter*, December 1948, p.28.
48. 'Mr Gillie', Joy Manning (student 1948-51), *Erinna*, 1951, p.12.
49. Miss Janet Fookes MP to Caroline Bingham.
50. Mr Richard Hardy, 'Memorial Address for Miss Dorothy Hustler, MBE, Secretary 1948-1964', RHCA *College Letter*, 1977, pp.8-9.
51. 'Report of the Visitation of Members of the University Grants Committee on 1 June 1960', RHC Archives GB/110/20, *Minutes of the Council No. 10*, pp.994-7.
52. 'A Draft Plan for the Building Development of Royal Holloway College', Professor Sir Leslie Martin MA, Ph.D. FRIBA, in conjunction with Colin St John Wilson MA, ARIBA, October 1960. Ibid., p.1011.
53. Ibid., p.1080.
54. Sir Douglas Logan to Dr Edith Batho, 13 February 1961, Ibid., p.1121.
55. 'Note on the Meeting between the Planning Committee and Professor Sir Leslie Martin and the Principal of the University and the Clerk of the Court on Monday, February 20 1961', Ibid., pp.1127-31.
56. Sir Douglas Logan to Dr Edith Batho, 24 May 1962, RHC Archives, GB/110/21, *Minutes of the Council No. 11*, p.1359.
57. Sir Douglas Logan to Dr Edith Batho, 4 July 1962. Ibid. p.1444.

CHAPTER NINE

1. Mr P. Vianney Waters (student 1965-8), one of the original men undergraduates, to Caroline Bingham, 15 May 1985.
2. Dame Marjorie Williamson to Caroline Bingham, 12 November 1986.
3. Dame Marjorie Williamson, interview with Caroline Bingham, 1985.
4. Ibid.
5. Ibid.
6. Negley Harte, *The University of London, 1836-1986* (1986), p.260.
7. Ibid.
8. Ibid., p.269
9. Ibid. Table 7:1 No of students 1960-85.
10. RHC *Annual Report* 1984-5 p.9. In this year Royal Holloway College was in process of merging with Bedford College, and there were in addition

580 students registered as Bedford students but already resident at Egham.

11. Dame Marjorie Williamson, interview with Caroline Bingham, 1985.
12. Ibid.
13. Mr A. J. Boog, interview with Caroline Bingham, 1985.
14. Ibid.
15. Ibid.
16. Dame Marjorie Williamson, interview with Caroline Bingham, 1985; also quoted by Mr Bert Sealey, recorded interview with Chrys Salt, 1985.
17. Dame Marjorie Williamson, interview with Caroline Bingham, 1985.
18. Mr P. Vianney Waters to Caroline Bingham, 15 May 1985.
19. Dame Marjorie Williamson, interview with Caroline Bingham, 1985.
20. Ibid.
21. Dr Roy Miller (Principal of Royal Holloway College 1982-5) to Caroline Bingham, 4 September 1986.
22. Ibid.
23. Dr Lionel Pike, 'One Hundred Years of Music at Royal Holloway College', RHC Centenary Lecture, typescript p.16.
24. Mr Mike Bayliss to Caroline Bingham, 22 July 1985.
25. Mr P. Vianney Waters to Caroline Bingham, 15 May 1985.
26. Ibid.
27. RHCA *College Letter*, December 1967, p.19.
28. Mr Richard Hardy, recorded interview with Chrys Salt, 1985.
29. Mr P. Vianney Waters to Caroline Bingham, 15 May 1985.
30. RHCA *College Letter*, December 1965, pp.32-3.
31. RHCA *College Letter*, December 1966, p.30.
32. Mr Mike Bayliss to Caroline Bingham, 22 July 1985.
33. Miss Felicity Lott to Caroline Bingham, 5 September 1985.
34. RHCA *College Letter*, December 1966, p.32.
35. Ibid.
36. This point was made to the author by Miss Norma Miller, Mrs Fowles (Miss S. P. Jenkins), Mr Robert Latham and Mr Roger Lockyer, *inter alia.*
37. RHCA *College Letter*, December 1969, p.27.
38. Ibid., p.12.
39. RHCA *College Letter*, December 1970, p.28.
40. Mr A. J. Boog, interview with Caroline Bingham, 1985.
41. Ibid.
42. Ibid.
43. RHCA *College Letter*, December 1968, p.25.
44. RHCA *College Letter*, December 1968, p.24.
45. RHCA *College Letter*, December 1970, p.27.

46. 'The Expansion', *Royal Holloway College* (September 1964), no pagination.
47. RHCA *College Letter*, December 1966, pp.20-1.
48. RHCA *College Letter*, December 1970, p.23.
49. Ibid., p.24-5.
50. RHC Annual Report, 1971/2, 'Report of the Council for 1971/2', p.1.

CHAPTER TEN

1. Dr Lionel Butler's words, quoted in his obituary in RHCA *College Letter*, May 1982, p.5.
2. *Higher Education: Report of the Committee appointed by the Prime Minister under the Chairmanship of Lord Robbins, 1961-3* (1963), pp.223-4.
3. Negley Harte, *The University of London 1836-1986* (1986), p.262.
4. Ibid., p.264.
5. Ibid., p.265.
6. *Final Report of the Committee into the Governance of the University of London* ('Murray Report', 1972), para. 146, p.55.
7. Negley Harte, op.cit., pp.266-7.
8. Ibid., pp.268-9.
9. Memorial Address for Dr Lionel Butler (died 26 November 1981), given at a Thanksgiving Service for his life and work in the Chapel of Royal Holloway College, on 6 March 1982, by Professor J. S. C. Riley-Smith. *RHC Annual Report, 1981/2* pp.4-7.
10. Ibid.
11. Ibid.
12. Professor Katharine Worth, interview with Caroline Bingham, 1986.
13. The author was fortunate to see the notes of Dr Butler's lecture 'Emily Penrose and the New Century', which greatly assisted her in writing Chapter Four, 'The Larger Life of a University'. This appears to be the only set of notes surviving from this series of lectures; they will be deposited in the College Archives, together with notes of the sermons which Dr Butler preached from time to time in the College Chapel, transcribed by Miss Janet Christie.
14. Verse and accompanying explanation given to Caroline Bingham by Miss Janet Christie.
15. RHC *Annual Report*, 1973/4, p.3; RHC *Calendar* 1973/4, pp.xi-xvii.
16. RHC *Annual Report*, 1973/4, p.23.
17. RHCA *College Letter*, May 1981, 'Professor F. Berry', p.7.
18. RHC *Annual Report*, 1974/5, p.21.

19. RHCA *College Letter*, May 1983, 'Dr Enid Stoye', p.11.
20. RHC *Annual Report* 1973/4, pp.36-8.
21. RHCA *College Letter*, May 1977, 'Professor K. Wilson', p.5.
22. John D. Dodge, *History of the Royal Holloway College Botany Department, 1893-1985* (privately printed by the Department 1985), pp.11-13.
23. Dr Lionel Butler, Memorial Address for Professor E. J. Bourne (died 30 November 1974), given at a Service of Thanksgiving for his life and work, held in the College Chapel, 22 January 1975. RHCA *College Letter*, May 1975, pp.8-11.
24. Helmut Weigel, 'Edward John Bourne 1922-1974: Biographical Notes', *Advances in Carbohydrate Chemistry and Biochemistry*, vol 34 (1977). (Off-print of 22 pages, with complete bibliography of papers published by Professor Bourne and his research associates, loaned to Caroline Bingham by Dr Helmut Weigel.)
25. Ibid., p.6.
26. Ibid., p.11
27. RHCA *College Letter*, May 1982, 'Professor Trevor G. Bonner', p.8.
28. Dr Roy Miller to Caroline Bingham, 4 September 1986. (Dr Helmut Weigel was generous in giving me information on the work of his predecessors in the Chemistry Department, but, modest about his own work, he requested me to ask Dr Roy Miller for details, which the latter was kind enough to give in the letter quoted. CB)
29. RHC *Annual Report*, 1979/80 p.40. Professor McDowell's published research papers and contributions to books can be found in the departmental lists of publications which are attached to these reports.
30. RHCA *College Letter*, May 1981, 'Dr Mary Bradburn', p.8.
31. RHCA *College Letter*, May 1983, 'Dr Barbara G. Yates', pp.10-11.
32. RHCA *College Letter*, May 1977, 'Professor E. H. Hutten', p.5.
33. RHCA *College Letter*, May 1978, 'Professor P. A. Jewell', p.5.
34. RHC *Annual Report*, 1973/4, p.60.
35. RHC *Annual Report*, 1983/4, p.77.
36. RHC *Annual Report*, 1973/4, p.34.
37. Ibid.
38. Ibid., p.35.
39. RHC Annual Report 1983/4, p.47.
40. RHC *Annual Report*, 1973/4, p.64.
41. Ibid.
42. Dr Lionel Butler, Memorial Address for Professor E. J. Bourne, RHCA *College Letter*, May 1975, pp.8-11.
43. RHC *Annual Report*, 1973/4, p.1.

44. Ibid., p.2.
45. Miss J. L. Hurn, interview with Caroline Bingham, 1985.
46. RHC *Annual Report*, 1974/5, p.1.
47. Ibid.
48. RHC *Annual Report*, The Principal's Report on behalf of the Council for 1975/6, p.1.
49. Ibid.
50. RHC *Annual Report*, Report by the Principal for 1977/8, p.2.
51. Ibid., p.1.
52. Miss Alison Chard (student 1978-81) to Caroline Bingham, 9 April 1985.
53. Dr Roy Miller, interview with Caroline Bingham, 17 December 1985.
54. Negley Harte, *The University of London, 1836-1986*, p.280.
55. Ibid., p.281.
56. Dr Roy Miller, interview with Caroline Bingham.
57. Ibid.
58. 'Reply to the Swinnerton-Dyer Committee', June 1980, RHC *Annual Report*, 1979/80, pp.1-4.
59. Ibid.
60. Liaison Planning Group Papers (unclassified), loaned to Caroline Bingham by Dr Roy Miller.
61. Negley Harte, op.cit., p.283.
62. Ngaio Crequer, 'Room with a different view', *Times Higher Education Supplement*, 29 September, 1983, p.8.
63. Manuscript verse by Dr Lionel Butler; copy given to Caroline Bingham by Miss Janet Christie.
64. *Minutes of the 109th Meeting of the Senate of Brunel University, held on Tuesday, 20 October 1981*, copy given to Caroline Bingham by Professor R. E. D. Bishop, 18 November 1986.
65. Ibid.
66. *Guardian*, 22 October 1981.
67. Liaison Planning Group Papers, copy of 'Discussion Paper for Brunel-RHC talks' issued by Professor R. E. D. Bishop, 3 November 1981.
68. Negley Harte, op.cit., p.282
69. Dr Roy Miller, interview with Caroline Bingham.
70. Ibid.
71. Ibid.
72. Professor Sir Randolph Quirk, interview with Caroline Bingham, 6 April 1987.
73. Dr Roy Miller, interview with Caroline Bingham.
74. 'A Bedford View of the Merger', written by Miss Marigold Packenham-

Walsh (Assistant Secretary of Bedford College 1968-82; Deputy Secretary 1982-5) for Caroline Bingham, 16 October 1986.

75. Professor Sir Randolph Quirk, interview with Caroline Bingham.
76. Ibid.
77. 'A Bedford View of the Merger'.
78. Dr Roy Miller, interview with Caroline Bingham.
79. 'A Bedford View of the Merger'.
80. Philip Howard, 'Double Egham and Chaps', *The Times*, 22 February 1986.
81. Dr Roy Miller, interview with Caroline Bingham.
82. Mr Richard Hardy, interview with Caroline Bingham, 1985.
83. Professor Sir Randolph Quirk, interview with Caroline Bingham, 1987.
84. Professor Dorothy Wedderburn, Foreword to *College Lives: A Celebration of the Past, Present and Future of Royal Holloway and Bedford New College*, researched, compiled and edited by Chrys Salt and Liz Bennett (RHBNC, 1986).
85. Professor K. C. Bowen, copy of poem given to Caroline Bingham, 7 March 1986.

## NOTE ON SOURCES

My chief source for this History has been the Royal Holloway College Archives, catalogued by Derryan Paul in 1973, and reorganized with the catalogue brought up to date by Elizabeth Bennett in 1985/86. The second most important group of sources comprises the manuscript material contributed by former students, listed in the acknowledgements, and the transcripts of interviews with college staff, past and present, academic, administrative and domestic, collected by the author and Chrys Salt. All these materials will be deposited in the College Archives.

The relatively small number of printed books, periodicals and pamphlets consulted will be found in the Notes and References.

# INDEX